· E. E. BILBROUGH ·

NUMEROUS ILLUSTRATIONS & MAPS

'TWIXT FRANCE AND SPAIN.

L 30
159

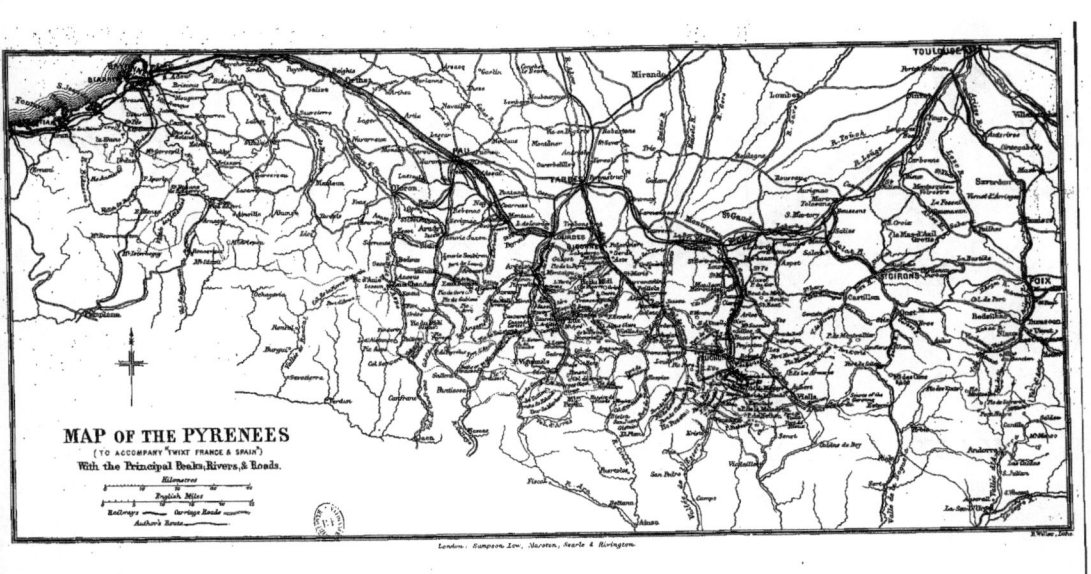

'TWIXT FRANCE AND SPAIN;

OR,

A Spring in the Pyrenees.

BY

E. ERNEST BILBROUGH.

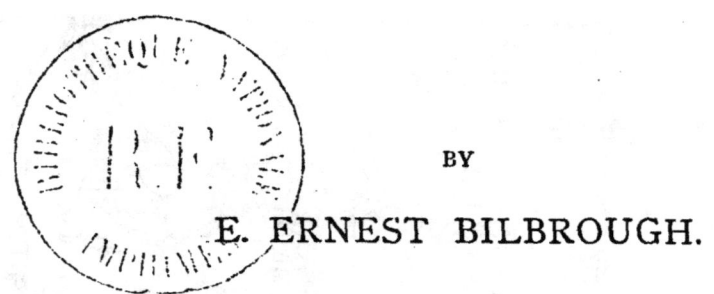

ILLUSTRATIONS BY DORÉ AND MISS BLUNT.

LONDON:
SAMPSON LOW, MARSTON, SEARLE, & RIVINGTON,
CROWN BUILDINGS, 188, FLEET STREET, E.C.
1883.
All rights reserved.

LONDON:
PRINTED BY WILLIAM CLOWES AND SONS, LIMITED,
STAMFORD STREET AND CHARING CROSS.

PREFACE.

It has been my endeavour in this volume to provide an illustrated gossiping Guide to the Spas of the Pyrenees. Unlike previous books on the same region, it deals with the resorts in spring, when they are most charming. A certain amount of detail—which is unavoidable in all guide-books—has been unavoidable here, and the rhymes have been introduced in the hope of lightening the reading. These rhymes, as a rule, have a distinct bearing on the subject under discussion; but they are inserted in such a manner that the reader can omit to read them —if he objects to such frivolities—without losing the sense of the prose.

Very little really fresh information has been gained about these beautiful mountains since Mr. Charles Packe published his 'Guide to the Pyrenees' in 1867: a few more springs have been discovered, a few more mountains have been successfully ascended, and the towns have gradually increased in size. There have been very few of those melancholy accidents that we so often hear of from Switzerland, because, probably, considerably fewer tourists attempt these mountains than attempt the Alps. In this volume no descriptions of scaling ice-walls, searching for the lammergeiers' nests, or any other great feats, will be found. It contains a plain account of what may be seen and done by any party visiting the mountain resorts in spring, without much trouble or fatigue; and the narrative form has been adopted throughout.

M. Doré's illustrations speak for themselves; and Miss Blunt's spirited sketches are a valuable acquisition.

The Appendices have been compiled with great care; and—at the suggestion of an experienced M.D.—brief comments on the chief springs at the various Spas, and their healing properties, have been included in the general information.

I beg to acknowledge my indebtedness to M. Joanne's 'Pyrenees' and Mr. Black's 'Summer Resorts;' and I have also great pleasure in thanking Miss Blunt for her sketches, and my friend Mr. A. H. Crow, F.R.G.S., for his kindly assistance in correcting inaccuracies. As, however, it is extremely difficult to completely avoid them, I shall feel obliged for the notification of any others that may happen to exist.

E. E. B.

CONTENTS.

CHAPTER I.

PAU.

PAGE

Trains and steamers—Bordeaux and its hotels—Lamothe —Morcenx—Dax—Puyoo—Orthez—First impressions of Pau—The hotels and pensions—Amusements—Pension Colbert—Making up parties for the Pyrenees—The Place Royale and the view—The castle of Pau and its approaches—Origin of name—Historical notes—The towers—Visiting hours—The tapestries—The wonderful bedstead—The delusive tortoiseshell cradle—The " Tour de la Monnaie "—The park—The Billères plains —Tennis and golf—The Route de Billères and the Billères woods—French *sportsmen*—Hunting—Racing —Lescar and its old cathedral—Fontaine de Marnières —The bands—The Parc Beaumont—Ballooning—The Casino—Polo—The cemetery—The churches of St. Martin and St. Jacques—The "old world and the new"—Rides and drives—to Bétharram—The start— Peasants and their ways—Vines trained by the roadside—Sour grapes—The " March of the Men of Garlic " —Coarraze—Henry IV.'s Castle—Bétharram—The ivied bridge—The inn—The "Via Crucis"—Assat and Gélos—The Coteaux—Perpignaa—Sketching with a donkey-cart—Over the Coteaux to Gan—The drive to Piétat—Picnicking and rejected attentions—The church —Feather moss—Bizanos—Carnival time—" Poor Pillicoddy "—" Idyllic Colbert."   1

CHAPTER II.

BAGNÈRES DE BIGORRE.

Backward spring—Hôtel Beau Séjour—Effect of the war of '70 on the English colony—The "Coustous"—The Church of St. Vincent—Géruzet's marble works—Donkeys—Up the Monné—Bains de Santé—Bains de Grand Pré—Salut Avenue and baths—" Ai-ue, Ai-ue "—Luncheon—Daffodils—The summit and the view—The " Castel-Mouly "—The Tapère—Mde. Cottin—Mont Bédat—Gentians—The Croix de Manse—" The Lady's Farewell to her Asinine Steed "—Market-day—The old iron and shoe dealers—Sunday—A cat fight—The English Church—To the Col d'Aspin—" The Abbé's Song "—Baudéan—Campan, its people and church—Wayside chapels—Ste. Marie—The route to Gripp, &c.—Payole—The pine forest—The Col d'Aspin—The view from the Monné Rouge—" The Plaint of the Weather-beaten Pine "—The Menu at Payole—Hurrah for the milk!—Departures—Divine music—Asté—Gabrielle d'Estrelle—The ivied ruins—The church—Pitton de Tournefort—Gerde—The pigeon traps—The cattle market—The Jacobin tower—Theatre—Grand Etablissement des Thermes—Hospice Civil—Eglise des Carmes—Mount Olivet—Madame Cheval, her cakes and tea—Bigorre in tears 32

CHAPTER III.

LOURDES.

The journey to Tarbes—The Buffet and the Nigger—Lourdes station in the wet—Importunate " Cochers "—Hôtel des Pyrénées—" Red tape " and Porters—Lourdes in sunshine—Sightseeing—The " Rue de la Grotte "—" The Cry of the Lourdes Shopkeepers "—Candle-sellers—The Grotto—Abject reverence—The Church—Saint Bernard—Interior of church—The panorama—Admirable effect—Rue du Fort—The castle—The view from the Tower—Pie de Mars, or Ringed Ousels . . . 52

CHAPTER IV.

ARGELÈS.

Road v. rail—Scenes, sublime and ridiculous—Hôtel d'Angleterre—Questions and "The Argelès Shepherd's Reply"—A forbidden path—The ride to Ges, Serres, Salluz, and Ourous—Argelès church—Route Thermale—Ges—The tree in the path—"A regular fix"—Serres—"It's a stupid foal that doesn't know its own mother"—A frothing stream—A fine view—Pigs in clover—Salluz—Ourous—Contented villagers—The high road—The bridge on the Pierrefitte road—Advice to sketchers—"Spring's Bitters and Sweets"—The "witch of the hills"—Large green lizards—"Jeannette's Lamb"—Round the Argelès valley—Château de Beaucens—Villelongue—Soulom—The old church—Hôtel de la Poste, Pierrefitte—St. Savin—The verger and the ancient church—Cagots—"The Organ's Tale"—St. Savin's tomb—The Château de Miramont—Jugged Izard—Market-day—Sour bread and the remedy—Arrival of the first parcel . . . 60

CHAPTER V.

CAUTERETS.

Hôtel de la Poste, Pierrefitte—The Gorge—Its majestic beauty—The resemblance to the Llanberis Pass—Mrs. Blunt becomes poetical—Zinc mines—Le Pont de Médiabat—Entering the town—The Rue Richelieu and Hôtel du Parc—Winter's seal upon them still—Thermes des Œufs—Thermes de César—The Casino and Esplanade des Œufs—A good dinner and the menu—The start for the Col de Riou—The Grange de la Reine Hortense—The pines—Miss Blunt's "Exhortation to the First Snow"—The dogs and their gambols—Defeated, but not discouraged—To the Cérizey Cascade—The baths of La Raillère, Petit St. Sauveur, and Le Pré—Cascade de Lutour—The Marcadau Gorge—Scenery—Pic de Gaube—At the Cérizey Cascade—The Pont d'Espagne and Lac de Gaube—Pont de Benqués—Lutour valley—

Various excursions up same—The " Parc "—Allées de Cambasque—The Peguère—The " Pagoda " villa—Promenade du Mamelon Vert—The road's up again—Blows and blasts—The bishop's arrival—Enthusiasm, pomposity, and benedictions—The pilgrims at large—They start on an excursion—The market and Hôtel de Ville—The grocer's opinion—Pyrenean dogs and their treatment—The dog-fancier—Smiles and temper—Bargaining displaced—No dog after all ! . . .   77

CHAPTER VI.

LUZ AND BARÈGES.

Rain at starting—A blighted view, yet lovely still—Pont d'Enfer—Nature's voice—Sère and Esquiez—Luz—Its situation and status—An old house—The ancient church of the Templars—La Chapelle de St. Roch—Pyrenean museum—Hôtel de l'Univers—Château de Ste. Marie—" The Jackdaw's Causerie "—A new " diet of worms "—The new bathing establishment—To Barèges—Pic d'Ayré—Esterre—Viella—Betpouey—Mill conduits—Cercle des Etrangers—Opinion of the town—Grand Etablissement—Promenade Horizontale—Hospice de Ste. Eugénie—" The Jay of Barèges "—Wood anemones—Hepaticas—Valley of Lienz—Pic de Lienz—Pic d'Ayré's summit—Pic de Néouville—Mountain rhododendrons—*Anemone vernalis*   95

CHAPTER VII.

ST. SAUVEUR.

Pont de Pescadère—Sassis—Gave de Gavarnie—St. Sauveur—Hôtel de France—Pont Napoléon—Napoleon's pillar—Bee orchids—Chapel of Solferino—The view from thence—Ne'er a hermit but for gold—Luz cemetery—Luz post-office—Short cuts—Pharmacie Claverie—Jardin à l'Anglaise—Ascent of Pic de Bergons—Villenave—The shepherds' huts—Lunch—Snow, its use and abuse—On foot—" Excelsior "—Dangerous footing—The last

PAGE

crest but one—The view—Gavarnie and Argelès in sight—A lazy guide—A "fast" bit—Mountain flowers—Mr. Sydney to the fore—A short walk and a good view—To Sazos and Grust—The bathing establishments—Sazos: the old church—The belfry—Chiming extraordinary—Various promenades—Gems of hill and vale 108

CHAPTER VIII.

GAVARNIE.

A "falling glass"—The wonderful echo—Cascade Lassariou—Sia and its bridge—Pont de Desdouroucat—"Changing scenes"—Bugaret torrent—The Piméné—Bué—Gèdre—Brêche de Roland in the distance—The "Grotto"—Scenery at fivepence per head—Daffodils—Lofty summits—Cascade d'Arroudet—Chaos—Valley of the "Ten Thousand Rocks," Amoy—A dirty avalanche—The Sugar-loaf—Travellers' troubles—Importunate females—Hotel des Voyageurs—Poc—Guide or no guide—Chute de Lapaca—The guardian summits of the Cirque—Cascade du Marboré—Chandelles du Marboré—The Cirque—Its marvellous beauty—Reluctantly returning—"The Guide's Auction"—"Two women enough for a market, and three for a fair"—A Yankee tale—Sketching and flowers—Tempers and appetites . . 119

CHAPTER IX.

FROM LUZ AND ST. SAUVEUR TO BAGNÈRES DE LUCHON.

A smiling valley—Lourdes again—The chapel in the crypt—St. Peter's statue—Burnished toes—Solemn quietude—Preparing for the great pilgrimage—"Ornamented" crosses—Mr. Sydney's new vocation, "Guide, Philosopher, and Friend"—Bigorre again—An open-air concert—Harmonious echoes—Paying through the nose—The fête at Payole—Sport à la française—Costumes—The view from the Col d'Aspin—Arreau—Quaint houses—La Chapelle de St. Exupère—A whining "gardien"—

Eglise de Notre Dame—The river Neste—Hôtel de France—Bordères—Avajan—Louderville—Oxslips and cowslips—Wild narcissus—Col de Peyresourde—The view—Garin—Cazaux—St. Aventin—Lovely avenues—Our destination. 132

CHAPTER X.

BAGNÈRES DE LUCHON.

The bathing establishment and its surroundings—The lovely *Allées*—Montauban church and cascade—The Villa Russe and its genial host—Various excursions—Orphanage of Notre Dame de Rocher—The Vallée du Lys—The Rue d'Enfer and cascades—A lively scene—The view from Superbagnères—Loading wood—"The Oxen's Appeal"—Visit to the Orphanage—A "holy" relic—To Bosost—St. Mamet—"A stumbling-block"—Cascade of Sidonie—Horse tricks and jockey dodges—Lizards in flight—Fashion on a donkey—On the Potillon 'twixt France and Spain—The valley of Aran—Snug Bosost—A curious inn—Children with artistic bent—A bright pathway—Missing much, but thankful still 141

CHAPTER XI.

ST. BERTRAND DE COMMINGES.

Keeping to old friends—Valley history—Entering the Garonne valley—The picturesque St. Béat—St. Béat to Viella—Memories of the lovely Thames—Baths of Ste. Marie—Loures—The cross-roads—Weak walls—Entering St. Bertrand—An ancient house—The inn—A charming garden—The cathedral—A national disgrace—"The Crocodile of St. Bertrand"—The tomb of Hugues de Chatillon—Travelling desecraters—St. Bertrand's rod—The ruined cloisters—Desolation—Swine feeding—Montrejeau—The buffet—No milk!—French railway officials—Trying experiences . . 159

CHAPTER XII.

EAUX BONNES AND EAUX CHAUDES.

Carriage *v.* diligence—Early birds—Height of absurdity—Diminutive donkeys—A whitened region—" Crystal clear "—Washerwomen and their gamps—A useful town-hall—A half-way house—Moralising—A much-loved pipe—An historic ruin—A noteworthy strong box—" Ici on rase "—Where are the bears?—Women in gaiters—Picturesque costumes—A lovely road—A " perfect " cure—A spring scene—A billiard-playing priest—A well-placed pavilion—The Valentin and its cascades—Through solid rock—Gaps in the road—A grand scene—Wanted, an artist—A fine torrent—Professional fishers—Lucky guests—Musings—Poor Mr. Tubbins—Bonnes *v.* Chaudes—Over the Col de Gourzy—Peculiar teams—Guelder roses—Spinning 170

CHAPTER XIII.

BIARRITZ.

A warm ride—Bayonne—A " Noah's ark " landscape—Amusements—Bathing—Shells—Cavillers—A canine feat—The pier and rocks—A restless sea—" The Three Cormorants "—Dragon's-mouth Rock—To the lighthouse—Maiden-hair ferns—Mrs. Blunt's adventure—The drive round the lakes—*Osmunda regalis* ferns—The pine-woods near the bar—St. Etienne and the Guards' cemetery—Croix de Mouguère—Cambo and the Pas de Roland—Anemones—A fat couple—A French scholar—Hendaye—Fuenterabia—A quaint old-world town—The Bidassoa—Pasages—San Sebastien—The Citadol and graves—The " Silent Sisters "—Raised prices—Parasols and spectacles. 194

CHAPTER XIV.

CONCLUSION.

	PAGE
"Where duty leads"—Resorts in the Eastern Pyrenees—Caen—"Riou"—Our paths diverge—"The Lesson of the Mountains"—Farewell	214

APPENDIX A	221
APPENDIX B	250
APPENDIX C	255
APPENDIX D	257
INDEX	263

LIST OF ILLUSTRATIONS.

	PAGE
MAP OF THE PYRENEES . . . . *Frontispiece*	
DAX	4
THE TOWER OF MONCADE, ORTHEZ	5
PAU (FROM THE JURANÇON SIDE OF THE GAVE . .	10
THE CASTLE COURTYARD	14
IN THE CASTLE PARK.	16
THE PINE FOREST NEAR THE COL D'ASPIN . . .	43
THE "PALOMIÈRES DE GERDE".	49
LOURDES (A SMALL GENERAL VIEW)	54
THE "OLD FORT" AT LOURDES	58
ON THE ROAD TO ARGELÈS	61
A "RÉGULAR FIX" (by Miss BLUNT) . . .	64
A PRETTY BIT AT ARGELÈS	69
CAUTERETS.	80
THE ASCENT OF THE COL DE RIOU (by Miss BLUNT) .	84
THE LAC DE GAUBE	88
THE GORGE NEAR PIERREFITTE	96
THE ANCIENT CHURCH OF THE TEMPLARS AT LUZ .	99
THE CASTLE OF STE. MARIE	102
BARÈGES	104
ST. SAUVEUR	109
PONT NAPOLÉON, ST. SAUVEUR (by Miss BLUNT) .	110
THE VILLAGE OF GÈDRE	122
THE CHAOS NEAR GAVARNIE	124
THE CIRQUE OF GAVARNIE (IN SUMMER) . . .	128
"ON THE TARBES ROAD".	135
THE PEARL IN THE PEERLESS VALLEY . . .	142
THE CHURCH OF MONTAUBAN (by Miss BLUNT) .	143
THE RUE D'ENFER AND THE CASCADES . . .	147
ON THE ROAD TO SUPERBAGNÈRES	149
ST. BERTRAND DE COMMINGES	162
THE CROCODILE OF ST. BERTRAND (by Miss BLUNT) .	165

LIST OF ILLUSTRATIONS.

	PAGE
IN THE OLD CHURCH AT LARUNS	177
CASCADE DU VALENTIN	181
CRABÉ BRIDGE, IN THE EAUX CHAUDES GORGE	184
THE BIOUS-ARTIGUES	188
THE PIC DE GER	191
THE ROCKS OF BIARRITZ	200
THE VILLA EUGÉNIE	202
MRS. BLUNT'S ADVENTURE (by Miss BLUNT):—	
SCENE I.—BEFORE THE START	203
SCENE II.—THE ANCIENT STEED GREW YOUNG ONCE MORE	203
SCENE III.—WHO'S MY DRIVER?	203
"MY PAW IS ON MY NATIVE HEATH, AND MY NAME IS 'RIOU'" (by Miss BLUNT)	215
"SEE MORNING'S GOLDEN RAYS," &c.	218
"TOWERING ABOVE THE PLAIN"	219
PANORAMA OF THE CIRQUE OF THE VALLÉE DU LYS	*facing* 239
PANORAMA OF THE PIC DU MIDI DE BIGORRE	*facing* 231

INTRODUCTION.

CONSIDERING the number of English and Americans who yearly visit Switzerland and the Riviera, it is astonishing that so few, comparatively, ever think of approaching nearer to the Pyrenees than Pau. And it is more astonishing still, that those who have been enabled to enjoy the beauty of these mountains from the Place Royale at Pau, should ever think of leaving their vicinity without a more intimate acquaintance with them.

It may be, that since the various resorts have gained celebrity for the healing powers of their waters, healthy travellers are of opinion that they will be surrounded by a crowd of sickly individuals, whose very appearance will spoil all the pleasure that they might otherwise experience. That this *might be* the case *in the season*, at a few spas, is not to be denied, but *in spring* not an invalid of that kind is to be met with, and the bathing establishments have no customers; but the scenery is everywhere at its best. Dr. Madden writes: "The attractions of the Pyrenees are not, however, confined to the invalid traveller, but even for the pleasure tourist offer inducements for a pedestrian excursion in some respects superior to any in Switzerland;" and there can be no doubt that they have a beauty of their own quite distinct from the grandeur of the Alps, and yet equally as wonderful in its style.

Extending for nearly 300 miles from the foaming billows of the Biscay to the azure waters of the Mediterranean, they form a huge barrier "'twixt France and Spain"; gaining their name of Pyrenees from the words "Pic Nérés," which in the *patois* of the country signifies "black peaks!" That this title is a misnomer for all but three months of the year—viz., from July to October—must be already a well-known fact; for who would call them "black" when clothed in their garments of snow?

The highest summits are in the Maladetta group, and the Pic Nethou (11,170 ft.) is the highest of all; while the average height of this magnificent range of mountains is between five and six thousand feet.

Luxurious valleys branch out in all directions, fed by the mountain streams, and among the central heights the wonderful natural amphitheatres known as Cirques stand in majestic solitude. The Cirque of Gavarnie—the best known—possesses on a bright day in spring such a charm, in its snowy imperial splendour, as the Alps would fail to surpass. In scenes where a lake adds such wonderful effect, Switzerland is quite supreme; we know of no view in the Pyrenees, of a comparable nature, that could pretend to vie with the harmonious loveliness of the panorama that can be seen at sunset from Montreux across Lac Leman, when the water is rippleless and the mountains are bathed in a rosy flood. But for all that, in other ways— in flower-clothed slopes, in luxurious valleys, in winding rivers and foaming cascades—the Pyrenees present pictures that, with the freshness of springtime to aid them, cannot fail to delight and charm.

Four roads cross the Pyrenees from France to Spain: the Route Nationale, from Paris to Madrid *viâ* Bayonne; the Route Departementale, from Bayonne to Pampeluna *viâ* the Col d'Urdax; the Route Nationale, from Perpignan to Barcelona *viâ* Gerona; and the route from Pau to Jaca *viâ* Oloron. There are other ways of entering Spain by the Cols (passes), but over these a horse track is the broadest path.

The principal bathing resorts on the French side are connected by the splendid Route Thermale, which extends for 70 miles; but, owing to its exposed position in some parts, especially between Eaux Bonnes and Argelès, and Barèges and Ste. Marie, it is only wholly open three or four months in the year!

Of the mineral springs it is sufficient to state here that, within the same extent of country, no other part of Europe can present such a wonderful choice. There are three principal kinds—the sulphurous, the saline, and the ferruginous; and over 200 springs contribute to them. Some resorts have waters of each of these classes, and many have at any rate two out of the three.

Of these, fuller information is given in the Appendix, as well as the chief uses of each, and the affections for which they have been successfully used.

As regards sport, unattended by much labour or fatigue, the Pyrenees can hardly be recommended, except perhaps for fishing. There is very good fishing in several of the rivers, but unhappily French conservancy laws are so lax—if indeed they have any at all—that peasants may frequently be seen at the waterside with a rod in one hand and a capacious net in the other, so that if unsuccessful with the first, they will at any rate not come home empty-handed; unless some brother "sportsman" has just preceded them over the same pools!

Though the wolves have nearly all been poisoned, there are still some bears to shoot in winter, and izard (a species of chamois) and capercailzie to pursue in autumn; but the "sportsmen" are many and the game few, and the way to their haunts lies by bad and unfrequented paths; so that "le jeu ne vaut pas la chandelle." To the botanist and the geologist, however, there is a splendid field, which, varying in richness according to the locality, is more or less rich everywhere; and besides these, the entomologist will not visit this territory in vain. To the mountaineer these almost numberless summits offer attractions of all kinds, from the wooded slope with its broad mule-path, to the ice-wall only to be scaled by the use of the rope and the hatchet. There are ascents which a child almost might attempt in safety, and there are others where the bravest men might well quail.

For the ordinary pedestrian, beautiful walks abound in the vicinity of nearly every Spa, but near St. Sauveur, Luchon, Eaux Chaudes, and Argelès they are, we think, most charming. The roads on the whole are excellent, and the hotels, with hardly any exceptions, particularly clean and comfortable; and, with the one drawback of the bread (see Appendix D) —which can be easily remedied—the food is well cooked and well served.

It must be understood that the succeeding chapters only describe—or attempt to describe—scenes that every one in moderate health can go and enjoy for themselves, and it is in the hope that a few more may be induced to visit the region about which they speak, that they have ever seen the light. For accurate information about the mountains and the best means of ascending them, no better guide-books could be wanted than Count Russell's 'Grandes Ascensions des Pyrénées'* in French and English, and Mr. Chas. Packe's 'Guide to the Pyrenees'; † while for information of all kinds Monsieur P. Joanne's 'Pyrenees,'* in French, could hardly be surpassed. For the ordinary traveller Mr. Black's 'South of France Summer Resorts, Pyrenees,' &c., is a compact and useful companion; and for guidance in matters medical, Dr. Madden's 'Spas of the Pyrenees' and Dr. Lee's 'Baths of France' are exceedingly valuable.

With these preliminary remarks we beg to refer the reader to our experiences of 'A Spring in the Pyrenees.'

* Hachette et Cie., Paris.
† Longmans and Co., London.

'TWIXT FRANCE AND SPAIN.

CHAPTER I.

PAU.

rains and Steamers—Bordeaux and its Hotels—Lamothe—
Morcenx—Dax—Puyoo—Orthez—First impressions of Pau—
The Hotels and Pensions—Amusements—Pension Colbert—
Making up parties for the Pyrenees—The Place Royale and
the view—The Castle of Pau and its approaches—Origin of
name—Historical notes—The Towers—Visiting hours—The
Tapestries—The Wonderful Bedstead—The Delusive Tortoiseshell Cradle—The "Tour de la Monnaie"—The Park—
The Billères Plains—Tennis and Golf—The Route de Billères
and the Billères Woods—French *Sportsmen*—Hunting—
Racing—Lescar and its old Cathedral—Fontaine de Marnières
—The Bands—The Parc Beaumont—Ballooning—The Casino
—Polo—The Cemetery—The Churches of St. Martin and
St. Jacques—The "Old World and the New"—Rides and
Drives—to Bétharram—The Start—Peasants and their ways—
Vines trained by the roadside—Sour Grapes - The "March
of the Men of Garlic"—Coarraze—Henry IV.'s Castle—
Bétharram—The Ivied Bridge—The Inn—The "Via Crucis"
—Assat and Gélos—The Coteaux—Perpignaa—Sketching
with a Donkey-cart—Over the Coteaux to Gan—The Drive to
Piétat—Picnicking and Rejected Attentions—The Church—
Feather Moss—Bizanos—Carnival time—"Poor Piliicoddy"
—"Idyllic Colbert."

FEW Winter Resorts have gained a greater celebrity
than Pau, and its popularity yearly increases. Fifty
years ago its English visitors might have been
counted by tens; to-day they must be reckoned by
thousands. But this is only during the winter and

spring; in summer it is almost entirely deserted by foreigners, few people in fact, unless compelled by circumstances, staying after May has passed into June.

For many reasons it has become a favourite resort for invalids, an important one being, its exceedingly accessible position. Notwithstanding that it is 776 miles distant from London, fewer changes are requisite than for many a journey of less than a quarter of the distance. The quickest way from London is *viâ* Dover, Calais, Paris, Bordeaux and Dax; and as a through sleeping carriage can be obtained from Paris to Pau, that part of the journey is anything but formidable. For those who prefer the sea route, the fine boats of the Pacific Steam Navigation Company which start from Liverpool are the most preferable conveyance, though the less expensive steamers belonging to the General Steam Navigation Company, sailing from London, are comfortable enough in fine weather. The former land their passengers at Pauillac, whence they proceed to Bordeaux by tender or train; but the latter boats, being smaller, can come right up to Bordeaux, which is a decided advantage.

Though the third port in France, Bordeaux can certainly not be recommended as a stopping-place unless necessity requires it, for the hotel-keepers generally succeed in reaping a rich harvest from travellers passing through.

The Hôtel de Nantes is the nearest to the quay, but the Hôtel Richelieu will be found more moderate and more comfortable. In the town, the grand Hôtel de France has the best reputation, but "birds of passage" have apparently to pay for it, whereas old stagers concur in saying that for *gentlemen*—especially those who appreciate a good dinner—the best place is the Hôtel de Bayonne.

Bordeaux has many fine buildings and objects of interest over which a week can be easily spent, and for this length of time the hotel prices are in proportion considerably less per diem; but in winter it is especially bleak and cold, and travellers are advised to get on to Dax or Pau as quickly as possible. The railway journey of one hundred and forty-five miles to Pau occupies as a rule about six hours, passing Lamothe, Morcenx, Dax, Puyoo, and Orthez. Lamothe* (25 miles) is the junction for Arcachon,* the celebrated winter station among the pines, situated on the shores of a landlocked bay; and Morcenx* (68 miles), is likewise the junction for the Tarbes line and Bigorre.

Dax* (92 miles) has a well-deserved reputation for its baths, and possesses several mineral bathing establishments, of which the "Grand Etablissement des Thermes" stands first. The mud baths are perhaps more celebrated than those of steam or water, being especially efficacious in severe, and often apparently otherwise incurable, cases of rheumatism. There are also some pleasant walks by the River Adour, and in the neighbourhood there is a bed of fossil salt.

Puyoo* ($111\frac{1}{2}$ miles) is the junction for the Bayonne line, but is without other interest.

Orthez* ($120\frac{3}{4}$ miles) is of historic interest and possesses some noteworthy remains. M. Doré has represented the Tour de Moncade, built in 1240, with mediæval surroundings, and not quite as it may be

* See Appendix.

DAX.

seen now. It was the scene of many of Gaston Phœbus' greatest crimes. The old fourteenth-century bridge over the river, with its central tower, could tell some tales too, if we could discover "sermons in stones"; and the plain below the town was the scene of one of Wellington's many victories in 1814.

Two coaches start from Orthez, one to Salies (10

THE TOWER OF MONCADE, ORTHEZ.

miles), celebrated for its salt springs, and the other to Mauléon-Licharre, a picturesque spot where fine views, cascades, and ruins abound.

Passing the ancient town of Lescar (140½ miles)—of which we shall have more to say later—the train is soon drawn up in the station of Pau, and directly the traveller shows his face outside, he is hailed by the "cochers" from the various hotels in a bewildering chorus. This is the same, *more* or *less*, at every French town where English people congregate, and Pau only inclines, if anything, towards the "*more*."

The first impression conveyed when leaving the station and passing along the Avenue de la Gare, is, that the town is mainly composed of the castle and magnificent hotels which tower above the station. This, to a certain extent, is correct, for they occupy a large area, and the views from the windows of the hotels, as well as from those of the castle, are the finest in the town. Issuing from the Avenue into the "Place de la Monnaie," the ruins of the "Mint" tower, and above them the castle itself, come into full view, after which the road continues along the Rue Marca for a short distance, branching afterwards to the right into the most ancient square of the town, the Place Grammont.

The hotels de la Poste and Henri IV. are here situated, but the roads to the various other hotels and pensions diverge in different directions. To the right up the Rue Bordenave and along the Rue Henri IV. is the route to all the finest hotels, of which the "France" is the best, and the "Gassion" the most imposing; the others are the Belle Vue, Splendide, Beau Séjour, and de la Paix, all with the exception of the last possessing the magnificent mountain view, but although from the windows of the "Paix" only a side glimpse can be obtained, yet at the same time this hotel faces the "Place Royale," the popular resort of all classes in Pau. From the left-hand corner of the Place Grammont a narrow street leads to the fine church of St. Jacques, which is also the nearest way to the grand Hôtel Continental near Trinity Church, and the Pension Hattersly in the

Rue Porte Neuve. But the route more to the left still, leading up the hill and joining the Route de Bordeaux, past the Haute Plante parade ground, is the usual one followed, especially for the Pensions—Lecour, Nogués, and Maison Pieté, in the Rue d'Orléans; Pension Etcherbest, in the Passage Planté; Hôtel de Londres, on the route de Billères; and Maison Colbert, in the Rue Montpensier.

Well knowing the comfort of a good pension, and intending to make a long stay, we drove straight from the station to the well-known Maison Colbert, and were soon as comfortable as we could wish. There are many people we are aware who detest " pensions." " We don't approve," say they, " of meals at fixed hours, of a drawing-room common to all, and of such a small house that everybody must know everyone else before the first dinner is over!" Well! why should they? They can go to the hotels; but let all those who are suffering or delicate put away thin-skinned feelings of superiority, till they have a good enough constitution to support them, and in the meantime seek peace and kindness, such as may be experienced at the Pension Colbert.

If, on the other hand, it can be taken as a criterion that those living in hotels are not invalids, then the visitor contingent of Pau must consist principally of healthy people, who prefer a good climate and lively society to the attractions that England and America have to offer from October to May. This is hardly correct, but there can be no doubt that more than half the foreigners* who come for that period, do so for comfort and pleasure alone. And it is not to be wondered at. Who, that was untrammelled by the

* From the French standpoint—i.e., English and American.

cares of business, or shortened purse-strings, but would not gladly exchange the bill of fare England has to offer, of London fogs, east winds, Scotch mists, and Irish dynamite, for the handsome menu awaiting him at Pau? Drives, kettledrums, dinners, balls, lawn tennis, polo, pigeon-shooting, golf, racing and hunting; and, if he particularly wishes it, a balloon ascent as well. This last-named is an expensive pleasure, as the aeronaut, judging by the prices on the bill, requires a substantial fee, and it is besides an amusement life insurance companies do not readily countenance.

Of course, if one comes to Pau merely for enjoyment, hotel life may be preferable to that in a pension, though our experiences of the latter mode have been very pleasant ones. It is so easy to make up a small party for a drive or a picnic, and being all in one house there is but little chance of any mishaps before starting, such as individuals forgetting the time that had been fixed and keeping the rest waiting. Above all, when planning a tour into the Pyrenees, it is essentially necessary to form a party of some sort, if the trip is to be carried out in the spring; for although, as we shall endeavour to show later, the scenery is then at its best, still, since it is not *the* season, only one or two hotels are open in each resort, and society is "nil."

Then further, when people are going to travel in company for several weeks it is well that at least they should know something of one another, for if they all commenced "pulling different ways" up in the mountains, the safety, or at any rate the composure of each, would be likely to suffer. My own relations, who were with me at first, left for England long before the mountain trip was arranged, but we made up a very pleasant quartette before the time for starting arrived, and accordingly visited Pau in company as well as the mountains. This quartette consisted of Mrs. and Miss Blunt, Mr. Sydney and myself, and though it will be seen by subsequent chapters that the trio decided on staying a fortnight at Biarritz in preference to following my example and spending the time at Bagnères de Bigorre, yet we made arrangements to meet either at Lourdes or Argelès and thenceforward to travel in company.

To see Pau in its beauty, winter must have given place to spring. When the grass once more begins to grow, the trees to unfold their tender leaves, the rivers to swell, and the birds to sing; while yet the sun's rays cannot pierce the snowy garment on the distant heights; then Pau is in her beauty. Passing— as we so often passed—down the Rue Montpensier and the consecutive Rue Serviez, into the Rue du Lycée, then turning from it to the right for a short distance, till, with the English club at the corner on our left, we turned into the Place Royale, and, with the fine theatre frowning on our backs, quickly made our way between the rows of plane-trees, but just uncurling their leaves, to the terrace whence the whole enormous expanse of mountain can be viewed, our admiration at the magnificent scene unfolded before us never diminished. But our favourite time was at sunset, especially one of those warm ruddy sunsets that tint the heavens like a superb red canopy.

Then, leaning on the terrace wall, we admired in silence. Beneath us lay part of the town and the railway station, the river beyond, in one part divided and slowly flowing over its stony bed among the alder bushes; at another, gathered together again,

PAU (FROM THE JURANÇON SIDE OF THE GAVE).

rushing furiously along as though impatient to lose itself for ever in the depths of the ocean.

Beyond the river, amid the varied green of tree and meadow, nestled the scattered villages, with the hills above, here brown with bare vineyards, there vying with the meadow's green; and in the background behind and above all, the mighty range of snow mountains extending as far as eye could reach, and fading in the dim haze of distance. Then, as the sun sank lower, the soft rosy hue shone on the castle windows, glinted through the trees of the Château Park, dyed the swift waters of the river, and tipped the snowy crests afar. There are few, we think, who would not, as we did, enjoy fully the contemplation of such a scene.

From the Place Royale to the Château is a very short distance; turning to the right past the Church of St. Martin—a fine well-built edifice—and the Hôtel Gassion, it stands in full view, and the broad walk passing beneath the side arches leads into the courtyard. In order to obtain a good view of the entrance and the towers that guard it, it is preferable to approach the castle by the Rue Henri IV. (a continuation of the Rue du Lycée that passes between the theatre and the end of the Place Royale), which, when the shops are left behind, suddenly curves to the left, to the foot of the bridge leading direct to the main entrance. It is worth while to stand on the bridge for a short time, and survey the whole scene, which can hardly fail to carry the thoughts back to olden times, and as the castle is so intimately connected with the town of Pau, a few explanatory historical facts will not, we trust, be considered out of place before continuing the inspection of the edifice.

The origin of the name of Pau is the Spanish "Palo," a "stick" or a "stake," and takes us back to the time when the Saracens had taken possession of a large part of Spain and were making raids beyond the Pyrenees. Feeling their unprotected position, the inhabitants of the Gave Valley made over a piece of ground to a Prince of Bearn, on the condition that he should erect a fortress for their defence thereon. This he agreed to do, and as the extent of his allotment was marked out by "stakes," the castle became known as the castle of "stakes" or Palo, which in time became Pau.

Its commanding position and appearance inspired confidence, and houses soon sprang up around; and, at least a century before the birth of Henry IV., Pau had become an important place. In time it became the capital of the kingdom of Navarre, and later, when Navarre, Bearn, and the "Pays Basques" were constituted as one department in 1790, it still retained its position as chief town.

Now to resume our inspection from the bridge. The two towers in full view on either side of the sculptured façade, are the finest and most prominent of the six that flank the castle, but there is one in the interior of the court of more interest. The highest of these two is the donjon on the left, built of brick, and known as "La Tour de Gaston Phœbus" (112 feet). Its walls are over eight feet in thickness. The tower on the right is known as "La Tour Neuve," while the most interesting is that known as "La Tour de Montaüset" or "Monte-Oiseau," in which are the ancient dungeons and oubliettes. The porter has rooms on the ground-floor of the Gaston Phœbus Tower, and his wife sells photographs singly and in books. Outside, underneath and adjoining the same tower, is a small modern (1843) chapel.

The hours for visiting the interior of the Château are between 10 and 12 and 2 and 4 daily, and the entrance is free, though the guide expects a gratuity, say of one franc for one person, two francs for three. As we were always lucky enough to be the only people wanting to inspect, at the particular hour we went—which was always as near ten as possible—we managed by judicious means to calm the impetuosity of the guide, and induce him to tell his tale slowly. If, as usually happens, other people are there at the same time, he rattles off his lesson at such a pace that it requires very good French scholars to even *follow* him; to remember what he says is out of the question. Whether by "more judicious means," it would be possible to induce him to go round out of hours, we do not know, never having had occasion to try, but we certainly think it would be worth an attempt, if the visitors could not otherwise manage to hit a time when they could go over alone.

Passing under one of the three arches of the façade, we traversed the courtyard to the extremity, and while waiting for the guide to come to us at the small side door, examined the curious sculptures surrounding the window on the left. On the door being opened we passed into the Salle des Gardes, and from that into the Salle à Manger, where stands a statue of Henry IV., supposed to be more like him than any other. Then through a succession of rooms and up flights of stairs, and through rooms again, to describe which as they deserve would alone fill up a small volume, but this we do not intend to do, contenting ourselves with simply mentioning as much of what we saw as we hope may induce everyone to follow our example, and see them for themselves. To any lovers of a grand view, that which may be seen from the upper windows of the castle is almost alone worth coming for, and the tapestry which lines the walls of many of the rooms is simply exquisite.

The "Sports and Pastimes of the various Months" of Flanders work, in the "Salle des Etats"—the six pieces of Gobelin work in the Queen's Boudoir on the

THE CASTLE COURTYARD.

first floor—the five pieces of the same work, including "Venus's toilet," in Queen Jeanne's room on the second floor, and the four pieces of Brussels in Henry IV.'s bedroom—also on the second floor—are only a few of the many wonderful pieces of tapestry.

In the "Grand Reception Room," in which the massacres took place in 1569, is a fine mosaic table and Sèvres vases, besides the Flanders tapestry.

There are several objects of interest in Henry IV.'s room, in which he is said to have been born 13th

December, 1553, including the magnificently carved bedstead; but the chief attraction is the tortoise-shell cradle, which as a rule Frenchmen come only to see. Why they should come is quite a different matter, seeing that although a tortoise's shell might make a very comfortable cradle for even such an illustrious infant as was Henry IV., yet as he never had anything to do with the one in question, it is rather absurd that year after year they should flock to see it out of respect to him; and the absurdity is greater, since in a statement on the wall hard by this fact is made known. None of the northern rooms are open to the public, but the chief objects of interest have been transferred to the other wing!

Leaving the courtyard by the road under the side arches that leads to the terrace, the tasteful gardening of the surroundings is noticeable, and as soon as the lower walk is reached, the "Tour de la Monnaie" lies in full view below. No efforts are made to keep these ruins, in which Calvin used to preach, from crumbling into dust. "*O tempora! O mores!*"

From the terrace on the other side of the Castle, the remains of the old fosse may be seen, though houses are now built where the water used to lie. A broad pathway encircles the edifice, and a bridge leads from the extreme end over the Rue Marca into the Castle Park, called also "lower plantation" (basse plante) in distinction from the "upper plantation" (haute plante), which surrounds the barracks. Near the road the trees are planted stiffly in rows, but when another and smaller bridge has been traversed, the beauty of the Park is manifest.

Following the course of the river, and filled with the finest trees and shrubs, through which the

IN THE CASTLE PARK.

beautiful little nuthatch may occasionally be seen flying, and among which many other birds sing — it is indeed, with its long cool walks and pleasant glades, a lovely promenade. The Bayonne road is the boundary on the opposite side from the river, and just beyond the limits of the Park a path branches off river-wards to the Billères Plains, where tennis and golf are played. In the opposite direction another leads up under the shadow of an old church, and joins the Route de Billères, which, starting from the Bordeaux road, passes the Villa Lacroix and other handsome houses, and descending throws off another branch into the Bayonne road. It then curves in an opposite direction, and ascends, while at the same time skirting the grounds of the Château de Billères, to the favourite Billères woods. From the woods it communicates in a nearly straight line with the Bordeaux road again, so that in reality it describes three-quarters of a circle.

These woods, though sadly disfigured by the demand for fire-wood, are pleasant to ramble in when the soldiers are not in possession, and there are drives through them in all directions. At one time wild duck, pigeons, and woodcock were plentiful there, but that time has passed, though the gallant French *sportsmen* may still be seen trooping through with their dogs after blackbirds and tomtits!

Pau dearly loves excitement. Three times a week in the winter the hounds meet in the vicinity, and many are the carriages and many the fair occupants that congregate to see the start. It is generally a very gay scene, with no lack of scarlet coats and good steeds, pretty dresses and sometimes pretty faces too; and though afterwards they enjoy many a good run, there are but few falls and fewer broken heads. But it is over the races that Pau gets really excited. Hunting only attracts the well-to-do, but all who can hire or borrow even a shandry make a point of not missing the "races." And these meetings are not few and far between, but about once a fortnight, for there is no "Jockey Club" at Pau, and consequently it pleases itself about the fixtures.

The course, which is some two miles from the town on the Bordeaux road, is overlooked by an imposing grand stand, which generally seems well filled, though the betting is not very heavy on the whole.

We drove over one afternoon, and after waiting for three events which to us were not very exciting, proceeded towards Lescar. The nearest way would have been by turning to the right by a white house on the Bordeaux road (not far from the race-course), but we continued along it instead for some distance, finally turning off down a narrow lane without any sign of a hedge. After following this for a length of time, we took the road at right angles leading between fields covered with gorse, and later, descending one or two steep hills with trees on either side, we re-ascended and entered the ancient town of Lescar, only to dip under the tottering walls of the ancient castle—a few minutes later—and mount again under a narrow archway to the church.

P. Joanne in his excellent guide-book calls it "the ancient Beneharum, destroyed about the year 841 by the Normans, rebuilt in 980 under the name of Lascurris. In the old chronicles it was called the "Ville Septénaire," because it possessed, it is said, seven churches, seven fountains, seven mills, seven woods, seven vineyards, seven gates and seven towers on the ramparts." The church now restored was formerly a cathedral, and there are some fine old mosaics (11th century) to be seen under the boarding near the altar. Jeanne d'Albret and other Béarnais sovereigns are buried there.

The Castle is very old, though the square tower dates from the 14th century only.

The whole town, so curious and ancient-looking, is well worth a visit, and forms a contrast in its fallen splendour to Pau's rising greatness, such as cannot fail to strike any intelligent observer.

Passing through the town, we took the road to the

right homewards, which joins the Bayonne route, but instead of continuing along the latter all the way, we branched off into the route de Billères, and came by the Villa Lacroix and the Hôtel de Londres back to the pension.

Another road leads from the Villa Lacroix over a brook, and past the establishment of the "Petites Sœurs des Pauvres" into the country, and in fact to Lescar. The brook is known as the Herrère, and by following the path to the left which runs beside it, the "Fontaine de Marnières" is reached. The water of this fountain is considered very pure and strengthening, and many people drink it daily.

The band is another attraction at Pau; twice a week in the afternoon they play in the Place Royale, and twice in the Parc Beaumont. The music is of a very good order, and excessively pleasing to listen to from beneath the shade of the trees. The Parc Beaumont is quite near the Place Royale, the principal entrance being at the end of the Rue du Lycée, close to the Hôtel Beau Séjour.

Balloon ascents were often the chief attraction on Sundays, which "all the world and his wife" went out to see. There is *a* casino in the Park, used occasionally for concerts, but *the* casino is behind the Hôtel Gassion, and though it was hardly finished enough for comfort when we saw it, that defect will soon doubtless be remedied.

Polo is generally played in the "Haute Plante" (in front of the Barracks), and bicycle races take place there also occasionally. It is only a step from this pleasure-ground to the cemetery, and though this nearness never affects the joy of the children on the roundabouts or the young people swinging, yet it is another practical example that "in the midst of life we are in death."

The Rue Bayard—on the left of the Haute Plante—leads to the cemetery gates, and the tombs extend behind the barracks; those of Protestants being divided from the Roman Catholics' by a carefully kept walk leading from the right-hand corner of the first or Roman Catholic portion!

There is a charm about this last resting-place in spite of its mournfulness, and the many flowers load the air with a delicious perfume. The marble statue of a Russian lady in fashionable costume, over her tomb, is considered a fine piece of sculpture, and many people go there simply to see it.

The two principal French churches are those of St. Martin and St. Jacques, but the latter is in every way the more beautiful. The "Palais de Justice" stands close to St. Jacques, but facing the Place Duplaa, where many of the best houses are situated. The Rue d'Orléans, communicating with the Place Duplaa and the Route de Bordeaux, contains many good French pensions, which have been previously mentioned.

By following the Rue St. Jacques past the church of the same name, and turning down the street which cuts it at right angles, called the "Rue de la Fontaine," the ancient part of the town can be reached. It may be here remarked that this mingling of the old with the new is one of the peculiar characteristics of Pau, and yet probably seven visitors out of ten fail to notice it. The other end of "Fountain Street" leads into the Rue de la Préfecture. This is one of the very busiest streets in Pau, and if after leaving one of the magnificent new hotels we traverse this busy street, and then suddenly plunge down the Rue de la Fontaine to what was once the bed of the castle fosse—where the houses are small and dirty, and the walls and slates barely hold together, so wretchedly old and tottering are they—where, instead of bustle and grandeur, there is only gloom and poverty, and in place of the enjoyment of the present, there is the longing for a lot a little less hard in the future ; we feel as though we had gone back several centuries in as many minutes, and have a decided wish to return to nineteenth-century civilisation again.

We did not find the rides and drives the least pleasant of our enjoyments, and there are so many places to visit, that picnics are plentiful as a matter of course.

The chief excursion from Pau is to Eaux Bonnes and Eaux Chaudes, but as there is a slight danger of damp beds there—if you get any beds at all—early in the year, we postponed this grand trip for another time.

Another long drive is to Lourdes and back, but this we did not take, as we meant to stop a night there later ; but one day we made up a party for Bétharram, which is a long way on the same road, and, under ordinarily kind auspices, a delightful day's outing.

If it was less pleasant than it might have been to us, the weather had a good deal to do with it, and the other causes may develop themselves in narration. There were ten of us, and we started in a grand yellow brake with four horses and a surly coachman. The morning was excessively warm, and some of the party were of such rotund proportions, that the thin ones were nearly lost sight of, if they chanced to sit between them, while the warmth approached to that of a cucumber frame with the sun on it. We attracted a good deal of attention as we *crawled* down the Rue Serviez and passed the entrance to the Parc Beaumont, down the hill to Bizanos; but as soon as the château that takes its name from the village was reached, we met with little admiration, except from the good people jogging along in tumble-down carts and shandries. The peasants seemed on the whole a good-natured lot, taking a joke with a smile often approaching a broad grin, and occasionally, but only very *occasionally*, attempting one in return. The following is an instance of one of these rare occasions:—We were walking beside the Herrère stream in the direction of the Fontaine de Marnières; several women were busy washing clothes at the water's edge, and above, spread out in all their glory, were three huge umbrellas—umbrellas of the size of those used on the Metropolitan 'buses, but of bright blue cloth on which the presence of clay was painfully evident. We asked the price without smiling, and the women, wondering, looked up. We said they must be very valuable, and we would give as much as *six sous* for any one of them. At this moment another woman, who had been listening to the conversation from a little garden behind, came up and said: "Those umbrellas belong to me, and they *are* worth a lot of money; but I will sell you one cheap *if you promise to send it to the Exhibition!*"

But to resume. After crossing the railway line beyond Bizanos, and leaving the pleasant little waterfall on the right, the sun began to pour down on us very fiercely, and all we could do, wedged in as we were, was to appear happy and survey the country.

It was curious to note the method of training the vines up the various trees by the roadside. The simplicity and efficacy of the method seemed plain enough, but with memories of the difficulty experienced in guarding our own fruit even with glass-tipped walls to defend it, we were forced to the conviction that in the Pyrenees fruit stealers are unknown. Perhaps, however, the "grapes are always sour," or sufficiently high up to give the would-be thief time to think of the penalty, which probably would be "higher" still.

The road continues nearly in a direct line through Assat (5 miles), but when that village was left behind, the mountains seemed to be considerably nearer, and even the snow summits—a bad sign of rain—appeared within a fairly easy walk.

The painful odour of garlic frequently assailed our nostrils passing through the hamlets, and though it is not quite as bad as the Japanese root *daikon*, yet to have to talk to a man who has been eating it, is a positive punishment. We would fain bring about a reform among the people, getting them to substitute some other healthily-scented vegetable in place of the objectionable one. To this end we composed a verse to a very old but popular tune, styling it

"THE MARCH OF THE MEN OF GARLIC."

>Men of Garlic—large your numbers,
>Long indeed your conscience slumbers,
>Can't you change and eat cu-cumbers?
>   Men of Garlic, say!
> They are sweet and tender,
> Short and thick or slender.
>Then, we know well your breath won't smell
>   And sickness' pangs engender.
>Men of Garlic, stop your scorning,
>Change your food and hear our warning,
>See the day of Progress dawning,
>   Give three cheers—Hurray!

Doubtless the fact of the verse being in English will militate against its efficiency, but before we had time to turn it into French, we had passed to the right of the quaint old town of Nay, and were entering Coarraze (10½ miles). As we bore off to the right across the river, the old castle—where Henry IV. spent a great part of his childhood like any peasant child—towered above us, and the scenery around became considerably more picturesque than any we had passed through that morning. The banks of the river were more shapely, and the alternation of bushes and meadow, with the varying lights and shades on the distant peaks and the nearer slopes, would have seemed more than beautiful, if our wedged positions and the accompanying warmth had not somewhat evaporated our admiration. Though the heat remained, the sun had disappeared behind huge banks of clouds, as we at length entered Bétharram (15 miles), so, instead of pulling up at the hotel, we drove on to the beautiful ivy-hung bridge, a great favourite with artists. This really belongs to the hamlet of Lestelle, which adjoins Bétharram, and is so picturesque that the villagers ought to be proud of it; doubtless in the old days, when Notre Dame de Bétharram's shrine was the cherished pilgrimage —now superseded by the attractions of N. D. de Lourdes—many thousand "holy" feet crossed and recrossed this ancient bridge!

In order to reach the hotel we had to ascend slightly to turn the vehicle, much to the consternation of one of the party, who, clasping the back rail with both hands and endeavouring to look brave, could not withhold a small scream which escaped from the folds of her veil.

The dining-room of the hotel smelt decidedly close, so we spread our sumptuous lunch on tables outside; but Jupiter Pluvius soon showed his disapproval of our plans, and forced us to go within, where a fine specimen of a French soldier had done his best to fill the place with smoke. However, we managed fairly well, in spite of some sour wine which we tried, under the name of "Jurançon vieux," for the "good of the house" and the "worse of ourselves." As the rain passed off ere we had finished, we afterwards repaired to the "Via Crucis," where there is a small chapel at every turn till the "Calvary" is reached at the summit. The first chapel is beside the road, midway between the hotel and the bridge, and the view from the summit on a fine day is said to be very good; but when only half-way, the rain came down in such torrents that we were glad to return to the inn for shelter. For two hours the downpour lasted, but it cooled the air and rendered the return journey a little more supportable; and when we arrived at the house, we also arrived at the decision that never again to a picnic, as far as we were concerned, should thinness and rotundity go side by side!

There is no doubt that a landau is the most comfortable vehicle for a drive of any length, although some very comfortable little T-carts, with good ponies between the shafts, can be hired too. We often used the latter for drives to Assat and over the suspension-bridge—so old and shaky—and home by Gélos and Jurançon; while at other times, taking the necessaries for afternoon tea, we drove as far as Nay, crossing the river to enter its ancient square—in which stand the Townhall and the Maison Carrée, of historical fame—and then leaving the tanneries and houses behind, sought some quiet spot down by the water, for sketching and enjoying our tea.

Rides or drives on the coteaux (hills) in the vicinity are very pleasant, as the views from certain points are particularly fine. Of these the most popular is to Perpignaa, two hours being sufficient for the drive there and back. It is a nice walk for an average pedestrian, and the road is easy to find. We generally started in the afternoon, passing across the bridge and through Jurançon, and where the road forks, bearing along the Gan road to the right. Then, taking the first turning to the right, leading between fields, we reached an avenue of trees, with a village beyond. We then followed the road across the bridge to the left, and kept bearing in that direction till we reached the foot of the coteau, where there is only one route, and consequently no chance of taking any but the right one! We heard of a case of two young ladies going off in a donkey cart, intending to sketch the view above Perpignaa, who, when they reached the avenue, turned down to the right and wandered along the bank of the Gave as far as the donkey would go, and then sketched a church steeple in despair. But such a mistake is quite unnecessary; and they would doubtless have remedied theirs, if they had not found it obligatory at last to push behind in order to make the donkey move homewards. Although very hoarse and tired when they arrived, they had voice enough left to say they "wouldn't go sketching in a donkey cart again!"

From the foot of the hill the road zigzags, making a fairly easy gradient to the summit, on which stands a house whose owner kindly allows visitors to walk about his grounds and participate in the view. When riding, we followed the road that continues on the right for several miles, in order to prolong the pleasure produced by the exercise and the view.

Another pleasant ride is by way of the coteaux to Gan, and back by the road, or *vice versâ;* but we always preferred the former, as the horses had the hill work while fresh, and then the level home. In the first instance we found this track by accident. We had passed through Jurançon, and at the spot where the road forks debated which to take, finally deciding on the left one, but this we only followed for a few yards, taking again the first turning to the right, which brought us over the railway line direct to the hills. Winding up through the trees, we passed a tricyclist pushing his machine before him, who informed us that we were on the way to Gan. Of this, after we had ridden up and down, wound round hillsides and passed through pleasant dingles, we were at length assured by descending into that village, from which we got safely home in spite of a " bolting " attempt on the part of one of the " fiery " steeds.

To thoroughly enjoy the longer drive to Piétat it is better to make a picnic of it. We started about ten one lovely morning, turning to the left beyond Jurançon, crossing the line to Oloron—on the main road—and later on, bearing more round in the same direction, and beginning to ascend. As on the hills to Gan, we were perpetually mounting only to descend a great part of the distance again, but ever and anon catching glimpses of the valley in which Assat and Nay lay, and of Pau itself, besides the lovely snow hills stretching as far as eye could reach. When Piétat was arrived at, there was but little to interest us in what we saw there of a half-finished church and two cottages; but the view on all sides after we had walked along the grassy plateau was very lovely, especially as the lights and shades were everywhere so perfect. Having selected a cosy spot and spread the luncheon, we were besieged by children anxious to sell us flowers and apples, and to share whatever we would give them. They were hard to get rid of even with promises of something when we had finished, and when at last they did go, an elderly female took their place with most generous offers of unlocking the church for us. There was an old sweet-toned bell in front of the western door, and a half-finished sculpture of the " Descent from the Cross" over it. The interior of the edifice was sufficiently roofed for a portion to be utilised for prayer, and the high altar and two lateral ones were already erected.

After culling a quantity of the beautiful feather moss from the hedgerows, we re-entered the carriage, and descended the hill into the Gave valley, crossing the suspension-bridge by Assat, and through the village into the main road, and home by Bizanos. It was the time of the carnival, and on the following day Bizanos—which has an evil repute for bad egg-throwing on festive occasions—was to be the scene of the mumming. Luckily they did not attempt to practise on us, though as we drove up through the town we met bands of gaily-dressed individuals parading the streets.

These bands consisted of about thirty, mostly men decked in a preponderance of red, white, and blue, and usually accompanied by a tableau arrangement on a cart. Every twenty yards they stopped, went through a series of antics, supposed to be country dances, to the tune of the cornet and a fiddle, and then brought round the hat, frequently embracing any woman who objected to give her sous.

A carnival such as this combines a holiday with money-making to the mummers, and as long as they can get money in this fashion, they certainly cannot be blamed for taking their amusement in such a highly practical manner.

There are several private coaches at Pau, which turn out in grand style on race days; and balls, concerts, and kettledrums abound, with private theatricals occasionally. We attempted to get up "Poor Pillicoddy," but were very unlucky about it. Firstly, when in full rehearsal, our Mrs. O'Scuttle became unwell, and we had to look for another, and when we had found her and were getting into shape again, her nautical husband put the whole ship on the rocks and wrecked our hopes by losing his voice.

However, our departure was very nigh, and packing is an excellent cure for disappointment, though we were interrupted in that one morning with a request to write "something" in the visitors' book. With the memories of our pleasant stay upon us, we do not think we can err in reproducing one contribution, which was styled

"IDYLLIC COLBERT."

(*With apologies to* Mr. W. S. GILBERT.)

If you're anxious for to dwell in a very fine hotel
  By the mountain's wide expanse,
You at once had best repair to that house so good though *chère*
  Called the "Grand Hôtel de France."
Or if for food your craze is, you still can give your praises
  To the *chef* of its *cuisine*.

Your taste you need not fetter, for 'tis said in Pau, no better
    Has ever yet been seen.
But this I have to say, you will not like your stay
    As much as if at Pension Colbert you the time had spent,
And such a time, I'm very sure, you never would repent.

If I'm eloquent in praise of those most peculiar days
    Which now have passed away,
'Tis to tell you, as a man, what awful risks I ran
    Lest my heart should chance to stray.
I never would pooh-pooh! 'tis cruel so to do,
    Though often weak and ill,
For they my plaints would stop, with a juicy mutton-chop,
    Or a mild and savoury pill!
And this I have to say, you're bound to like your stay,
    And never in your life I'm very sure will you repent
      The time in Pension Colbert's walls and well-trimmed garden spent.

And if a tantalizing passion of a gay lawn tennis fashion
    Should fire your love of sport,
On the neat and well-kept lawn, a net that's *never* torn
    Hangs quiv'ring o'er the court.
Or if your voice you'd raise in sweet or high-tun'd lays,
    You'll find a piano there,
And *birdies* too will sing, like mortals—that's a thing
    You'll never hear elsewhere—
And then you're bound to say that you have liked your stay,
    And never in your life I'm very sure will you repent
      The time in Pension Colbert's walls and well-trimm'd garden spent.

If for hunting you've a liking, you can don a costume striking,
    And proceed to chase the fox.
Or if you're fond of driving, *perhaps* by some contriving
    You may mount a coach's box.
If picnics are your pleasure, you can go to them at leisure,
    And lunch on sumptuous fare,
And though maybe, perforce, you'll get lamb without mint sauce.
They never starve you there.
And always you will say, that you've enjoyed your stay,
    And never in your life I'm very sure will you repent
      The time in Pension Colbert's walls and well-trimm'd garden spent.

As Mrs. and Miss Blunt and Mr. Sydney had definitely decided to spend the time at Biarritz while

I stayed at Bigorre, I turned my attention to discovering if any other acquaintances were proceeding in the same direction as myself. In this I was successful, and in company with Mr. H—— and his two daughters, and Mrs. Willesden and Miss Leonards, bade "au revoir" to Pau, with the prospect of a long spell of beautiful scenery if the clerk of the weather could only be controlled, by longings and hopes.

CHAPTER II.

BAGNÈRES DE BIGORRE.

Backward Spring—Hôtel Beau Séjour—Effect of the war of '70 on the English Colony—The " Coustous "—The Church of St. Vincent—Géruzet's Marble Works—Donkeys—Up the Monné—Bains de Santé—Bains de Grand Pré—Salut Avenue and Baths—"Ai-ue, Ai-ue"—Luncheon—Daffodils—The Summit and the View—The " Castle-Mouly "—The Tapêre—Mde. Cottin—Mont Bédat—Gentians—The Croix de Manse—" The Lady's Farewell to her Asinine Steed "—Market-day—The Old Iron and Shoe Dealers—Sunday—A Cat Fight—The English Church—To the Col d'Aspin—" The Abbé's Song "—Baudéan—Campan, its People and Church—Wayside Chapels—Ste. Marie—The route to Gripp, &c.—Payole—The Pine Forest—The Col d'Aspin—The View from the Monné Rouge—" The Plaint of the Weather-beaten Pine "—The Menu at Payole—Hurrah for the Milk !—Departures—Divine Music—Asté—Gabrielle d'Estrelle—The Ivied Ruins—The Church—Pitton de Tournefort—Gerde—The Pigeon Traps—The Cattle Market—The Jacobin Tower—Theatre—Grand Etablissement des Thermes—Hospice Civil—Eglise des Carmes—Mount Olivet—Madame Cheval, her Cakes and Tea—Bigorre in Tears.

WE had a bright day for our journey to Bigorre, and the country looked pretty, though very backward for April, but this was owing to the late frosts, which had been felt everywhere. Bigorre itself was no exception, and instead of all the charms of spring ready to welcome us, the leaves were only just taking courage to unfurl. Our first impressions were consequently anything but favourable, though our comfortable quarters in the Hôtel Beau Séjour compensated us to a certain degree. To the French and Spaniards, Bigorre is only a summer resort, but as it is considered to possess a very mild climate, many English reside there all the year round. In fact, before the war of 1870 there was quite an English colony there, but the chance of a Prussian advance dispersed it, and many were the hardships endured by some of those who had stayed to the last moment, in their endeavours to reach the coast.

Our first two days were more or less wet, and by reports of heavy snowstorms around us, we were unanimously of opinion that we had come too early. However, with a little sun the place soon began to look more cheerful, and a few days' fine weather wrought quite a change.

The hotel looks down on the Place Lafayette and the commencement of the avenue known as the "Coustous." This name puzzled us! We tried to find its derivation in French, without success, and Greek and German were no better. Latin seemed to solve the difficulty with the word "Custos," since it is said that the ancient guardians of the town formerly marched up and down beneath these fine old trees; so we decided to hunt no further but to translate "Coustous" into the "Guards' Walk." Having settled that knotty point, we took a stroll in the avenue, and later, paid a visit to the parish church of St. Vincent which is close by. It is particularly chaste inside, some portions dating from the 14th century, but the 15th and 16th have each had a share in the construction. Some of the altars are made of fine Pyrenean marble, and the Empress Eugenie is said to have given the wooden image of the Virgin on the pedestal.

As the various marbles obtained in the vicinity are

exceedingly interesting, and in many cases very beautiful, a very pleasant half-hour can be spent at one of the many marble works which the town possesses. Fired with this idea ourselves, one gloomy day after lunch we sallied from the hotel, down the road to the left of the church, through the public gardens, and—attracted by the marble pillar—down the lane to the right of it, which at length brought us to the works of Monsieur Géruzet. The huge blocks of the rough stone were first inspected, then we saw the various processes of cutting, ornamenting and polishing, and finally were ushered into the show-room, where all kinds of articles from a sleeve-stud to a sideboard were on sale. The cigar-trays and letter-weights were most reasonable, but it is not necessary to buy at all—and gratuities are not supposed to be permitted.

There were some fine turn-outs in the donkey line which deserve notice, the peculiarity of these animals here being, to go where they are wanted, and even to trot about it. Looking out of the window one morning, we were immediately attracted by the tiniest of donkeys galloping across the "place" with two big men behind it; and later on in the day, a neat specimen of the same tribe passed down the "Coustous," dragging a small dogcart, almost completely filled by the form of a French female, two or three times as large as her donkey.

But like other things, the "genus asininus" is very variable, almost as much so as the barometer, and those "on hire" for riding purposes were quite as obstinate as their relations in other countries; at least so the ladies declared who tried them, and they ought to know. Their bitter experience was gained in a trip up the Monné, the highest mountain in the immediate vicinity, being 2308 feet above Bigorre, or 4128 above the sea. Our party was seven in all, supplemented by a broken-winded and coughing horse (called Towser; French, *Tousseux*), two very obstinate donkeys, and a particularly polite donkey boy. Add to these, three luncheon-baskets and various sticks, umbrellas, and parasols, and the cavalcade is complete. We left the hotel and passed up the Coustous in rather mixed order, which improved as we turned into the Rue d'Alsace, and leaving the Great Bathing Establishment * and French Protestant Church on the right, and the Baths of Santé and Grand Pré on the left, entered the "Salut" avenue, which in due time brought us to the baths of the same name. The ascent, which by the road is most circuitous and easy, commences from thence. But though easy, the donkeys did not attempt to conceal their dislike for the work at a very early stage, and when the blasting in the quarries was hushed, "the voice of the charmer" (i.e. donkey boy) might have been heard, painfully resembling the sounds made by the traveller with his head over the vessel's side, urging them on, "Ai-ue—Ai-ue." As we rounded the last of the minor peaks, "the keen demands of appetite" were not to be resisted; so on a nice green plateau, with the object of our desires in full view, we discussed the luncheon. Shawls were spread, plates handed round, bottles gurglingly uncorked, and chicken and "pâté de foie gras" distributed until everyone was steadily at work.

The mountain air seemed to affect the "vin ordinaire"; everyone averred it was as good as "Margaux,"

* Grand Etablissement de Thermes.

while the chicken was voted delicious, and the pâté superb.

This important business over, a start was again made, and though the donkeys were still obstinate, we managed to make progress. Daffodils were growing in profusion as we neared the summit, making the hill crest seem crowned with gold At last, after one or two nasty narrow bits of path, barely affording sufficient footing for the animals, we gained the top, anxious to enjoy the view. Unhappily, the tips of the highest peaks were hidden in the clouds, but the general view was excellent, so we endeavoured to be content. With our backs to Bigorre, we had the Pic du Midi (9440 ft) and the Montaigu (7681 ft.) right before us, with the small Val de Serris and the finer Val de Lesponne beneath. More to the left, the continuation of the Campan Valley leading to Luchon, in which, as far as Ste. Marie, the route is visible. On the extreme left lay the four villages of Gerde, Asté, Baudéan and Campan, with the Pêne de l'Heris (5226 ft.) and the Ordincède rearing above them. Looking in the direction of Bigorre, we could see on our right the trees fringing the hills above Gerde, and known as the Palomières; and slightly to the left Lourdes and its lake, with the entrance to the Argelès valley further round in the same direction, and close to the wooded hill known as the Castel-Mouly (3742 ft.). The Tapêre (a small stream) flows from this last-named hill into a narrow glen, on the left side of which Madame Cottin wrote the "Exiles of Siberia." The hill above, known as "Mont Bédat," and surmounted with a statue of the Virgin, is a favourite walk from the town, the ascent for a moderate walker taking about forty-five minutes.

After twenty minutes to enjoy this panorama we began the descent on the Castel-Mouly side, and were very soon forced to make short and sometimes slippery cuts, to avoid the banks of snow lying in the path. We easily managed to strike the proper path again, however, and soon found ourselves at our "luncheon plateau." We now bore along to the left, finding several large gentians, and gradually, by dint of short cuts, we reached the Croix de Manse—a plateau where four roads meet. Taking the one leading from the Bédat, we were soon deposited at the hotel in safety.

The ladies were inexpressibly glad to give up their donkeys, and Miss Leonards considered her experiences so bitter as to wish them to be handed down to posterity under the title of

"THE LADY'S FAREWELL TO HER ASININE STEED."

My donkey steed! my donkey steed! that standest slyly by,
With thy ill-combed mane and patchy neck—thy brown and
    cunning eye,
I will not mount the Monné's height, or tread the gentle
    mead
Upon thy back again: oh slow and wretched donkey steed!

The sun may rise, the sun may set, but ne'er again on thee,
Will I repeat the sorry ride from which at length I'm free;
I'd sooner walk ten thousand times, though walking would
    be vain,
Than ever mount, my donkey steed, upon thy back again.

Perchance in *nightmare's* fitful dreams thou'lt amble into
    sight,
Perchance once more thy cunning eye will turn on me its
    light.
Again I'll raise my parasol—*in vain*—to make thee speed,
A parasol is nought to thee, my wretched donkey steed.

'Twas only when at my request some kindly hand would
  chide,
Or sharply thrust a pointed stick against thy shaggy side,
That the slow blood that in thee runs would quicken once
  again,
For though my parasol I broke, my efforts *still* were vain.

Did I ill use thee? Surely not! such things could never be!
Although thou wentest slowest when I fain would haste to
  tea,
Creeping at snail's pace only—while I couldn't make thee
  learn
That donkeys' legs were never made to stop at ev'ry turn.

At ev'ry turn!—such weary work—I knew not what to do:
Oh nevermore!—no, nevermore!—would I that ride renew.
How very wide thy jaws were kept—how far thrown back
  thine ears,
As though to make me think thee ill and fill my soul with
  fears.

Safe and unmounted will I roam with stately step alone,
No more to feel, on thee, such pains and aches in ev'ry bone:
And if I rest beside a well, perchance I'll pause and think,
How even if I'd brought thee there, I couldn't make thee
  drink.

I couldn't even make thee move! Away, the ride is o'er!
Away! for I shall rue the day on which I see thee more!
They said thou wert so meek and good, and I'm not over
  strong,
I took their *kind* advice, but oh! their *kind* advice was
  wrong.

Who said I'd gladly give thee up? Who said that thou
  wert old?
'Tis true! 'tis true! my donkey steed! and I alas was *sold*.
With joy I see thy form depart—that form which ne'er again
Shall bear me up the mountain-side and fill my soul with
  pain.

After such a potent warning posterity will doubtless avoid "donkey steeds" altogether.

Saturday is the great market-day of the week, and not only then is the "Place de Strasbourg," at the end of the "Rue du Centre," well crowded, but even—as happens on no other day—the Place Lafayette, in front of the hotel, and the top of the Coustous as well. The first-named is the fruit, flower, and vegetable market; the second, the grain and potato; and the third, the iron and old shoe market. The amount and variety of old iron and cast-off shoes exposed for sale is astonishing. And if the vendors were given to crying their wares they might indulge in something like the following—of course translated:—

" Now who's for an 'upper,' a 'heel,' or a 'sole'?
  This way for some fine rusty chain!
The sum of ten halfpence will purchase the whole,
  And surely you cannot complain!

" Just glance at this slipper, whose fellow is lost;
  Here's a boot that was only worn thrice;
A hammer, your honour, at half what it cost;
  I'm sure that's a reasonable price."

The curious characters loafing, begging, buying and selling, quite defy description, though the resemblance of many to the ape tribe was conspicuous. One ancient individual, presiding over an " umbrella hospital," presented an interesting spectacle surrounded by *adult* shoe-blacks whose trade did not appear to be too lucrative.

Sunday is usually a very quiet day out of the season, but on our first Sunday morning the Place de Strasbourg was the scene of a real cat-fight. The combatants quite tabooed spitting and scratching, and went to work with their teeth. After a few squeaks and a great deal of rolling in the dust, a magnaminous dog appeared on the scene, and after separating them, pursued the victor down the street. The rest of the day, as usual, passed peacefully, and the pleasant services in the pretty little English Church were much enjoyed. It is situated near Dussert and Labal's marble works, just off the Rue des Pyrenées, leading to Campan, about a hundred yards beyond the Coustous, and is reached by crossing a small wooden bridge.

Monday broke very fine, and as the market people had notified that the Col d'Aspin was now open, we made up a party of ten, just filling two landaus, for this fifteen-mile drive. We did not start till eleven, and by that time the clouds had commenced to show themselves, but hoping for better things, we went ahead. Following the Campan road, we soon left Gerde and the Palomières above it, in the distance, and in a few moments the village of Asté as well. A little further on we met a barouche, lolling back in which sat a priest. His hands were clasped o'er his breast, his spectacled eyes were fixed upwards, and judging by the expression of his mouth and the movement of his lips, he was endeavouring to put some pleasant, self-contented thoughts into words. We took the liberty of guessing what he was saying, and set it down as

"THE ABBÉ'S SONG."

Oh! I am an Abbé, an Abbé am I,
   And I'm fond of my dinner and wine.
Some say I'm a sinner, but that I deny,
   And I never am heard to repine.
'Tis said what a pity I can't have a wife,
   But I'm saved from the *chance* of all naggings and strife,
While in my barouche I can ride where I will,
   Feeling life not half bad, though the world may be ill.

I always wear glasses, but that's to look sage,
   And not 'cause my eyesight is dim,
For when sweet maids I view of a loveable age,
   I contrive to look over the rim.

> And when I'm alone with the glass at my lips,
>   I am ready to swear, as I pause 'twixt the sips,
> That as long as the world does not hamper my will,
>   I think I can manage to live in it still.

A short distance before reaching Baudéan a road strikes to the right up the Vallon de Serris, and a short distance beyond, another, in the same direction, strikes up the Vallée de Lesponne, *en route* for the Lac Bleu (6457 ft.) and the Montaigu (7681 ft.). When Baudéan and its quaint old church were left in our rear, and we were nearing Campan, we witnessed a fierce struggle between a young bull-calf and a native. The calf objected very strongly to the landaus, and wished to betake itself to the adjacent country to avoid them. To this the native very naturally objected in turn, and a struggle was the result, in which the calf was worsted and reduced to order.

Campan is a curious old town, with a quaint market-place, whose roof rests on well-worn stone pillars. Turning a corner, we came on a somewhat mixed collection of men, women, oxen, and logs of wood. The French flag was fixed against a tree, and painted on a board underneath it were the familiar words, "débit de tabac," with an arrow or two pointing round the corner, but no tobacco shop was in sight.

The peasants thronged the windows as we drove down the street, but the greater number were weird and decrepit females, with faces like the bark of an ancient oak-tree.

The old church, which stands near the market-place is well worth a visit. Passing under an archway on the right side of the road, we entered a court-yard, in which stands a marble statue erected in honour of the late curé, and on the right of this is the entrance into the church.

After leaving Campan the road ascends slightly through several small hamlets, each possessing a proportionately small chapel at the wayside, till Ste. Marie (2965 ft.) is reached. Here the road bifurcates, the branch to the right leading to Gripp, Tramesaïgues, the Col du Tourmalet, and Barèges; the branch to the left, along which we continued, to the Col d'Aspin, Arreau, Bordères, Col de Peyresourde (5070 ft.), and Luchon (2065 ft.). From Ste. Marie the grandeur of the scenery increases. Besides the Montaigu and the Pic du Midi on the right, on the left are the Pêne de l'Heris (5226 ft.) and the Crête d'Ordincède (5358 ft. about), with their wooded crests uplifted above the range of lower hills, dotted with the huts of the shepherds. Still ascending slightly, we passed Payole (3615 ft.), where a head thrust out of the window of the Hôtel de la Poste showed us it was at any rate occupied, and as we drove past at a good pace, visions of a pleasant tea rose before us.

We were soon mounting the zigzags through the splendid pine woods, and enjoyed the delicious glimpses down the deep moss-grown glades, with the scent of the rising sap in our nostrils. The glimpses on the mountains up and down the road were very felicitous also. On emerging from the forest the road was rather narrow for the carriage for several yards, the snow being two to three feet deep on either side, but as soon as this was passed, another three-quarter mile of open driving brought us to the Col d'Aspin (4920 ft.). The view from this spot is very fine, but to really enjoy the scenery to the fullest extent, we mounted the crest on the left, called the Monné Rouge (5759 ft.),

THE PINE FOREST NEAR THE COL D'ASPIN.

and were well rewarded. Although, as too often happens, the highest peaks were in the mist, we could see the whole extent of the valleys, and the tops of the lower mountains. The range of sight is magnificent; the Maladetta (10,866 ft.) only just visible to the east, the huge Posets (11,047 ft.) standing out frowningly to the south-south-east, as well as the Pez (10,403 ft.) and the Clarabide (10,254 ft. about), and many others. While not only the valley of Séoube, just passed through, and the valley of Aure, in which Arreau lies, are visible, but to the north-west even the plain of the Garonne as well. As the clouds were gradually obscuring the scene, we made our way at a smart pace through the pines back towards the inn at Payole. One weather-beaten old fir, hung with lichen, devoid of all its former garb of green, seemed to appeal to us for pity; we noticed it both when ascending and descending, and its misery at dying when all the trees around were growing anew, we have set down as

"THE PLAINT OF THE WEATHER-BEATEN PINE."

Behold I stand by the Aspin road, an old and worn-out Pine,
The years I cannot recollect that make this life of mine:
The snows have fallen o'er my crest, the winds have whistled high,
For tens of years the winter's frost I managed to defy;
But now the fiat has gone forth, the flame of life is dead,
And nevermore I'll feel the storms that beat about my head.

I've watch'd the carriage travellers pass so gaily on their way,
I've heard the capercailzie's note at early dawning grey;
But now, alas! my doom is sealed, I have not long to wait,
For when the axe has laid me low the fire will be my fate.
Farewell to sun, farewell to storm, to birds and travellers all,
—Oh sad to think that one so great should have so great a fall!

As some of the party had gone on earlier, we found the table spread when we reached the Inn de la Poste; and after a warm at the kitchen fire proceeded to discuss the repast, of which the following is the *menu* :—

MENU.

SOUP.

Tea.

FISH.

Cold Minnows.

ROASTS.

Remains of Cold Chicken.   Remains of Paté de Foie Gras.

COLD.

Household *Bread*—very sour.

MADE DISH.

Butter.

SWEETS.

Sponge Biscuits.

DESSERT.

Apples and Oranges.

WINES AND LIQUEURS.

Vin Ordinaire, Water with very little Whisky, Kirschwasser.

We were unable to procure any addition to our meal from the innkeeper, except sour bread and sugar. Our tea had to be drank without milk, as the cow had gone for a stroll up the mountain and was out of reach of the post-office. Having suggested to our host that a telegram might be of use, he disappeared grinning, and in about ten minutes the servant entered with a bottle containing the precious liquid. The shout of joy that rose to the rafters rather startled the quiet female, but it was spontaneous, not to be suppressed, and told of a happy finish to our not over sumptuous tea.

The drive from thence home was decidedly chilly, but nothing exciting happened, though occasional glimpses of the snow peaks were enjoyed, and many fine specimens of the genus bovus, dragging carts laden with trees (or all that remained of them), were passed by the way.

The entire excursion occupied six hours and a half.

A few days afterwards our sociable circle at the hotel was much reduced, and among others the Clipper family departed. We missed Mr. Clipper greatly, for though bearing strong evidence to Darwin's theory about the face, he was a chatty companion and capital "raconteur," while his facility for remembering names, even of places visited in his youngest days, was really remarkable.

Nor could we easily spare the four sylph-like Misses Clipper, for with them vanished all hopes of delicious music in the evening. Ah, that was music! The way they played together the "Taking of Tel-el-Kebir" took us by storm. The silent march through the dead of night, the charge, the cheers, the uncertain rifle fire, and then the thunder of the cannon was so effective, that the landlord rose in haste from his dinner, and anxiously inquired if the pier-glass had fallen through the piano; reassured, he went back to his meal, but whether the "taking of the redoubt," or the "pursuit of the fugitives," or even the capital imitation of the bagpipes—which followed in due course—interfered with his digestion (it might have been a regard for his piano), we never learnt, but his face showed unmistakable signs of annoyance for the rest of the evening.

The next morning—which was Saturday—Miss Leonards, Mrs. Willesden, and myself took a walk to the villages of Asté and Gerde. They lie on the opposite side of the river Adour, and are within an easy walk. The market people were coming in a continuous stream along the Campan road, some in long carts crowded sardine-like, some in traps, some on donkeys, but the majority on foot. We stopped two of the most crowded carts and asked them to make room for us. The inmates of the former took it as a joke and drove off chuckling; but those in the second took the matter-of-fact view and began squeezing about, till, having a space of about four inches by three, one man said he thought they could manage; however, not wishing to "sit familiar," we thanked him, but declined to trouble him any further.

The first bridge over the river, built of stone, leads to Gerde and Asté, but we preferred to take the longer route, which continues along the Campan road, till, after passing several smaller wooden bridges, it turns to the left between two houses over an iron bridge, and strikes straight into Asté. Before entering the town we glanced over in the direction of Campan, and caught a fine glimpse of the Houn Blanquo (6411 ft.), and the Pic du Midi, with a bit of the Montaigu. Asté is interesting, formerly a fief of the Grammont family; it has been associated with not a few celebrated characters, and though that does not enhance the value of the surrounding property (since the Grammont estate is now in the market), yet of course it renders the village more worthy of a visit.

The picturesque and ivy-covered ruin is all that remains of the feudal castle where Gabrielle d'Estrelle* lived and loved, and whither the renowned Henry IV. (the object of that love) came over from his castle at Pau on frequent visits.

The church, with its Campan marble porch, is celebrated for the image of the Virgin which it contains, and which is greatly reverenced in the neighbourhood.

Asté was honoured with a long visit from Pitton de Tournefort, a celebrated French naturalist, and the fact is commemorated by an engraved tablet affixed to the house in which he passed his nights.

The tablet is on the left-hand side of the main street (going towards Gerde), and the inscription—which is in verse—runs as follows:—

> " Pitton de Tournefort dans cet humble réduit,
> De ses fatigues de jour se reposait la nuit.
> Lorsqu' explorant nos monts qu'on ignorait encore,
> Ce grand homme tressait la couronne de flore."
> MDCCCXXXII.   M. B.

Which might be translated—

> " Pitton de Tournefort when tired for the day,
> In this hole made his bed, on a shakedown of hay.
> Our hills, long despised, he was pleased to explore,
> And we thank him for lib'rally paying the score!"
> 1832.

Taking the path leading to the right, we managed by dint of a little wading to reach Gerde, a village possessing little internal interest besides the neat church, but otherwise known to fame from the "palo-

* So the oldest inhabitant said!

mières," or pigeon-traps, worked between the trees which fringe the hills above it. During the autumn, when the pigeons are migrating, huge nets are spread between the trees, and on the approach of a flock, men, perched in a lofty "crow's nest," throw out a large wooden imitation of a hawk, at the sight of which the pigeons dip in their flight and rush into the nets, which — worked on the pulley system — immediately secure them. There are three species taken in the traps: the wood pigeon, the ringed wood pigeon, and the wild dove.

Leaving Gerde by the principal thoroughfare, we came back to Bagnères by the Toulouse road, passing the Cattle Market — held in a triangular space shaded with trees — on the left; and the Géruzet Marble Works, and later the Parish Church, on the right.

With the exception of the baths or Thermes, we did not find many places

PALOMIÈRES DE GERDE.

of interest in the town. The old Jacobin tower, surmounted by a clock, in the Rue de l'Horloge, is all that remains of a convent built in the 15th century, but is in a good state of preservation. The theatre is part of what was formerly the "Chapel of St. John," used by the Templars. The porch over the doorway was erected in the 13th century, and is of the Transition style, utterly incongruous to the use now made of it; but this kind of sacrilege is unhappily now becoming of common occurrence! Leaving the theatre, in a short space we were in the "Place des Thermes," where the New Casino is being built among the shrubs on the right. The "Grand Etablissement," which occupies the centre of the "Place," contains seven different springs, and there is another in the circular building outside, the latter being only used for drinking purposes. On the first floor of the building are the library (to the left), the geological room (in the centre), and the picture gallery (to the right). The corridors leading to the first and last are panelled with good specimens of the Pyrenean marbles, and in the same room with the pictures is a supposed model of a section of the Pyrenees—anybody gaining any information from it deserves a prize.

To the left of this establishment stands the "Hospice Civil," a fine building in grey stone.

The Carmelite Church, on the left of the road leading to Mount Olivet, where several pleasant villas are situated, is now closed, the "order" having been dispersed two years ago; so nothing is to be seen there of interest except the sculpture representing the "miracle of the loaves" over the door.

One institution must not be forgotten, viz., the afternoon tea or coffee at Madame Cheval's.

This good lady presides over a confectioner's shop opposite the end of the Hôtel (Beau Séjour), in the Rue du Centre. Her cakes and coffee are good, and, thanks to our enlightened instructions, anyone taking some tea to her can have it properly made, and be provided with the necessary adjuncts for enjoying it ; cream even being attainable if ordered the previous day. We spent many a pleasant half-hour there, and can well recommend others to follow our example.

Towards the end of the month Mr. H—— and his daughters moved on to Luchon, as their time was limited ; and the last week saw the departure of Mrs. Willesden and Miss Leonards for England, whereat Bigorre was as tearful and miserable as a steady downpour could make it. I had serious thoughts of moving on to Luchon for two or three days myself, and a driver who had brought two men thence over the Col d'Aspin, offered to take me back for twenty francs, but learning next day that there were five feet of snow on the Col, and that Luchon was wretchedly cold, I decided to wait till later on, a decision in no way regretted.

Although during the latter part of our stay the weather was agreeable, and the influence of spring manifest, I was not sorry when the day for moving forward arrived, and though Madame Cheval, when I broke the news to her over my solitary cup of coffee, looked as concerned as she could, and murmured something to the effect that "all her customers were going away," yet with the assurance that some day soon a party of us would pay her a visit, she managed to smile again !

CHAPTER III.

LOURDES.

The Journey to Tarbes—The Buffet and the Nigger—Lourdes Station in the Wet—Importunate "Cochers"—Hôtel des Pyrénées—"Red tape" and Porters—Lourdes in Sunshine—Sightseeing—The "Rue de la Grotte"—"The Cry of the Lourdes Shopkeepers"—Candle-sellers—The Grotto—Abject Reverence—The Church—St. Bernard—Interior of Church—The Panorama—Admirable Effect—Rue du Fort—The Castle—The View from the Tower—Pie de Mars, or Ringed Ousels.

THE railway run from Bigorre to Lourdes is by no means a long one, the actual distance being only twenty-six and a quarter miles, and actual time in the train about one and a half hours, but the break at Tarbes considerably prolongs it.

The early morning had been wet, and showers continued till the afternoon, but the sun condescended to come out as the train wound slowly out of the station, and the lights and shades up the valley and hillsides were delightful. Having the anticipatory pleasure of meeting Mrs. and Miss Blunt and Mr. Sydney again at Lourdes; and a lovely view of the beauties of spring when I looked out of the window, the time did not take long to pass. One particularly pretty bit of meadow, trees, and stream led to the building of an airy castle, which the sudden appearance of the spires and roofs of Tarbes—suggesting the return to bustle and the haunts of men—soon banished, and the arrival in the station and the necessary change eradicated completely.

Thirty-five minutes to wait. Too little to see the town, too much for twiddling one's thumbs. Then what? Glorious inspiration! The Buffet! Capital; and into the Buffet I accordingly went. Seated at a table, a nigger, slightly white about the finger tips, but otherwise quite genuine—no Moore and Burgess menial—appeared to do my bidding. "What would Monsieur take? Café?"—"Oui." "Café noir ou café au lait?" I decided on taking the coffee with milk, adding that anything in the biscuit line would not be amiss, and away he went grinning. He soon returned with cakes and coffee, and by dint of taking my time I had barely finished when it was time to start.

Again I managed to secure a carriage to myself, but this time it proved a very badly coupled one which jolted considerably. Lourdes was reached in a wretched drizzle, and the benefit conferred on passengers by having the station *quite* free from any covering whatever, was *apparent* to all. A sudden activity on the part of the "cochers" to entrap me to their respective (but by no means necessarily respectable) hotels, as I emerged from the station—which proved useless—and I was jolting onward to the Hôtel des Pyrénées. When arrived, inspected rooms, ordered fires and dinner, and whiled away an hour till it was time to repair again to the station, to meet Mrs. and Miss Blunt and Mr. Sydney. "Red tape"-ism dominant there, as it is everywhere in France. In fact, "red tape" is the French official's refuge. Whenever a system is weak or underhand, they seek protection behind a maze of stupidity and fuss. I wanted to see the station-master, to obtain permission to perambulate the platform till the arrival of the train. No porter would bestir himself to find this great official, but whichever way I turned one was always ready with his "Où allez-vous, Monsieur?" to which the only sensible reply would have been "Pas au ——, comme vous," but silence and an utter indifference were better still, and armed with these I ran the gauntlet of the pests, and finding the "Chef de Gare" in his "bureau," at once received the desired permission. There was not much time for perambulation, as the train soon steamed in, though without Mr. Sydney, who was detained for a day or two longer, and once more, but now a triangular party, we jolted

back to the hotel. The rest of the evening was passed with dinner, and an endeavour to get warm; the rain and wind still enjoying themselves without.

However, with the morn all these miseries vanished, and the sun shone from a blue sky flecked with a few films of snow. Lourdes looked very charming under such auspices, and Miss Blunt availed herself of the balmy air of the morning to wander round the stables and garden with a speckled pointer and a Pyrenean puppy, between which and the mountains her attention was divided, though the last named had certainly the least of it.

Then out we sallied to see the sights, which are

more of quality than quantity. Turning to the right from the hotel door, through the Place de Marcadal, where the fountain was playing in delightful imitation of the previous night's rain, we gained the commencement of the Rue de la Grotte (which bears sharply to the left by the Hôtel de Paris), and followed its muddy ways with more or less danger owing to absence of footpath, and presence of numerous carriages. However, having passed the Hôtel d'Angleterre and the end of Rue du Fort (leading to the ancient castle), footpaths came into view, but the joy of the discovery was much minimized at the sight of the shops and shopkeepers, as the latter gave us no peace. It was one ceaseless bother to buy, mostly in French; but one damsel, confident of success assailed us in whining English, running up and down before her wares, and seizing different objects in quick succession, while continuing to praise their beauty and cheapness. Every shop or stall we passed—and there were a good many—had an inmate more or less importunate, but as what they had to say was very similar, it can be all embodied in the following

"CRY OF THE LOURDES SHOPKEEPERS."

This way, if you please, miss; and madame, this way;
 Kind sir, pause a moment, and see.
Oh! tell me, I beg, what's your pleasure to-day?
 Pray enter—the entrance is free.

Some candles? I've nice ones at half a franc each,
 Or thirty centimes, if you will.
Some tins, each with lids fitted tight as a leech,
 For you, with blest water to fill.

And look at these beads, only forty centimes,
 All carved, and most beautif'ly neat.
I've "charms" that will give you the sweetest of dreams,
 And *bénitiers* lovely and sweet.

    A cross of pure ivory. Photographs too.
      —No good?—You want nothing to-day?—
    Alas! what on earth must poor shopkeepers do?
      Oh, kindly buy something, I pray!

    One candle? You must have *one* candle to burn
      When into the grotto you tread.
    Not one? Not a little one? Onward you turn!
      Bah! may miseries light on your head!!

As soon as the shops were passed, and even before, women besieged us with packets of candles, and it was with great difficulty we made them understand the word No! Then, leaving the Hôtels de la Grotte and Latapie on the right, and the "Panorama" on the opposite side, we wound down towards the river and the grotto.

To us, it would be hard to conceive anything more pitiable or repulsive than the scene which met our gaze as we passed at the base of the church and came in full view of the grotto. An irregular opening in the dull grey stone going back only a few feet, with the moisture oozing over it here and there, and the ivy and weeds adding picturesqueness to what would otherwise be commonplace; in an elevated niche on the right, a figure of the Virgin in white robes and blue sash; in front, on the left, a covered marble cistern, with taps; and innumerable crutches and candles, were all the unsuperstitious eye could see. But to those poor wretches gathered round in prayer, influenced by the "light-headed" dreams of a poor swineherd, the spot was the holiest of holy ground. The abject reverence of their attitudes, the stand of flaming and guttering candles, the worship and kissing of the rough wet stones, the pious drinking of the cistern's water as they came away—a few pausing to buy some "blest" token of their visit at the adjacent shop—and the solemn silence that reigned over all, were the chief features that made the scene one from which we were only too glad to turn away. Taking the zigzag path among the pleasant trees and shrubs, on the right, we soon reached the level of the Gothic church, which we entered from the farther end. Ascending the steps, the two statues on either side of the porch came in view, but neither repaid a nearer inspection; St. Bernard, on the left, looking about as dejected and consumptive as anyone, priest or layman, well could. The church itself, from a Roman Catholic standpoint, must be considered very fine, but the adoration of the Virgin to the almost complete disregard of her subjection to "Our Saviour" is most apparent. The windows and many of the altars are beautiful, and so are many of the banners, while the high altar is a great work of art; but the *unreligious* tone that this striving after effect produces, but without which the religion—or so-called religion—would soon cease to exist, struck us as we entered, and increased with every step. It was as if to say, "Look at these lovely things, feast your eyes on them, and let their beauty be the mainspring to inspire you with faith." There was no appeal to the true religion of the soul, that springs from the heart in a clear stream, and which no tinsel banners, no elaborate statues, and no flaming candles, can quicken or intensify!

Leaving the church by the high road, with the Convent and "Place,"—with its neat walks and grass plots,—on the left, we proceeded to the "Panorama," where, our admiration having been tempered by the payment of a franc each, we spent an enjoyable quarter of an hour. The painting as a whole—representing

Lourdes twenty-five years ago—is most effective, and the effect is heightened by the admirable combination with real earth, and grass, and trees. The grouping of the figures round the grotto, representing the scene at the eighteenth appearance of the Virgin to Bernadette—who is the foremost figure kneeling in the grotto—is particularly fine; but how that huge crowd standing there were content with Bernadette's assertion that she saw the vision, when none of them saw anything but the stones, is a practical question

that few probably could answer, and least of all the priests. Returning by the way we had come, we bore up the Rue du Fort to inspect the old castle—or all that remained of it—and enjoy the view. After some two hundred yards of this narrow street, painfully suggestive, in the vileness of its odours, of Canton's narrower thoroughfares, we reached the steps leading up on the left, and commenced the ascent. As it was, we did not find it very difficult work, though if a rifle had been levelled from every slit in the two-foot walls, it is probable that before *two* of the nearly two hundred steps had been surmounted, we would have been levelled also. Passing between once impregnable walls (where English soldiers also passed in days of yore), we crossed the now harmless-looking drawbridge and rang the bell. A woman opened the door and requested us to enter, a request which evidently met with the approbation of two diminutive youngsters, whose faces were dimpled with smiles wherever the fat would allow. Keeping along the right wall in the direction of the pig-sties (O! shades of the Black Prince!!!) we were greeted with the musical tones of the " porkers " and many *sweet* odours. Having entered one of the prisons at the base of the tower for a moment, we next followed the ever-winding steps till fairly giddy, and reached the top. Thence the view was exceedingly fine. We seemed to be at the meeting-point of four valleys, and the snow peaks in the direction of Argelès were free from clouds. The whole of Lourdes lay like a map beneath ; the church with the "Calvary" on the hill over against it, the river sparkling in the sunlight, the Pic de Jer with its brown sides, and the winding roads with the green fields and budding trees, joining to make a pleasant picture.

Descending again to the hotel, we partook of a capital lunch, of which the "pie de mars," or ringed ousel—a bird of migratory habits, little known in our isles (except in a few parts of Scotland), but considered a great delicacy here—formed a part. After this, Miss Blunt once again devoted herself to the Pyrenean puppy, till the carriage came round and we took our departure.

CHAPTER IV

ARGELÈS.

Road v. Rail — Scenes, sublime and ridiculous — Hôtel d'Angleterre—Questions and " The Argelès Shepherd's Reply " —A forbidden path—The ride to Ges, Serres, Salluz, and Ourous—Argelès church—Route Thermale—Ges—The tree in the path—" A regular fix "—Serres—" It's a stupid foal that doesn't know its own mother "—A frothing stream—A fine view—Pigs in clover—Salluz—Ourous—Contented villagers—The high road—The bridge on the Pierrefitte road—Advice to sketchers—" Spring's Bitters and Sweets "—The " witch of the hills "—Large green lizards—" Jeannette's Lamb "—Round the Argelès valley—Château de Beaucens—Villelongue—Soulom —The old church—Hôtel de la Poste, Pierrefitte—St. Savin—The verger and the ancient church—Cagots—". The Organ's Tale "—St. Savin's tomb—The Château de Miramont—Jugged izard—Market-day—Sour bread and the remedy—Arrival of the first parcel.

ALTHOUGH the railway line takes very nearly the same route as the carriage road, the drive is decidedly preferable, and when it can be undertaken for ten francs—as in our case—there is little to choose between the modes of conveyance on the score of cheapness, especially as a landau can carry a very fair quantity of luggage. We considered ourselves amply repaid for our choice as we wound underneath the rocky crags and by the side of the river, anon ascending the curve of a small hill with the fresh fields below, a little church or ivied ruin standing out on the mountain-side, and high above all, the snowy summits so majestic and so intensely white. There was occasionally a ridiculous side to the picture too, when we put a flock of sheep in rapid motion in a wrong direction and the luckless shepherd had to start in hot pursuit—using the politest of language ; or, again, when some natives on tiny donkeys or skittish mules came by, their faces breaking into a respectful grin as they wished us "bon jour." Skirting the railway line for a short distance, we drove into Argelès rather unexpectedly, our ride having seemed all too short. However, there was our hotel—the Grand Hôtel d'Angleterre (everything is grand now-a-days)—

standing boldly by the road, with the quaint, though poor-looking village about it, and for another few days that was to be our abode. This hotel, though possessing less of a reputation than the Hôtel de France, nevertheless commands a finer view on all sides, and is a pleasanter abode on that account. The afternoon was still young when we arrived, so as soon as we had stowed our luggage we sallied out for a walk along the road to Pierrefitte. A short way from the hotel, an old shepherd was standing in the middle of the road leaning on his staff, with his flock of sheep all round him, and the dog lolling idly on the grass.

The tall poplars by the roadside waking into life, the merry stream meandering at their feet, and the back ground of mountains tipped with snow, filled up the scene. We accosted the old man with a good-day, and asked him several questions about the weather and himself, all of which he answered in a genial way, and which strung together made up

"THE ARGELÈS SHEPHERD'S REPLY."

Good-day, sir! The weather, sir; will it be wet?
  You see, sir, I hardly can say,
We gen'rally know at the earliest dawn
  What weather we'll have in the day;
But at night—in these mountains—I couldn't be sure,
  And I'd rather not tell you, sir, wrong.
And yet, what does a day here or there make to you?
  If it rains, 'twill be fine before long.
Have I always looked after the sheep, sir? Why, No!
  I've served in the army, sir, sure.
Let me see—ah!—it's now thirty summers ago
  Since those hardships we had to endure.
Ay, I fought with your soldiers 'mid bleak Russia's snow,
  Half numb'd in the trenches I worked,
And suffered what few of you gents, sir, would know,
  But somehow, we none of us shirked.
Was I wounded, sir? No, sir! thank Goodness for that,
  Though I've seen some stiff fighting, 'tis true.
In Africa 'twasn't all sunshine and play,
  And in Austria we'd plenty to do.
Do I like being a shepherd, sir, roaming the hills,
  Just earning enough to buy bread?
Well, I wouldn't have cared all my days, for the ills
  And the life that as soldier I led.
No, sir! no! though 'twas well enough then, Peace, you see,
  Is the best when one's hair's turning grey!
Will I drink your good health, sir? Ay, proud I shall be,
  And, thanking you kindly—Good-day!!!

Strolling on, we soon reached the bridge over the River Gave d'Azun, and leaving the old structure "whose glory has departed" on the right, we crossed over and continued along the road for a short distance, till we noticed a lane leading off to the left, which we followed. This in time bore further round in the same direction and suddenly ended at the entrance to a field. However, keeping straight on, we came in view of the river's bank and to this we kept, recrossing by the railway bridge below, and then back by the fields home, completing a round none the less pleasant because a captious critic might have called it trespassing.

As lovely a ride or walk as can well be imagined, even by an imagination as fertile as this lovely valley, passes by way of the four villages of Ges, Serres, Salluz, and Ourous. Although the weather was rather unsettled, we started one morning about 9.15, and following the road towards Lourdes for about two hundred yards, took the sharp turn to the left (with the telegraph wires) up into the town. Gaining the church, we bore along to the right into the open "Place," at the left corner of which the Route Thermale to Eaux Bonnes and Eaux Chaudes begins. For about half a mile this was our road also, but after that distance, the Ges route branched off to the right, and the views of Argelès, and the rest of the valley from it, as we wound upwards, were particularly lovely. The horses were very fresh, having only lately been brought from the mountains, after a winter of idleness, and they walked at a fast pace fretting at any stoppage whatever, which they did not endeavour to disguise, any more than their inclination to shy at anything they possibly could. As far as Ges the way is easy to follow, but it is wise to inquire frequently afterwards, as so many equally important (this importance is decidedly on the negative side) looking paths branch off in every direction. The good people we saw in Ges, a village of thatched cottages looking the worse for rain, said we should find the "road vile," but this did not daunt us, and with a "bon jour" we passed on. We had not gone very far, however, when to our dismay we saw a huge tree right across the road. Our position was an awkward one. The road was rather narrow and without any protection; there was only the steep hillside above, and the steep hillside below. To go up was quite impracticable, to go down was destruction! My horse

approached the impediment very quietly, and allowed me to break off several of the worst branches, and then scramble by. Miss Blunt's horse came close up to it as though intending to pass quietly, but, instead, wheeled round on the extreme edge of the path in anything but a pleasant fashion, either for the rider or the observer. Dismounting and tying my steed to one of the branches on the near side of the road, I held back as many of the others as possible, and the horse came up quietly again, but repeated the disagreeable business, still more dangerously. Having broken off several more, and again pulled back the others, the skittish animal consented to pass. But in passing he bent down a very pliant bough, which, when released, flew back and hit my peaceful steed sharply on the legs. For a few seconds his efforts to get free were—to put it mildly—unpleasantly severe, especially as he became with each effort more entangled in the tree. When the reins were at length unknotted, he quieted a little, and after being led a few yards, submitted to be mounted very peaceably, and we descended, with the fresh leaves above and below us, into Serres. Here we had occasion to remark that "It's a stupid foal that doesn't know its own mother," as one pretty little thing would persist in following our steeds, until a sturdy "paysanne" turned it back. The correct route all this time was the upper one (or that to the left), and we now came to a very lovely bit, where two swift frothing streams dashed down beneath the trees, near a small saw-mill. A fine view up the valley behind us, to the snow peaks towering over the ruddy hill-tops, was enjoyed, as we continued along the ascending and uneven path. In the fields above, some shepherds were driving a flock of sheep, and a woman, reposing under a huge blue gingham, was watching the vigorous onslaught of several pigs in a small clover patch. A few villagers, in their Sunday best, stood by the wayside discussing some topic with languid interest, which they dropped, to wish us "bon jour" and tell us the road. More lovely effects of light and shade over the hills towards Pierrefitte, with filmy clouds shrouding the tallest summits, and here and there a glimpse of the blue sky, and we passed into the straggling hamlet of Salluz, after which the path branched up—still to the left—through the trees. Winding down again, we came to Ourous, to which apparently the inhabitants from all the other villages had come, dressed in their Sunday best, to mass. "Young men and maidens, old men and children," women tottering with extreme age, were all assembled round about the old church, looking contented and happy, smiling, and wishing us a "bon jour" as we rode in a circular direction through the village, till we reached a spot where the road forks, the one to the right leading to Argelès, the one to the left to Lourdes. The former looked so stony that we chose the other, and had not gone very far before a smooth and broader path to the right (from which a grand view of the whole valley opened before us) brought us down to a few houses, between which we passed, and reached the high-road. A good trot along this, by the side of the railway line, and we were back at the hotel, convinced that the badness of the road and all drawbacks were amply—and more than amply—outweighed by the succession of beautiful scenery.

Two walks, one ending in rather a scramble, branch off immediately below the bridge, on the Pierrefitte road. The one we took, at a respectable hour of the morning, which ascends the left side of the mound, is the prettier by far, as it discloses lovely glimpses at every turn. We followed it till it branched off in two directions (the one to the left being the real continuation), but at this point we turned off into a field, deep in grass and studded with flowers, where some comfortable-looking boulders invited us to rest. Miss Blunt,—whose soul thrills with delight at the vastness and beauty of nature,—never allowed opportunities of committing the choicest bits to canvas or paper, to escape her; and, some picturesque display having caught her eye, directly she had located herself on an accommodating boulder, she was at work. Herrick's good advice, "Gather ye rosebuds while ye may—Old Time is still a-flying," might be adapted, she thinks, to sketchers in mountainous regions, and she speaks from bitter experience when she suggests:

> "Paint in your snow-peaks while you may,
>   If clouds are quickly flying,
> For those heights now in bright display
>   May soon in mist be lying."

The beauty of the scene was without alloy, the colouring splendid, and up the road above us, beyond which rose the hill, a shepherd was leading his flock of sheep, now and then clapping his hands or shouting to a straggler, but as a rule walking quietly on, the whole flock following in a continuous line. Not wishing to be idle, I took out my pencil to indulge in a poetic eulogy. How far I succeeded may be judged from the following lines, which might be called

"SPRING'S BITTERS AND SWEETS."

> Here on a moss-grown boulder sitting,
> Watching the graceful swallows flitting,
>   Hearing the cuckoo's note.
> Sheep on the hills around me feeding,
> While in their piteous accents pleading,
>   The lambkins' bleatings float.
> —Oh, dear! a fly gone down my throat.
>
> Spring's gentle influence all things feeling,
> New life o'er hill and valley stealing:
>   Buttercups, daisies fair,
> Studding the meadow, sweetly smiling,
> Bees with their hum the hours beguiling,
>   Breezes so soft and rare.
> —Oh, what a fearful wasp was there!

> Grand is the view from this grey boulder,
> Each high snow-peak, each rocky shoulder :
>   Charming, yet wild, the sight.
> Cherry-trees, with white blossom laden,
> And 'neath their shade a peasant maiden,
>   Comely her costume bright.
> —Oh, how these impish ants do bite!
>
> Onward the winding river's flowing,
> Its spray-splashed stones in sunshine glowing,
>   The peaceful oxen by.
> From the tall trees the magpies' warning,
> As on their nests intent, our presence scorning,
>   From branch to branch they fly.
> —Oh! there's an insect in my eye.
> I've done : such pests one really can't defy.

Miss Blunt couldn't defy them either, so, as it was getting near luncheon-time besides, we retraced our steps, but had not gone very far before we suffered a severe disappointment. Some fifty yards below us in the path stood a seeming counterpart of "Madge Wildfire"; a wild, weird, wizened looking creature, whom we immediately recognised as a "witch of the hills." Her hair unkempt, her bodice hanging in tatters from her shoulders, her patched and threadbare petticoat barely fastened round what should have been her waist (and a *waste* it was) by a hook and eye held by a few threads—even such as this, up the path she came. But what a miserable failure she was! When she came close to us, instead of pouring out a torrent of mad words, telling of her woes and wrongs, or at any rate breaking into a disgusting whine such as

> " Oh, gentles, I am mad and old,
>   My dress is worn and thin ;
> Oh, give me one small piece of gold!
>   To clothe my wretched skin ;"

she didn't even offer to tell our fortunes, but passed timidly by. It was enough to have disappointed a saint! and we were only restored to a pleasant frame of mind by finding Mr. Sydney at the hotel on our return.

In the afternoon we took the other path—previously mentioned as branching off below the bridge over the Gave d'Azun,—which leading sharply to the right, passes beside the river for a short distance, and then leads among the fields, finally—like others in

Argelès—losing itself there. Just as the poplars which run with it ceased, we had a lovely view up a dip between two fertile hills, to the snow-peaks near Barèges; a narrow path skirts the side of the hill, on the right, in the direction of the morning's sketching ground, but this we did not take, making, instead, for the hill standing immediately above the river. Up this a certain distance we clambered—scaring a few large green lizards that were sunning themselves on the stones,—by a sheep track we managed to discover, till we could look down on a mass of tangled brushwood by the riverside. Scrambling down to this through the wild vines and briars, we succeeded, after many fruitless attempts, in gaining the water's edge. There was no place to cross and the current was far too swift to attempt jumping, so we had to turn back. While deliberating on the right path, a little girl, looking very wretched, with blurred face and torn clothes, came round a corner, and asked us if we had seen a lamb anywhere. We were sorry we hadn't, very sorry indeed; all we could do was to endeavour to recollect a rhyme and adapt it to her case, that we learnt in the nursery when we were something under fifteen, and, although it didn't seem to assuage her grief much—probably because she didn't understand a word of English—we think it ought to be quoted in case it should be useful to others.

JEANNETTE'S LAMB.

Jeannette had a naughty lamb,
  That looked like dirty snow;
And wherever Jeannette went
  That lamb would never go.

It wandered from her care one day,
  (Oh, stupid little fool!)
It made her cry her heart away
  While searching brake and pool.

And Jeannette tore her dress to rags,
  And scratched her hands and face;
But of her dirty little lamb
  She couldn't find a trace.

The lamb fell in the river deep,
  But Jeannette never knew.
Though Satan finds some mischief still,
  For little lambs to do.

However, she listened very submissively till we had finished, and then wandered off again still searching for her lamb, while we retraced our steps.

There is a drive round the Argelès valley, which on a fine day is simply splendid, and ought certainly not to be missed. At ten a.m. a landau with two good horses was at the door, and away we went towards Argelès station, across the line, over a new piece of road, and then across a rather shaky, but wholly quaint, wooden bridge (under which flows the Gave de Pau) to the base of the hills. As we continued along this road in the direction of Pierrefitte, the views of the mountains on the Argelès side were especially fine. The Pic d'Arrens (7435 ft.) and the Col de Tortes (5903 ft.), with the wild Pic de Gabizos (8808 ft.) with its toothed summits, behind it—in the direction of Eaux Bonnes: over Pierrefitte the Pic de Soulom (5798 ft.), the Pic de Viscos (7025 ft.), and far up the Cauterets valley the Cabaliros (7655 ft.), the Pic de Labassa (9781 ft.), and the Pyramide de Peyrelance (8800 ft. about). An especially interesting part arrives, as the road approaches the wonderful old ruin of the Château de Beaucens (with "oubliettes" towers, a "donjon" of the 14th century, and west walls of the 16th ditto), which stands on the left, not far from the village of the same name. Crossing the river again, we just managed to pass over some newly-laid road, to the village of Villelongue—above which, on the left, towers the imposing Pic de Villelongue—and soon after found ourselves beside the river again at the foot of the Pic de Soulom, where it is very lovely, and crossing another bridge, reached Soulom itself. It seemed to us an old and somewhat dirty town—not to say filthy—but the church is worthy of a visit. It was formerly fortified, and the construction of the belfry—if such it can be called— is curious. The inscription over the door, "This is the house of God and the gate of heaven," written in Latin, seems somewhat grotesque for such a building, although the dome is painted to represent the sky in all the "intensity" of a starlight night. A few yards along the road and we stood on the bridge over the "Gave de Cauterets," at the other side of which is Pierrefitte—and from which point the scenery is especially grand. Passing the Hôtel de la Poste (recommended) on the left, and the way to the station on the right, we bore up the hill in the former direction, towards St. Savin.

This old place—in fact the oldest village in the valley—is an easy walk from Argelès, and should certainly not be excluded from a visit. Having passed the dismantled Château de Despourrins and the statue at the roadside erected in the poet's (Despourrins') honour, we had a grand glimpse of the valley below; and, leaving behind the Chapelle de Piétad (16th century), which stands on a point above the road, we entered the village. The street leading to the ancient Roman Church is ancient too, reminding one, in the curious construction of the houses, of Chester, the style of supporting the upper part on wooden beams, reaching over the road, and leaving a passage beneath, being very similar. The church has been restored and is in capital preservation. As there were so many objects of interest, chiefly connected with the great St. Savin himself, we sent for the verger, sexton, bellringer, parish beadle, or whatever the "goîtreux" individual called himself, and paid great attention to all he had to say. Although a good deal was quite unintelligible, the following are some of the most interesting facts. Entering at the small side door, immediately within stands a curious and very old bénitier (font), with two curious individuals carved in the stone supporting the basin. These are supposed to represent two "Cagots," a despised race for whom the font itself was constructed. Very few people know anything about their origin, but they were greatly detested by the inhabitants of the country, and not even allowed to worship in the same church or use the same "holy water" as the rest. They still exist about Gavarnie and a few other spots, and we hope to learn more of them. The old battered organ next presents itself to the view, with the long flight of steps leading up to it, but as it wished to tell its own story, without further description behold

"THE ORGAN'S TALE."

Good people who gaze at my ruinous state,
    Don't lift up your noses and sneer:
I've a pitiful story I wish to relate,
    And, I pray you, believe me sincere.

I was young, I was "sweet," in the years that are gone,
    The breath through my proud bosom rolled,
And I loved to peal forth as the service went on,
    O'er the heads of the worshipping fold.

How time speeds along! Three whole centuries—yes!—
    Have passed since the day of my birth;
And, good people, I thought myself then, you may guess,
    The loveliest organ on earth.

Such pipes and such stops! and a swell—such a swell!!!
    My music rang under the dome;
And the way that I held the old folks 'neath my spell
    You should know; but alas! they've gone "home."

Then my varnish was bright, and my panels were gay
    With devices both script'ral and quaint;
I frightened the *sinner* with hair turning grey,
    But charmed into rapture the *saint*.

Those faces once painted so brightly would smile,
   And put out their tongues at my voice ;
As the pedals were played, they would wag all the while,
   And the children below would rejoice.

Now is it not sad to have once been so grand,
   And now to be shattered and old?
To look but a ruin up here, where I stand
   Decidedly out in the cold?

Each "pipe is put out," and my "stops" are no more,
   I belong to a "period" remote ;
And as to the tongues that wagged freely of yore,
   They have long disappeared down the throat.

My pedals are broken or gone quite awry,
   My "keys"—you may "note"—are now dust ;
No longer a "swell"—not as faint as a sigh—
   While my bellows, good people, are "bust."

I am twisted and worn, in a ruinous state,
   But prythee, good people, don't sneer !
My joys and my sorrows I've tried to relate,
   And in judging me don't be severe !!!

Leaving the organ, and passing behind the "high altar," we beheld the tomb of the redoubtable saint, who is supposed to have been shut up there at the end of the 10th century, though the gilt ornament (?) above is some four centuries younger. The set of old paintings to the right and left represent scenes in the good man's life, who, if he had only changed the *i* in his name to *o*—and the king would have agreed readily—by the perpetual allusion to *Savon*, would perhaps have done much for the natives generally. The robing-room, wherein the head of the revered man is kept in a casket, and the "Salle du Chapitre," with quaint carvings of the 12th century, beyond, are other places of interest.

The "Château de Miramont," which adjoins, is now used as a convent (or college), and visitors are not permitted to inspect it. We bought a lithographed print of the church and its environs for half a franc, from our round-backed guide, besides depositing a "douceur" in his horny palm, and consequently parted with him on the best of terms. The road for some distance being rather steep, we preferred to walk and let the carriage follow, but when nearing the junction with the Pierrefitte road, we mounted again and bowled along at a smart pace over the well-known bridge to the hotel.

There was nothing striking about our hotel life, although we found it pleasant, being a "parti carré." We were generally the sole partakers of the table-d'hôte, at which the food was excellent, the jugged chamois (izard) being especially good. Light, however, was at a premium. It may have been all out of compliment, to bear testimony to our being "shining lights" ourselves; still, for all that, we should have been glad to forego the politeness, and receive, instead, a reinforcement of lamps.

Argelès itself is a peculiar old place, though devoid of much interest, except on market-days. The curious houses and towers, the street watercourses (as at Bagnères de Bigorre), the church, and the strange chapel-like building now used as a diocesan college, are all that is noteworthy even, excepting the "State schools," built three years ago.

On a Tuesday, when the market is in full swing, the square in front of the post-office looks bright and cheerful, and vegetables flourish. We took a very pleasant walk after passing through the stalls, and down past the Hôtel de France. The route we followed leads to the right, close by the new State schools, among some poor cottages, where it turns sharply in the opposite direction, and runs down beside some fine old chestnut trees to the river. Continuing, the track leads up a fine glen, with views of the snow-peaks towards Eaux Bonnes, which well repaid our walk.

Returning again by the town, we wandered about through the narrow streets, taking a farewell survey before leaving for Cauterets, whither we were next intent.

There is another episode connected with Argelès, that will live in our memories, and it is one that future travellers, methinks, may have reason to appreciate, if not to endorse.

Everybody learns from unhappy experience how sour the bread is throughout the Pyrenees, only excepting two or three resorts, and as we were aware of the fact before leaving Pau, we arranged with Monsieur Kern, of the Austrian Bakery, Rue de la Préfecture, to send us a certain amount of bread every day. The first night at Argelès was spent without it, but on the evening of the following day a packet was brought into the drawing-room, where we were assembled, and at the magical word "bread" every eye brightened, and every face relaxed into a smile. Let no one cavil. This was one of the episodes that link Argelès to us with a pleasant charm.

CHAPTER V.

CAUTERETS.

Hotel de la Poste, Pierrefitte—The Gorge—Its majestic beauty—The resemblance to the Llanberis Pass—Mrs. Blunt becomes poetical—Zinc mines—Le Pont de Médiabat—Entering the town—The Rue Richelieu and Hôtel du Parc—Winter's seal upon them still—Thermes des Œufs—Thermes de César—The Casino and Esplanade des Œufs—A good dinner and the menu—The start for the Col de Riou—The Grange de la Reine Hortense—The pines—Miss Blunt's "exhortation to the first snow"—The dogs and their gambols—Defeated, but not discouraged—To the Cérizey Cascade—The baths of La Raillère, Petit St. Sauveur, and Le Pré—Cascade du Lutour—The Marcadau gorge—Scenery—Pic de Gaube—At the Cérizey Cascade—The Pont d'Espagne and Lac de Gaube—Pont de Benqués — Lutour Valley — Various excursions up same—The "Parc"—Allées de Cambasque—The Peguère—The "Pagoda" Villa—Promenade du Mamelon Vert — The road's up again—Blows and blasts—The bishop's arrival—Enthusiasm, pomposity, and benedictions—The pilgrims at large—They start on an excursion—The market and Hôtel de Ville—The grocer's opinion—Pyrenean dogs and their treatment — The dog-fancier — Smiles and temper — Bargaining displaced—No dog after all!

A LANDAU with four horses was ready after lunch, to transport us and our baggage to Cauterets; but having enjoyed Argelès very much, we were none of us particularly glad at the prospect of the change. The road as far as Pierrefitte, lovely as it is at this season of freshness, discloses no other views than those previously described, but when we turned sharply to the right, after passing the Hôtel de la Poste, and began the ascent towards Cauterets, then our eyes had indeed a rich treat. It would require the most dismal of dismal days, with sluicing rain and clouds low down on every beautiful crag and snow-tipped summit, to make anybody born with a soul above his dinner, complain of the grandeur of the gorge, or impugn the unceasing variety of dashing waterfalls, foaming river, freshly-opened leaves, white heather, and bright, flower-decked fields.

The same wild majesty as the Llanberis Pass presents, strikes one here: the enormous crags in threatening attitude far up the heights, the chasms and fissures brightened by a patch of young grass or a small tree, and, nearer the road, the scattered boulders luxuriantly covered with moss and fern, belong to both alike; and, while the bushes of snowy heather, the constant splash of the cascades falling over the rocks in feathery spray, and in the distance the hoary-headed monarchs of the range reaching up towards the sky, make this different from the familiar Welsh scene, it is only a difference that greatly intensifies the beauty and the charm of this Cauterets gorge.

Even Mrs. Blunt, who as a rule prefers the matter-of-fact to the poetical, was lifted out of herself, for she suddenly clutched me by the arm, and pointing in the distance, murmured something about "summits proudly lifting up to the sky," and being quite unused to that kind of thing, it took me some time to recover from the shock.

A little over three miles from Pierrefitte,—where a glimpse at the zinc mines and the wire tram in connection with them can be obtained—the road passes over the bridge of Médiabat, and some yards beyond becomes identical with the old route, which until then lay below us. The new portion (made in 1874) only extends for about two miles, as it does not commence till after the zigzag rise from Pierrefitte leads into the gorge, but the engineering of the whole has been admirably carried out, and the ascent of nearly 1,700 feet in the six miles does not tell severely on the horses. Now in an almost straight line, now by zigzags, we gradually neared the town, the gorge widening at the same time, though the peaks, some covered with trees, some snow-covered, seemed to bar the way completely at no very great distance.

We were quite close before we could really be said to have seen the town, and ere we could form any opinion of it we drove up the Rue Richelieu and found ourselves at the Hôtel du Parc. Monsieur Villeneuve, the jovial and experienced host, and his pleasant spouse, came out to welcome us, and although the hotel had only been open four days, made us as comfortable as they could.

Cauterets (3,254 feet) was only just waking into life, only two or three hotels, one or two hairdressers, one confectioner's, one tobacconist's, and one or two grocers' shops were open; while of the bathing establishments, the "Thermes des Œufs," the largest, and the Thermes de César, were the only ones showing signs of renewed life. The Esplanade des Œufs,* a large tree-planted space in front of the principal "thermes" (just mentioned)—which serves as casino, concert-hall, and theatre as well—seemed utterly deserted; whereas in summer, with the band playing, the trees in full leaf, the booths opened, and the crowds of visitors, the scene must be the gayest of the gay. We had just time to notice so much, on the

* "Œufs" because of the water's scent resembling "rotten eggs."

CAUTERETS.

afternoon of our arrival, before the sun set behind the huge mountains which surround this charming spot, and the hour of dinner arrived. This dinner was so excellent, so well cooked and served, that, although we despise with a deep-rooted scorn the wretched class of individuals who make their dinner their main object in life, we nevertheless consider that we are only paying a merited tribute to the *chef* in saying that the cooking was always of a high standard, and quoting as a specimen the evening's *menu* (May 1):

SOUP.

Gravy.

FISH.

Salmon, with sliced potatoes and melted butter.

MADE DISHES.

Hashed Veal.   Sauce Piquante.

Sweetbreads and green peas.

ROAST.

Chicken.

VEGETABLES.

Asparagus.   Potatoes (new).

PUDDING.

Sago.

ICE, &c.

Vanilla cream.

Cheese, Jelly, and Biscuits.

When we woke the following morning, the sun shining from a cloudless sky proclaimed an "excursion morning." Accordingly, we sent for a guide, to inquire if a visit to the Lac de Gaube was practicable. The guide arrived, and disappointment ensued. It was possible to go if we didn't mind a few miles of snow, two feet deep and upwards. But we did mind very strongly, and said so. Then the burly native spoke again, and said that the Col de Riou was an easy trip, that we could take horses to within a short distance of the summit, and that when we got there the splendid view would include St. Sauveur, Argelès, Barèges, Gavarnie, &c. &c. And we answered the burly native in his sister tongue (*patois* was his mother tongue), or as near to it as we could, and said, " Have three horses ready by half-past ten at this hotel, and we will start." Then, delighted, he smiled and bowed, and disappeared down the street.

At eleven o'clock the cavalcade started, and a noble cavalcade it was: Miss Blunt on a strong dark bay pony, Mr. Sydney on a similar-coloured horse, and myself on a grey, formed the van ; then came our burly friend (by name Pont Dominique), and another guide (Berret), carrying the lunch ; and the rear was brought up by a small brindled bull-dog, and a smaller specimen of unknown breed, which was nevertheless a capital harmony in orange and white. In this order we left the Rue Richelieu and ascended the Rue d'Etigny, passing under several wreaths and crowns, with which the streets were decorated. We had previously noticed these grand preparations on our arrival, and though sensible of the good feeling that apparently prompted these attentions, we thought they were somewhat superfluous. But that is (as they were) by the way. Having soon reached the last of the houses, we gained the Rue du Pauze Vieux, and turning sharply to the right, ascended to the two establishments known respectively as the Pauze Vieux and Pauze Nouveau. And here a paradox—pause, view, and be convinced! The Pauze Vieux is the Pauze Nouveau and the Pauze Nouveau is the Pauze Vieux. Should any well-educated citizen of any country under the sun (or daughter) be disposed to doubt, let him examine the buildings for himself, and he must agree.

Half-an-hour after starting we reached the cottage known as the "Grange de la Reine Hortense," the view from which is excessively fine. Looking down towards the town, the mighty Cabaliros (7655 ft.), forming a semicircle, stood above on the right; to the left of this semicircle reared up the Monné (8938 ft.), the highest mountain in the vicinity, from which other peaks make another similar formation, ending with La Brune, beside which, but more to the left and immediately over the town, rises the Peguère, covered with irregularly-heaped crags, and pines. The town itself looked very neat and compact: the Mamelon Vert (a small hill to the right) and the chief thoroughfares being easily distinguished. Far up the Lutour valley, to the extreme left, the Pic de Labassa, or de la Sèbe (9781 ft.), and the Pyramide de Peyrelance (8800 ft.), completed the chief points of the scene in that direction; but far away in the opposite one we could easily see the Argelès valley and the Gothic church of Lourdes. Behind us, seemingly facing the Cabaliros, were the Col de Riou (6375 ft.), our would-be destination, and the Pic de Viscos. Winding up the hillside, and passing banks blue with the large and small gentian, we entered the pines, which made a pleasant change. As at the Col d'Aspin,* the rising

* Vide Bigorre, p. 42.

sap filled the air with its refreshing odour, and the occasional glimpses of blue sky, mountain, and valley, through the gently waving branches, were very charming.

We had not proceeded very far through the trees when we reached a break, where one of the party felt

THE ASCENT OF COL DE RIOU.

that at least something had been gained. There, partly on the track, partly on the loose stones above it, lay a bank of snow, and so delighted was Miss Blunt at having attained the (present) snow-line—say about 4600 feet above sea level—that her feelings were not to be in any way damped or suppressed, as they burst forth in an

"EXHORTATION TO THE FIRST SNOW."

   Emblem of Purity,
   Chilly as Charity,
Oh, what a joy your deep whiteness to view!
   Something is gain'd at last,
   But you are melting fast,
Why does the cruel sun put you to stew?

   Tell me, O long-lain snow,
   What of the vale below?
What do you think about people and things?
   Do you love forest-trees?
   Or love you more the breeze?
Tell me what bird you think most sweetly sings?

   What? You've no heart at all?
   Cannot help where you fall,
Caring not if you swell to a huge size:
   Minding not how you rush,
   What you break, whom you crush?
Surely such feelings you ought to disguise.

   Ah, well! we won't discuss,
   Useless to make a fuss;
For, after all, I am glad that we met.
   Emblem of Purity,
   Chilly as Charity—
But I won't roll in you. No! you're too wet!

The two dogs were amusing in their absurdity. They were perpetually endeavouring to detach stones from the side of the pathway, so as to have the pleasure of pursuing them down the steep. At times, when the hill was thickly strewn with leaves or particularly steep, they completely disappeared, though violent pulsations among the scattered branches and the aforesaid leaves told us they were not lost, but only temporarily buried.

When we had barely mounted another 400 feet, we came upon regular banks of snow, right over the path. This was quite unexpected, and we had to decide whether to leave the horses and tramp through the snow, or to return. We chose the latter—although the Col de Riou stood out seemingly very practicable of ascent—and, returning on foot, the horses and guides following, with the dogs here, there, and everywhere, we reached the "Grange de la Reine Hortense" and proceeded to lunch. After giving a very good account of the *paté* sandwiches, and not forgetting the guides and the dogs, we made our way slowly back, defeated perhaps, but certainly not discouraged.

Although neither the Lac de Gaube nor the Pont d'Espagne were attainable, the Cérizey Fall, which is about one third of the distance to the lake along the same route, was kind enough to put itself at our disposal. Not wishing to appear ungrateful, we availed ourselves of a fine afternoon to order round the horses and our two guides, and started about two o'clock. For some time we followed the road known as the Rue de la Raillère, which leads to the baths of the same name from the Place St. Martin; crossing the river by a very unpretentious bridge, not far from the town. Leaving La Raillère behind, and passing in turn the drinking establishment of Mauhourat—near which the Gaves of Lutour and Marcadau form the Gave of Cauterets—and the baths of Petit St. Sauveur and Le Pré, and gaining as we mounted a good view of the "Cascade de Lutour" on the left, we entered the Marcadau valley, or (more properly) gorge. The scenery, similar somewhat to that at the entrance to the Cauterets gorge from Pierrefitte, is nevertheless wilder and more severe. The occasional bright fields and frequent mountain streams, with their merry music, disappear; but the lofty heights, the gloomy firs, the mighty crags and boulders, and the snow-peaks beyond, remain. After a great amount of very rough and steep ascending—the Pic de Gaube (7644 ft.) the while standing conspicuously before us—we reached the small hut that is intended as a shelter, near the fall. Dismounting and taking the narrow path to the right over the stones, immediately above the hut, we obtained a capital view of this noisy cascade. Other views were obtained by us from above, by clambering over the stones and boulders at the side of the torrent; but this is the best of all. From the hut (mentioned above) one hour's good walking, over anything but a pleasant track, brings one to the Pont d'Espagne, and it requires another forty minutes to reach the Lac de Gaube.* As horses can be taken for the whole distance when the road is free from snow, our feelings at not being able to proceed can be better imagined than described! By Mauhourat, whither we presently returned, the Pont de Benquès crosses the Marcadau, and the track to the left leads up the valley of the Gave de Lutour. We did not pursue it very far, as the workmen were busy repairing it, and it is also very rough and steep. Several favourite excursions, however, are reached by it, among which may be mentioned the Cascade de "Pisse-Arros" (forty minutes from Cauterets), the "Fruitière" (two hours from Cauterets), the Lac d'Estom, 5847 ft. (three hours from Cauterets), the Ravin d'Araillé (three hours forty-five minutes), the Lake of Estom Soubiran, 7632 ft. (four hours thirty minutes), the Lake of Estibaoute, 7744 ft. (four-hours forty five minutes),

* The lake is full of excellent salmon trout, and there is a small inn on its shores, where visitors can stop the night in summer. The Vignemale, from whose summit the view is wonderfully vast, rears up above the lake.

LAC DE GAUBE.

and the Col d'Estom Soubiran (six hours thirty minutes).

Instead of again crossing the bridge below La Raillère, we kept to the left, along what may have been *once* a Roman road, but which was *now* at any rate a track both unpleasant and dangerous.

For some distance, large boulders, soil, and smaller stones overhung it, and seemed as though the least rain or slightest push would bring them down. Gradually this unpleasantness ceased, and as the road widened we passed a few villas and entered the " Parc," which, according to the natives, is part and parcel of the Esplanade des Œufs, the great summer resort in front of the Casino, from the back of which a pleasant path of very gentle gradient ascends for about a mile to the " Allées de Cambasque," up the flank of the Peguère ; and to the Cabanes (huts) de Cambasque beyond.

Although there is but little level road for enjoying a ride, we nevertheless managed to pass a short time very pleasantly on horseback. Leaving the Esplanade des Œufs on the left, we took the road passing between the back of the Hôtel d'Angleterre and a curious châlet, built with a pagoda beside it, and little bridges in communication. Following this road, which is known as the Promenade du Mamelon Vert,* and in turn passing the " Café du Mamelon Vert "—near which the track to the Cabaliros branches off—and the commencement of the path to Catarabe, we bore down to the right at the back of the Mamelon, and crossed the Gave by a rickety wooden bridge—shortly to be superseded by one of stone—into the Pierrefitte road. Down this, through the fine gorge within sight of the

* The Mamelon Vert is a green hill near the entrance to the town.

mines, and then back to the hotel, constituted the remainder of the ride.

Our stay at Cauterets was not without excitement, though certainly that excitement was not of a pleasant kind. We soon discovered that the decorating of the streets was for the benefit of the "Confirmation Procession," for which the Bishop was coming from Tarbes. The Rue Richelieu was "up" all along one side for the laying of gas-pipes, and, by way of diversion, every now and then—usually when we were at dinner, or wanting to look out of the window—a penny squeaking trumpet would sound, then a lad would rush about and close all the shutters, leaving the rooms in darkness and the inmates in suspense, till it ended in a series of loud reports, accompanied by the distribution of various specimens of granite in all directions. The authorities stopped this nice performance when the Bishop was expected, as the mere chance of "blasting" a Bishop would have been too painful for the Catholic workmen's feelings, especially as they hoped for a benediction! As soon as word arrived of the approach of "Monseigneur's" carriage, the curé and chief dignitaries of the town, accompanied by a brass band, a detachment of firemen, and a small regiment of women—decked in hoods of blue or red or white—passed down the muddy street, bearing banners, and a gilded canopy with white plumes. In a few moments they returned, the band playing, the banners waving, the abbés and choir singing, and in the centre of the throng, with two curés in front of him under the canopy, came the new Bishop of Tarbes, resplendent in violet watered silk, trimmed with beautiful lace, gloves of the same hue, with ring on the outside of the right hand, which he perpetually kissed to the admiring spectators. Miss Blunt, who was for once able to look out of the window in safety, had a special one all to herself, and of course she didn't mind any amount of explosions after that!

Then we had other excitements, in the shape of wretched bands of pilgrims, who, having a spare day, came up from Lourdes to see the mountains. They invaded our salon, drank beer at eight o'clock in the morning, and looked on the whole—in spite of their rosettes of black, red, and yellow—as disreputable a lot of individuals as ever turned religion into farce. Whether it was quite worth while suffering their presence for the fun of seeing them mount, when starting for their excursion, is open to question, but that it was a unique and comic sight we were all agreed. The hotel garden, filled with guides, horses, donkeys, and pilgrims; the delicate exhibition of ankles and feet —such feet; the chairs to help the rotund damsels; the swarm of natives round one especially fat woman, who got down after all; the beaming face of the host, and the gloomy looks of a very fat man, just the size for a small pilgrim tea party; not omitting the priest, whose flowing robe nearly hid his *better half* (viz. the donkey), made a scene worthy of reproduction in the pages of 'Punch.'

Although we strolled about a good deal, we found but little of interest in the town itself; perhaps the most fascinating spot was the Patisserie Suisse, in the Rue César, just below the baths of the same name. The Hôtel de Ville is a fine building, and in summer perhaps, the market, which stands in a street to the left of it, may present an animated spectacle; but at this time it had the appearance of a large monkey cage, with good strong iron railings in front, a few cabbages and onions, and a small group of ancient and much-wizened native specimens inside.

We enjoyed our stay, however, in the midst of all the wild scenery immensely, and think that but few people, if they came during the month of June, would be prepared to differ from us. There are always some of course, and before coming we had the pleasure of meeting two of them, in the shape of a retired *grocer* (or something of that kind in the wholesale line) and his wife. They both declared that "Cauterets was a vile 'ole, with 'igh streets and showy 'ouses, and that a sensible 'uman being wouldn't stay there ha *h*our;" but it must be mentioned in their favour, that the day on which they went was rather damp, and there was only one grocer's shop open. If anyone should be disposed to take their verdict as more conclusive than ours, we can simply say, "Believe neither, but go and see for yourself."

There is one other subject worth mentioning, in regard to which we had a trifling diversion on the morning of our departure. The true breed of Pyrenean dogs may be seen at Cauterets, and puppies obtained by any people who wish to have a specimen of this fine race. The great secret in rearing them is to avoid meat of any kind, and feed them on bread with a little milk, or very thin soup. It is not the climate of England, as has so often been alleged, which gives them consumption, but the change to rich diet from the meagre fare which in the mountains they always receive.

The prices vary so much, that it is wisest for a stranger to enlist the services of some trustworthy native to arrange the purchase, rather than to do the bargaining himself. Pups from six weeks to three months sell at from ten francs to one hundred, but a really fine specimen of two and a half months ought to be bought for thirty-five francs. Dogs of six months and upwards are expensive; as much as five hundred francs being asked for them in the season.

As Miss Blunt had a great desire to become the possessor of one of these fluffy creatures, whenever any were seen inquiries were always directed at once with regard to their parentage and price. Happening to perceive a woolly tail disappearing behind a workshop in the Rue de la Raillère a few hours before we had to start, we passed up a short entry beside the aforementioned workshop, and asked to see the owner of the dogs. In a few seconds he stood before us, a weather-beaten Frenchman, who, as well as his clothes and his intellect, had seen better days—a man about five feet six inches high, with face deeply lined; moustache, goatee, and hair, all somewhat sparse and grizzled; a blue berret (the native hat) in his hand; his shirt fastened by a single stud, barely hiding what had been once a brawny chest; his loose trousers half-covered by a leathern apron; and his two coats both threadbare, and decorated with ribands in an equally worn-out state—such, bowing and smiling as he approached, was the proprietor alike of the dogs and the workshop. In spite of his poor appearance and idiosyncrasy—almost approaching to madness—he had a certain dignity of manner which we could not fail to notice. But he was very trying to deal with. Whenever the price was the object of our inquiry, he began in the following strain: "Very good, very good; which does Monsieur like? which does Ma'in'selle prefer? The finest of course? Ah yes, the finest! Ah, very good; take your choice, Monsieur; take which you please. The finest dogs in the world! See! see! Monsieur" (and here he pointed to the ribands on his breast), " I gained the prize at the Paris Exhibition!—at the Paris Exhibition!—the exhibition open to all the world—I, with the dogs I had brought down from the mountains and bred myself, I gained the prize. Ha! ha! there were two Englishmen, two of your fellow-countrymen, who thought they would beat me; but no, no, Monsieur, it was to me you see (pointing to his breast again), Monsieur, that they gave the prize." At last, however, he named fifty francs as the price of either, which was very excessive, and when I suggested ten—which was proportionately low—he proceeded to take off his apron, roll up his coat-sleeves, and then, looking at me fiercely, said, "So, Monsieur, you take me for a ten-franc man, do you? You think to mock me, do you? I, who gained the prize at the Paris Exhibition, the exhibition open to all the world, for the finest dogs, you think I will sell my puppies at ten francs, Monsieur? No, Monsieur. I will *not* sell you one for ten francs, and I do not wish to have anything more to do with you." And then he, who five minutes before had been shaking my hand with delight because I knew the owner of the parent dog (of his puppies), with a lofty wave of the hand motioned me to depart. Before doing so I soothed his offended dignity by a mellifluous explanation, and he once more, but somewhat loftily, offered me his hand as I bade him farewell. So, in spite of the pleasant diversion, Miss Blunt did not get her dog!

CHAPTER VI.

LUZ AND BARÈGES.

Rain at starting—A blighted view, yet lovely still—Pont d'Enfer
—Nature's voice—Sère and Esquiez—Luz—Its situation and
status—An old house—The ancient Church of the Templars
—La Chapelle de St. Roch—Pyrenean museum—Hôtel de
l'Univers—Château de Ste. Marie—" The Jackdaw's Causerie "
—A new " Diet of Worms "—The new bathing establishment
—To Barèges—Pic d'Ayré—Esterre—Viella—Betpouey—Mill
conduits—Cercle des Etrangers—Opinion of the town—Grand
Etablissement — Promenade Horizontale — Hospice de Ste.
Eugénie—" The Jay of Barèges "—Wood anemones—Hepaticas—Valley of Lienz—Pic de Lienz—Pic d'Ayré's summit
— Pic de Néouville — Mountain rhododendrons — *Anemone vernalis*. .

ALTHOUGH we had beautiful weather all the while we remained in Cauterets, directly we prepared to depart down came the rain, the mists descended over the hills, and until we reached Pierrefitte we were unable to obtain more than momentary glances at the beauty we had so delighted in, before. Having crossed the Gave de Barèges by the Pont de Villelongue, we were soon in the gorge, the rocks on the left of which were blasted for five miles, when the road was constructed. Notwithstanding that it still rained, the clouds were a little higher, and our view consequently less contracted.

The beauty of the scene was indisputable, and yet it was a beauty less wild and majestic, and more unequal,

THE GORGE NEAR PIERREFITTE.

than that of the Cauterets Gorge. The heights on the left had frequently the barest and most uninteresting appearance, when on the other side the eye was enchanted with the varied spring tints on the trees massed together up the slopes from the river, whose limpid green pools or foaming rapids gave such a charm to the picture. The old road is seen in many parts, and several of the old bridges, but the one about three and three-quarter miles from Pierrefitte, at a point where the Gorge widens—known as the Pont d'Enfer, and built partly of wood as well as stone—is by far the most interesting. The scenery in its vicinity was particularly beautiful. The wild quinces, with their white blossoms mingling with those of the cherry and the light green of the maples, larches, elms, birches, and limes; the bright fields above, and the ever-lovely river below; with the massive crags and a babbling waterfall, rendered this part especially—as well as several others in a lesser degree—enchanting.

An enthusiast might easily write a book on the beauty of this gorge alone, but in this age he would probably find few readers; of those who did look at his book the greater number would find it probably too highly-coloured, while the more enthusiastic ones would lament its lack of warmth. Not wishing to incur the displeasure of either, we refrain from saying a great deal about the splendour of this drive; knowing that to a lover of the beautiful in Nature, all we have left unsaid Nature will herself say ten times more impressively.

After passing the monument in honour of the "Reine Hortense," which is five miles from Pierrefitte, and crossing the Bridge de la Hiladère, we soon

H

caught sight of some villages on the left, where poplars —stiffly prominent in all directions—spoil much of the picturesqueness of the surroundings. The villages of Sère and Esquiez, that we saw when nearing Luz, are ancient and worthy of a visit. Together they formed a "chef-lieu" before the eleventh century, and the Roman church in each, but especially that of Sère, is exceedingly interesting. A few moments, during which we crossed a marble bridge over the Gave de Bastan, and, bearing to the left, we were in Luz.

Denominated by various titles, from a "poor village" to a "small rustic town," Luz is by no means an insignificant place. It doubtless owes a great deal to its situation in a pleasant hollow among the hills, with a pleasant landscape on all sides, and its appearance is certainly more quaint and rustic than poor. Undoubtedly there are several old houses, some looking particularly unsafe; undoubtedly the streets are often very narrow; and perhaps the inhabitants on the whole may be far from wealthy; but with all this Luz is not a poor looking village. On a market-day the streets in the vicinity of the old church, built—partly in the 12th and finished between the 15th and 16th centuries—by the Templars, assume a wonderfully gay appearance, and towards the back of the church we noticed one old house whose balconies, if a trifle warped and weather-beaten under the thin covering of white paint, were nevertheless bright with pots of geraniums, wallflowers, and stocks.

The church itself is most interesting, and was at one time very formidable also. Surrounded by a high wall pierced with loopholes in a double row, lies the graveyard, which is only a narrow strip between the ramparts and the church, the body of which lies between two towers. Under the higher of these, facing north, and built for defence with loopholes and embrasures, is one of the church doors, which leads to the high altar steps in a direct line from the entrance into the churchyard. Further to the right, but also facing north, is the most remarkable entrance, the inscriptions on the arch dating from the 12th century. On the extreme right is a door leading into the chapel, built in the 16th century, and dedicated to St. Roch. We found the inside interesting, without possessing any very striking features.

The effect from the main gallery is perhaps best, and the smaller ones running along the sides have a weird and aged appearance. Near the entrance to the church, low down, is shown what was once the door for that wretched race of beings, the "Cagots."* The Chapelle de St. Roch, which we passed into from the gallery in the main building, is the most striking of the two. The gallery and stairs were in a very shaky condition, and two candle-stands near the

* We found it difficult to obtain any reliable information about these creatures. They seem to have led an existence like the lepers in Palestine, being avoided and despised by the inhabitants generally, and they appear to have been both diminutive and ugly. (See St. Savin, p. 73).

latter seemed to have been in their prime many generations ago. The vaulted roof, with the curious wooden groins, and the ancient *bénitier* near the door, are worthy of inspection. Without scrambling up the tower to the "Pyrenean Museum," but not forgetting to examine the old bell-tower and its bells facing west, we walked down to the left and joined the main road.

The ancient Castle de Sainte Marie—a very interesting and historic ruin—being in the vicinity, we followed the principal highway to the right, and passing the much-recommended Hôtel de l'Univers, were soon in the promixity of the château, which, standing alone on the summit of a pointed hill, was charmingly conspicuous. The path, after winding up the hill, leads to an entrance at the back, which is locked, the castle being now the property of the Précepteur of Luz, who, however, is always willing to accommodate strangers by allowing them to enter, as well as to inspect his garden, and the very striking image of the Virgin which he has had perched on the front walls. A great number of jackdaws have taken up their quarters in the old towers, and as one of them kept continually cawing as though anxious to be heard, we append what we made out to be the meaning of his chatter (it is said they never speak without *cause*), which we call

"THE JACKDAW'S CAUSERIE."

Caw, caw! cried the jackdaw, and cawed again,
As he circled out of the ancient tower:
Caw, caw! and he circled thrice over the plain,
And cawed once more as he reached his bower.

Caw, caw! I was born in this fortress old,
As old as the hills, some folks might say;
Five hundred centuries, caw, have rolled
Since first it stood in the light of day.

Caw, caw! just to think I have built my nest
Where the Black Prince ruled in such royal state.
Caw, caw! I wonder if ever he guess'd
That this would in time be his castle's fate.

Caw, caw! but I never could quite perceive
Why one tower is round and the other square.
If I'd been the prince, I can well believe
I'd have made the architect build a pair.

Caw, caw! by-the-bye, there was old Coffite *
And Jean de Bourbon, that fought so well ;
And 'tis said that the prince underwent defeat—
At least my mother this tale would tell.

Caw, caw! they've finished with siege and fight ;
The castle's too old for that, of course ;
They go in for piety on the right,†
And we caw away till our voice grows hoarse.

Caw, caw! I'm a Catholic right sincere,
But somehow or other I cannot see
Why they put up the Virgin's statue ‡ here—
The place is as wrong as a place could be.

Caw, caw! I must see how my youngsters look
In their quiet nursery 'mid the stones ;
Next week they'll be able "to take their hook," §
And——but there they go with their squeaking tones.

Caw, caw! cried the jackdaw, the world is vain,
But I love to dwell in my ancient tower.
Caw, caw!—why the wretches want feeding again,
They've a "diet of worms" nearly every hour.
And he cawed as he flew to the nursery bower.

Leaving the jackdaw to pursue his paternal duties, we descended again to the town, and sheltered awhile from a shower under the balcony of the new and gaudy-looking bathing establishment, that stands in

* It is said that Jean de Bourbon, Comte de Clermont, and Auger Coffite of Luz, took this castle in 1404.
† The author does not hold himself responsible for the jackdaw's slang, which refers to the statue.
‡ This statue is in honour of " Notre Dame de Lourdes."
§ Again the jackdaw indulges in slang !

THE CASTLE OF STE. MARIE.

the outskirts, towards St. Sauveur. These baths, which are only opened during the summer, are supplied with water from Barèges, whither we were only waiting for a fine day to make an excursion. But fine days just then were rather hard to find, so we contented ourselves with one that did not look very ominous, and taking a good lunch with us, started in a landau and four at ten o'clock.

The road after leaving Luz follows the course of the Gave de Bastan, skirting in turn the base of the Montaigu * and that of the Pic d'Ayré, and, passing through the villages of Esterre (2 miles), Viella (2¼ miles), and Betpouey (3½ miles), winds in steep zigzags up to Barèges (4064 ft.).

This valley, after what we had seen, did not give us much pleasure; its appearance on the whole being sterile, though after leaving Luz as far as Esterre, the brightness of the fields and trees, and the splashing of the water overflowing the miniature mill conduits, made a pleasant landscape.

The actual distance from Luz to Barèges is barely four miles, and yet so great is the height of the latter (1600 ft. above Luz) that it was nearly one o'clock when we pulled up at the Cercle des Etrangers—the only specimen of a hotel or café open—for our lunch.

After a pleasant meal we made a move to inspect the town and its environs, and were not long in forming an opinion, at any rate, on the former, which we think most visitors at this season of the year would be inclined to endorse. One long ascending street lined with houses all shut up, occasional breaks where

---

* Not to be in any way confounded with the Montaigu near Bigorre. The French mountain vocabulary is so defective, they often call several heights by the same name.

BARÈGES.

a narrow alley or the roads to the hospitals and promenades branched off, the bathing establishments under much-needed repair, the dirty-looking river dashing down behind, on the left; the beech boughs clad in dead leaves rustling on the slopes, in the opposite direction; and a few natives here and there, very untidy and sleepy-looking, as though with difficulty awaking from the "dormouse" state, complete the picture of Barèges, which we need hardly add is in itself a most desolate and dreary-looking place. In mid-summer, with the sun shining and the trees in full leaf, an improvement in the scene would be noticeable; but very few, except invalids specially recommended for a course of the waters, are at anytime likely to stay there more than a few hours.

We took the road leading up, to the right of the

"Grand Etablissement," to the Promenade Horizontale, the great summer rendezvous, and passing the "Hospice de Ste. Eugénie" began the ascent up the easy zigzags of the "Allée Verte." We had not made much progress when we startled, from what was doubtless a contemplative mood, a very fine jay. He did not seem to like the disturbance at all, but kept flying from branch to branch in the vicinity, repeatedly uttering his guttural cries.

As the tenor of his thoughts—uttered in rather a shrill treble—seemed to bear considerably on topics of general interest, in spite of the apparent selfishness that was the key-note of the whole, we think it expedient to let posterity enjoy the enlightenment we received from

"THE JAY OF BARÈGES."

Lawks a mussy! and shiver my feathers!
  Why this is a wonderful sight;
In spite of my earnest endeavours,
  I can't quite get over my fright.

'Tis so long since the strangers departed,
  They ne'er would return, I had thought;
So no shame at their coming I started,
  Though perchance I felt worse than I ought.

Still to think through the days cold and lonely
  I've wandered about at my will,
With no one to chase me, and only
  The need to prevent getting chill.

Well, I say—when I think of the quiet
  And rest that is now at its close—
I have doubts of enduring the riot
  After such a long time of repose.

It is not that I hate to see pleasure,
  It is not that the world I detest;
But I like to have comfort and leisure,
  And not to be teased and oppress'd.

I don't mind the smell from the fountains,
 —Though a rotten-egg scent is not sweet—
For I always can fly to the mountains
 And seek some umbrageous retreat.

Then the season for shooting is over,
 So the sportsmen * will leave me alone,
And I'll pose as a Go(u)ld Jay in clover,
 Avoiding a *dollar*ous tone.

To my doctor, perhaps, 'twould be better
 The final decision to leave;
And I'll follow his choice to the letter,
 He's a bird I can always believe.

That reminds me 'tis time for my dinner,
 And as I don't wish it to wait,
As sure as I'm saint and no sinner,
 I'll be off at my very best rate.

And with a concluding chuckle the bright bird disappeared. We were by this time beyond the "Forest Administration" hut, and close upon the snow, which lay in narrow but deep drifts among the trees, the wood anemones and fine hepaticas growing in groups close by.

As we gradually progressed, the snow occupied the greater part of the way, and we were forced to betake ourselves to the extreme edge; and when at last we emerged into the Vallée de Lienz, trees and branches had to be scrambled over to avoid a wetting, although we were obliged to cross one or two drifts after all. Getting clear of the trees, we came in full view of the imposing Pic de Lienz (7501 ft.) on the left, and the rounded summit of the Pic d'Ayré (7931 ft.). Passing the two cabins constructed among the rocks in the open, we crossed the swift brook and began the ascent of the inferior but well-wooded hill below the Pic de

* The jay, with all its sophistry, did not apparently know that French sportsmen only kill what they can eat, and therefore its fears would in any case have been groundless.

Lienz. There is no proper path up to this Pic (as to most others), and the grass is rather bad for walking; but the views up the valley to the mighty Pic de Néouville (10,146 ft.), and the whole range behind the Pic d'Ayré, are very grand. We only went to the bend just before the summit of the Col, resting awhile among a huge pile of boulders, brightened by bushes of the mountain rhododendron, before commencing to descend. A fine specimen of the rather rare *Anemone vernalis* was a prize that fell to us as we carefully balanced ourselves on the slippery tufts which so often, carrying the feet along at an increased speed, cause the owner to find himself rather unpleasantly acquainted with mother earth. However, we reached the huts again in safety, and made considerably shorter cuts on our way back to the town, encountering a solitary sheep with a very young lamb at one of our sharp turns.

We arrived at the café just in time for tea, and then the horses were put in and we rattled back, having, in spite of the barrenness of Barèges, spent a very pleasant day.

CHAPTER VII.

ST. SAUVEUR.

Pont de Pescadère—Sassis—Gave de Gavarnie—St. Sauveur—Hotel de France—Pont Napoléon—Napoleon's pillar—Bee orchids—Chapel of Solferino—The view from thence—Ne'er a hermit but for gold—Luz Cemetery—Luz Post Office—Short cuts—Pharmacie Claverie—Jardin à l'Anglaise—Ascent of Pic de Bergons—Villenave—The shepherds' huts—Lunch—Snow, its use and abuse—On foot—" Excelsior "—Dangerous footing —The last crest but one—The view—Gavarnie and Argelès in sight—A lazy guide—A "fast" bit—Mountain flowers—Mr. Sydney to the fore—A short walk and a good view——To Sazos and Grust—The bathing establishments—Sazos : the old church—The belfry—Chiming extraordinary—Various promenades—Gems of hill and vale.

AT the bridge known as the Pont de Pescadère the road from Pierrefitte forks ; the branch to the left leads to Luz, while the road to St. Sauveur branches off to the right, and passes through the village of Sassis, above which is the more important one of Sazos. Then, keeping to the riverside till within half a mile of the town, it throws out a branch over the Gave de Gavarnie to Luz, and bending in the opposite direction, winds steeply past the baths to the hotels.

Like many of the villages in Japan, and especially along the great Nakasendo, St. Sauveur possesses one single street. The resemblance continues further with the fine scenery, but there it ends. The look of the houses and the comfort of the Hôtel de France find, alas! no parallel yet in the interior of that wonderful country.

We came to St. Sauveur direct without stopping at Luz, but as the latter is the larger town—in fact the mainstay of the former, and also the nearer to Pierrefitte—we have given it precedence. For situation and

ST. SAUVEUR.

all other qualifications, except as a residence in winter, St. Sauveur easily bears away the palm. The morning after our arrival, when the sun was shining brightly, we walked up through the remainder of the diminutive town to the Pont Napoléon, one of the most remarkable bridges in the Pyrenees. The

PONT NAPOLÉON, ST. SAUVEUR.

bridge itself is 216 feet above the river, and sixty-nine feet wide; but it is not so much the construction — though that is well carried out — as the position, which especially attracts on a lovely spring morning. The river, of a beautiful light green tint, wandering down the valley towards Pierrefitte, the trees with varied foliage crowding the slopes above, the glimpse of Saint Sauveur with its church, and the hills with the snow-peaks beyond, on either side — made such a glorious *ensemble* as we were not slow to appreciate.

But this was not all—nor nearly all—for not only had we the view of the grand rocky gorge from which the river issues above, but we could also take the easy gradient down to the riverside itself, which leads from the near side of the bridge, as well as survey the loveliness from the terrace at the base of the arch, on the side beyond. Having crossed this fine piece of engineering, and passed the pillar surmounted by an eagle erected in honour of Napoleon III. and the Empress Eugénie, we found the road led at right angles in both directions. The one to the right, to Gavarnie, we hoped to take thither later; the one to the left, leading to Luz, we followed there and then. After curving once or twice within view of the bridge, it bifurcates, forming an upper and a lower route, both of which lead to Luz, if desired. The lower, which is the direct route from Gavarnie to Luz, we abstained from taking, preferring the upper road to the right, which leads past fields resplendent with flowers (among which the "bee" orchid is noticeable), to the chapel of Solferino.

The view from the hill on which the chapel is built is an excellent one. Looking towards Luz, several small villages may be seen up the Barèges valley, with the Pic de Mont Aigu, and the Pic d'Ayré (7931 feet) on the right, and—immediately over against the town —the Pic de Néré on the left. Looking towards Pierrefitte, other small villages, and the whole of the Luz valley; on the left, St. Sauveur, and, above the almost indistinguishable village of Sassis, the Col de Riou, with the Pic de Viscos beyond. Looking towards the Pont Napoléon, the Pic de Bergons (6792 ft.) towers up on the left, and on the right may be easily noted the toothed Pic du Lac Grand the Col d'Aubiste, and the loftier Pic (8863 ft.) of the same name, besides a glimpse of pastures and foaming cascades as well. There is very little in the chapel itself except its history and its cold atmosphere. It is supposed to be an exact copy of the ancient Hermitage of St. Peter, which formerly stood on the same spot. The bones of the last good man, for whom "gaieties had no attraction whatever," and who consequently shut himself up for "years and years" in the dismal building, were collected by Napoleon III.'s command, and buried under the statue erected in front. There is a woman that calls herself the guardian (not angel) of the place, and demands a small gratuity in exchange for any amount of unnecessary talking; judging by her appearance, we decided she was *not* a hermit nor a particularly small eater either, though her stature was decidedly diminutive. Two tracks lead from this hill to Luz. One winding down on the left forms the branch route to St. Sauveur, the other, to the right—which we took—passes the cemetery, and leaving the new church in the same direction, leads to the back of the ancient fane of the Templars, through the town.

After transacting a little business at the post-office (there is none at St. Sauveur except in the season), which stands in one of the principal streets traversed on the route to Barèges, we returned to St. Sauveur by another way. The ordinary short cut from Luz to St. Sauveur crosses the bridge over the Gave leaving the Gavarnie road on the left, and turning sharply up a short distance beyond the river, joins the high road above the "Pharmacie Clavarie," near an ornamental pillar. We, however, bore up the Gavarnie road till, reaching a cottage, we pursued the narrow path obviously conducting to the river, over which a wooden bridge—whence a pretty view can be obtained,—leads to the Jardin à l'Anglaise. This garden, much frequented during the summer months, brought us in turn, by means of zigzags and steps, close to our hotel, and though it may be slightly longer than the "short cut," we certainly found it prettier and more agreeable.

There is one excursion from St. Sauveur, which is not very difficult nor laborious, and which well repays the certain amount of exertion that is at all times associated with ascents. This is the ascent of the Pic de Bergons. Although we could tell before we started that the snow would prevent us from reaching the summit, we nevertheless had hopes of arriving very near it; and finding a beautiful day, as it were, staring us in the face, we ordered round the horses and a somewhat aged guide, and were in motion by ten o'clock. Reaching the further end of the Pont Napoléon, we found the path striking off immediately before us, and the work began. The gradient for several minutes rose rather sharply, and as the road was anything but a pleasant or even one, the labour for the horses was considerable; but they went very willingly, until, at our arrival at a couple of cottages, we halted to give them a few minutes' rest.

Until then we had been winding up the face of the hill, but after leaving the cottages, the track bearing round to the side brought us above Luz, over which and the whole valley we had a splendid view. Not far from this point, the path from Luz, *viâ* Villenave, joined in, but no improvement in the general unevenness and stoniness of it was effected. With a barren

I

gorge on our left, and the green pastures with the snow-peaks of Bugaret and Maucapéra towering behind them, straight before us, we followed the disagreeable zigzags, our horses always on the very edge, as though courting our overthrow, till, finding on reaching the "cabanes" some shepherds kindly and well disposed, we repaired to the shelter that their cow-house wall afforded, to eat our lunch. The meal was a success, as such meals, when the victuals are good and the appetites hearty, usually are, and the *vin ordinaire*, cooled to a pleasant extent with snow from a neighbouring drift, tasted like nectar. But the same snow which was so delightful in the claret, interfered sadly with our locomotion, and having finished our luncheon, we had next to dispose of our horses, and commence the rest of the ascent on foot. Striking straight up from the hut, we soon attained a narrow track winding up the wooded hill to the left, and without much difficulty or exertion, found ourselves within view of St. Sauveur, and a great part of the mountains and valleys. However, we were yet some way from the summit, or even the highest attainable point (the summit being unattainable on account of snow), so we pulled ourselves into form, and whispering to one another to have "courage," we moved upwards again. A small rocky backbone was next attained, but still the higher crests remained, and seemed to say, "Excelsior." The guide got lazy, and preferred to study a little geology to mounting any higher, so we left him to pursue his researches and strode on. Between the next point, gained after some little work, and the last crête below the actual summit, several banks of snow lay, and rendered progress difficult. In two places a sharp decline, with no chance of clutching anything in case of falling, presented itself to dull our hopes, but by dint of using the alpenstocks well, and making deep tracks in the semi-melting snow, we reached the desired crest, with nothing but the white and inaccessible summit above. The view was a very fine one, and fully justified all expectations, although our lazy guide was effectually shut out from our gaze. The miniature town of St. Sauveur looked like a tiny model, with every accessory that could add to its charming position. To the left, high above us, the mighty Barbe de Bouch (9624 ft.) stood out just below the clouds, in which the still loftier and very stony Pic d'Ardiden (9804 ft.) was partially hidden. Further in the same direction the familiar forms of the Pics d'Aubiste and Litouèse, and further yet, the Tour and Casque of the Gavarnie Cirque, stood out as snowy and as clear as the most eager sightseer could wish. Over the town itself the Pic du Lacgrand, and down the valley to the right, the Col de Riou and the Pic de Viscos, were plainly visible; while the town of Argelès and the hills beyond it, required no glass to point out their position at the end of the splendid gorge. Over against Luz the Col d'Arbéousse and the Pic de Néré (7880 ft.); with the Pic Bugaret (8859 ft.), the Maucapéra (8893 ft.), and the massive Mont Arrouye (10,299 ft.), facing them, above the hut where we had lunched, added their attractions to swell the beauty of our view.

When we thought we had really taken in all that we could, we did not stay on our lofty perch much longer, fearing the result of our guide's geological researches; however, we found him still fairly well, and very little less lazy, so took him for a little jolting down a rather "fast" bit, which not only woke him up, but brought us quickly down to our shepherd's hut again. Partly riding and partly walking, the rest of the descent was successfully accomplished, including the gathering of gentians, bee orchids, mountain violets, and both *Polygalæ*;* while Mr. Sydney triumphed in the very laudable effort of showing the lazy guide how things could be managed, by arriving at the foot of the mountain some twenty minutes before him. A very short trot brought us to the hotel in time for some half-past five tea, having taken seven and a half hours over our trip, including the hour spent for lunch.

Between the Hôtel de France and the Pont Napoléon a narrow path strikes up to the right, almost opposite a large white house a short distance beyond the church; this we found a very pleasant quarter of an hour's walk, leading by an easy gradient to a good point of view. Box plants, with their bright leaves here and there changing into a rich red, lined the way, and many flowers, including gentians, added their charm. From the rock at which we terminated our walks, a fine view of the Pic de Bergons, two cascades, the gorge towards Gavarnie and St. Sauveur, the Pont Napoléon, and a small defile on the immediate right, was our reward.

Another pleasant promenade and not a very long one, which we much enjoyed, was to the villages of Sazos and Grust, in the direction of the ascent of the Col de Riou and the Pic de Viscos. We followed the high road down through the town, passing in turn the Roman-like and commodious baths, the path leading to the Hontalade establishment on the left, and the

---

* *Polygala rosea* and *P. amara.*

Pharmacie Claverie on the right; and just before the branch route from Luz joins in, took the left track up the side of the hill. Pretty views of the different valleys unfolded to our gaze as we continued on our way, while a splendid vista of villages lay before us when we reached the platform space on which an iron cross is erected, a short way below Sazos. The village itself, as well as that of Grust, which lies within easy distance above it, is a quaint, old-fashioned place. The church is the chief attraction; in fact, immediately Miss Blunt found herself within the ancient exterior portal, she demanded paper and pencil, and although all the paper forthcoming was the back of an envelope and a telegraph form, managed to turn out an efficient representation of the old Roman fane. In exploring it afterwards at our leisure, we were struck by several peculiarities which produced mingled feelings. Inside the doorway, two curious flights of steps lead to the narrow galleries and the belfry, the final flight being totally devoid of either "sweetness" or light. Having examined the bells and heard the clock strike three, we began the descent. In the darkness we certainly did clutch a vertical rope, but could that simple act—we ask in a whisper—have had such an unusual effect as causing the clock to repeat its striking? For, whether or not, before we reached the ground, the three strokes rang out again. The carving over the altar is good, and the general effect of the whole church is likewise; but the supposed model of the grotto at Lourdes, and the awful painting in the side altar on the left, certainly do not add to its beauty.

The children regarded us with inquisitive looks as we came away, but seemed to wish to keep at a safe distance. Whether the double striking of the clock had had a peculiar effect on them we did not, however, wait to inquire, but after taking a drink at the fountain, proceeded on our homeward way.

Any one making a lengthened stay can find out plenty of similarly enjoyable walks; in fact, one of St. Sauveur's chief charms lies in its favourable situation for such pursuits. The neighbourhood is very rich in flora, small jonquils, daffodils, oxslips, hyacinths, violets, *polygala*, *potentilla*, anemones, *Ramondia pyrenaïca*, *Primula farinosa*, large and small gentians, *linaria*, and bee orchids being among the easiest to find.

Before we started on the great drive to Luchon, we successfully accomplished a delightful day's outing to Gavarnie, but as it is full of interest and majesty, we give it a chapter to itself.

CHAPTER VIII.

GAVARNIE.

A " falling glass "—The wonderful echo—Cascade Lassariou—Sia and its bridge— Pont de Desdouroucat—" Changing scenes "— Bugaret torrent — The Piméné — Bué — Gèdre— Brêche de Roland in the distance—The " Grotto "—Scenery at fivepence per head—Daffodils—Lofty summits—Cascade d'Arroudet—Chaos—Valley of the " Ten Thousand Rocks," Amoy — A dirty avalanche — The Sugar-loaf — Travellers' troubles—Importunate females—Hôtel des Voyageurs—Poc—Guide or no guide—Chute de Lapaca—The guardian summits of the Cirque—Cascade du Marboré—Chandelles du Marboré —The Cirque—Its marvellous beauty—Reluctantly returning — " The Guide's Auction " — " Two women enough for a market, and three for a fair "—A Yankee tale—Sketching and flowers—Tempers and appetites.

THERE is no excursion from Luz or St. Sauveur for which it is so necessary to have a fine day, or which is so wonderfully unique, as that to the Cirque of Gavarnie. We were forced to wait several days; the barometer always, stupidly enough, wanting to fall, until on the third day of the moon it slowly began to rise, and gave us hopes for a start on the following morning. The following morning arrived, and with it a heavy fall of snow, decking the hills quite low down with a white mantle, and gloomily screening the view. However, about nine o'clock, the sun burst forth, the clouds rose, the blue sky appeared, and we felt that our opportunity had come. The lunch and the landau, with four horses, were ordered for ten o'clock, and at 10·15 we were on our way. Through the town, past the church and over the fine Pont Napoléon we went, our hearts—eager to appreciate—finding no lack of food.

Keeping along the base of the Pic de Bergons, with the Pic du Lac Grand rivalling it on the other side of the defile, we soon sighted the chasm and cascade of Rioumaou on our left, and reached the Pas de l'Echelle. At 1 metre 50 centimetres, or $4\frac{3}{4}$ feet, from the extremity of the ornamental facing which marks the place, we pulled up, to try the magnificent echo, and were in no way disappointed. Our voices came back particularly clearly, but from the coach-box the sound was stronger. On ahead again, still by the base of the Pic de Bergons, with the mighty Col and Pic d'Aubiste (8863 ft.) majestic across the river; till, at the foot of the Pic, where the sparkling Cascade de Lassariou comes tumbling down, the wretched hamlet of Sia, with its "quatre moulins" and very fine bridge, broke into view. Traversing the Pont de Sia—distant about three miles from Luz and built when the new road was made two years ago—we kept the right side of the Gave, and, with the Pic de Litouèse towering above us, reached the Pont de Desdouroucat ($4\frac{3}{8}$ miles), and again passed to the opposite bank, leaving the remains of the old route on the side whence we came. The sky was clearing more and more, and before us, over Gavarnie, it was one pure expanse of blue. The gorge was very wild, but with a wildness of piled-up crags and blackened sides that the beautiful winding river and the spring tints helped to beautify and subdue. Presently the massive Brada, up the grand Gorge de Bacheviron, came in sight on our left, and as we passed the insignificant hamlet of Pragnères (4¾ miles), where the torrent of Bugaret dashes down into the Gave, the Brada looked more massive still. Thus it continued all along the route, every bend of the road bringing something new—whether a cascade, a valley, or a lofty peak, always something to claim attention and praise. At such a bend, shortly after quitting Pragnères, the great snow-crowned Piméné (9193 ft.) seemed to bar the way; while at another, the hamlet of Bué and the Col de Bué appeared on the right, and at another, again, Mont Ferrat (10,575 ft.), up the Héas valley on the left. Not very much further, when bending into Gèdre, we obtained a splendid glimpse of La Tour and La Casque du Marboré and the Brêche de Roland. Gèdre (8 miles), like all the rest of the villages or hamlets in the vicinity, is a miserable, poverty-stricken-looking place, but with picturesque surroundings. It is a good centre for numerous excursions—notably that to the Cirque de Troumouse —and possesses an excellent botanist as well as a celebrated grotto.*

Stopping at the house by the bridge, we were escorted by the good woman into her garden and down some steps to a platform, whence the so-called grotto was to be surveyed. It is a very picturesque spot. The lofty walls of perpendicular rock, the overhanging bushes and flowers, the trees above, the field beyond, and the blue water of the Gave de Héas foaming beneath, are charming enough, with the aid of rays of sunlight, to make the spot famous, and the good woman chuckle as she pockets the half-franc per head.

* The grotto's notoriety is gained, perhaps, by its imposture; it is in reality no grotto, but a very pretty bit of scenery nevertheless, on a fine day.

THE VILLAGE OF GÈDRE.

Starting again, we commenced the zigzag ascent past the church—the road winding among fields golden with daffodils, mingling here and there with the lovely blue of the gentians and the pink *Primula farinosa*—towards the base of the Coumelie, the mule-path to the Cirque de Troumouse leading through a field above us, as we reached the zigzag's top. Still gently ascending round the foot of the Coumelie, the pointed summit of the lofty Taillon (10,323 ft.) came into view ahead, with the grandiose Campbieil (10,418 ft.) up the Héas valley; and the Pic de Saugué immediately above on the right, from whose height the splendid Cascade d'Arroudet, dashing past the shepherds' cottages, launches its foaming showers into the river below. A few more graceful curvings of the road and we entered the region so aptly termed "Chaos." Attributed to an earthquake at the end of the fourteenth century, rightly or wrongly, the fact nevertheless remains that one of the huge buttresses of the Coumelie became detached from the main summit, and dashed down in enormous blocks to the valley below. There they lie, the road passing between, in the wildest and most indescribable confusion. Here a heap piled one above another, there a mighty shoulder split in twain by a conical fragment which rests in the breach that it made; some towering above the road, others blocking the river below, a few isolated and many half-buried; but all combining to form as wild and wonderful a chaos as the eye could wish to gaze on, but which the pen must fail to describe. Far away on the shores of China, at the port of Amoy, is another scene which, though it must yield the palm to this, is nevertheless one of a similarly wild nature. The "Valley of the Ten Thousand

Rocks," as the spot is called, in the midst of which stands a joss-house (or temple), may be reached in a pleasant walk from the harbour of Amoy, by way of the wonderful Rocking Stone, and along paths lined with aloes and cacti. There the grass grows between the confusion of boulders, and the Chinamen's incense ascends to the blue sky; but these points of

difference from the Chaos of Gavarnie, though tending to subdue part of the barren wildness, nevertheless still leave a resemblance between the two scenes that is worthy of record.

Leaving this "boulder" region behind us, we passed through a huge avalanche that stood in frozen filthiness far above the carriage on each side of the road, while immediately over us on the left rose the mountain from which it had come—rightly named the Sugar-loaf—and opposite, on the right, the serrated summit of the Soum de Secugnac (8442 ft.).

At this point one of the many nuisances which ought to be classed under the head of "Travellers' Troubles," commenced. In the distance, but coming swiftly towards us, or rather as swiftly as a broken-winded, raw-boned, jolting apology-for-a-horse would allow, was *a* woman, and alas! in her train were several others; a few on or with donkeys, but more on foot. In vain we told them that we would engage no donkeys at all, and no horses till we reached our destination; in vain we bade them allow us to "pursue the even tenor of our way" in peace, and hush their high soprano tones. It was one perpetual babble in praise of their horses, their donkeys, and their capabilities as guides, with the constant repetition of the names of the surrounding peaks, which we already knew perfectly well. When we reached the gorge which opens up on the right, as though the earth had been split by some mighty shock, and through which the majestic Vignemale (10,821 ft.) was perfectly visible, the storm of voices directing our attention to the sight was as loud as it was unsolicited. But happily we were then close to Gavarnie, and crossing the bridge with a momentary glimpse at the Cirque, we drew up at the door of the Hôtel des Voyageurs.

After lunching and engaging our steeds, with an intelligent guide, who answered to the euphonious name of "Poc," we left the greatly disappointed donkey women still making a terrible clamour, and started for the Cirque.

As far as finding out the proper route goes, and that is a long way, no guide whatever is required, but in order to learn the names of the various peaks and other interesting facts, it is distinctly necessary to have one, unless the traveller possesses a very elaborate plan of the vicinity.

Leaving the new bridge to the left, as well as a very ancient one, and the plashing fall known as the "Chute de Lapaca," we turned round in the opposite direction, and passing the "Hôtel de la Cascade" and a wooden hut, again turned to the left, down what, though an execrable road, led, nevertheless, to the object of our desires. At this turn the Pic d'Aspé reared above us on the right, succeeded by barren hills covered with loose stones, but as we proceeded, the famous central excursion—the Piméné (9193 ft.) —came in sight on the opposite side, followed by the Brêche d'Allanz, the Pic Rouge de Pailla (9107 ft.), Pic d'Astazou (10,106 ft.), the Cylindre (10,916 ft.), and even the Marboré (9964 ft.) itself.

Between the Marboré and the Epaule de Marboré (10673 ft.), nearer the centre of the Cirque, the celebrated Cascade du Marboré, (1380 ft. in height) dashes during the warmer months. The curious summits known as La Tour (9902 ft.) and La Casque (9862 ft.), almost equidistant from the centre of the Cirque, on opposite sides, stood clearly before us, with the snow lying below each in the serrated shapes which give rise to the term "Chandelles du Marboré." The Brêche de Roland was—as it always is from this view—invisible, hidden behind the Pic de Sarradets (8993 ft.); but the Fausse Brêche beyond, and more to the right the magnificent Taillon (10,323 ft.), and the Pic de Gabiétou, with the Port de Gavarnie — a peculiar shoulder-like rock, below them both—filled up the semicircle in all its wonderful entirety. When at last we reached the point whence the whole can be viewed to most advantage, we did not require the assertion of the guide that we were in enjoyment of one of the best days of the year, to increase our admiration and delight.

The amphitheatre, standing before us like the ruins of some mighty arena, in which the throngs of eager men and women and the blood of the dying gladiator had long given place to the purifying snow; the summits around uplifted towards the blue sky; the cascade, no longer dashing as full of life and hope, but frozen in its course and hanging in icicles between the rocks; the few uncovered crags scattered here and there, relieving the dazzling whiteness of the "glace éternelle"; the sparse trees down the outer slopes struggling to free themselves from their winter cloak; the cloud of frost scintillating in the sunlight as a mass of loosened snow rushed into the depths below;—was not such a scene as this, presented to our gaze in unveiled splendour, more than sufficient to bewilder in the intensity of its majesty and loveliness?

Yet even this was not all. The silence, the solemn and perfect silence, that reigned over the whole, only broken by the dull sound of the falling avalanche or the shrill voice of the restless crow, was so evident and so powerful, and combined so impressively with the marvellous beauty of the surroundings, that the heart could not fail to recognise the sublimity of Nature and the omnipotence of Nature's God!

We stayed there for a long time, and with great reluctance turned our horses' heads from the scene;

THE CIRQUE OF GAVARNIE (IN SUMMER).

while even when we had done so, we stopped at nearly every bend of the road for another look.

The exact distance from the hotel to the extreme end of the Cirque is calculated at $3\frac{3}{4}$ miles, but we traversed little more than two-thirds of that distance, on account of the depth of the avalanches, which were then melting far too quickly to allow of dry walking any further.

Arriving again at the hotel, the chatter of the women over some new arrivals was as deafening as ever. Our good guide Poc considered it was not to be borne any longer, so having counted the women and their asses, he cleared a space in preparation for a mock sale at which they were all to be put up, and having got us in front as make-believe purchasers, proceeded with the business, which we called

"THE GUIDE'S AUCTION."

This way, sirs, this way! Will you please to walk up?
    The auction I'm ready to start:
I'm instructed to sell all these valuable lots,
    And the bidding I hope will be smart.

You see by the catalogue, forty clear lots—
    Thirty women; ten asses; some small.
To proceed then, we'll take them, sirs, just as they are,
    Say forty fine donkeys in all.

They've plenty of sinew, and as to their voice,
    I think about that you well know.
The first lot then, gents; shall we say fifteen francs?
    Well then, ten; but that's rather too low.

In our country for ladies we've heaps of respect,
    But we've fully enough and to spare;
And we know that "two women a market will make,
    And that three are enough for a fair."*

---

* His exact words were, "Dans mon pays, monsieur, nous disons qu'il faut trois femmes pour faire une foire, et deux pour un marché."

Now then, gents, please be sharp! No advance? No advance?
  The candle* burns fast to the end.
Ten francs for this wonderful native—ten francs!
  Why, surely, that's nothing to spend!

No bidding? Good gracious! Why what shall I do
  To oblige you? I'll class them as one:
Now what do you say for the whole forty lots?
  Make a bid, sirs, I want to have done.

Fifty francs for the lot; see the candle's nigh out:
  Fifty francs, take them all as they rise.
What! No one will buy them? Alas! I must say
  You're all most uncommonly wise.

They clamour and chatter the whole of the day,
  I believe they snore loudly at night;
Oh, if only a Barnum would take them away,
  You don't know how I'd dance with delight!

This last verse was very easy to understand, as the women are always anxious to obtain occupation for a lesser remuneration † than the qualified guides, who naturally dislike this interference between them and their earnings, although no bad feeling really exists on the matter.

After an enjoyable kettledrum, the tea being our own and made under personal supervision, Miss Blunt perched herself on a hillock to sketch, and Mr. Sydney explored the neighbourhood for flowers, of

---

* Alluding to the custom in France of burning bits of candle to denote the time in which the bidding may proceed; usually when the third piece goes out the bidding for the special lot is finished, and the next is proceeded with.

† There is a good tale told, *àpropos* of this, of a gentleman in San Francisco who wanted some wood chopped. An American offered to do it for a dollar, but a Chinaman asked only half. The gentleman, thinking it best to help his own countryman, gave the Yankee the job; but happening to pass the yard during the day, he found the Chinaman busily at work. "Hullo!" cried he, "I didn't give the job to you. Who told you to cut this wood?" "Melican man" (American man), responded the pigtailer. "And how much is he paying you?" "Hap dollar," replied the Celestial. And the swell went away resolved never to help his countryman again.

which gentians were the principal object of his search. Both having in a certain degree attained their ends, we started again at half-past four, and after a pleasant drive, which lasted two hours instead of three—the time occupied in coming—we reached our quarters in the best of tempers and not with the worst of appetites.

CHAPTER IX.

FROM LUZ AND ST. SAUVEUR TO BAGNÈRES DE LUCHON.

A smiling valley—Lourdes again—The chapel in the crypt—St. Peter's statue—Burnished toes—Solemn quietude—Preparing for the great pilgrimage—" Ornamented " crosses—Mr. Sydney's new vocation, " guide, philosopher, and friend "—Bigorre again—An open-air concert—Harmonious echoes—Paying through the nose—The fête at Payole—Sport à la française—Costumes—The view from the Col d'Aspin—Arreau—Quaint houses—La Chapelle de St. Exupère—A whining " gardien "—Eglise de Notre Dame—The River Neste—Hôtel de France—Bordères—Avajan—Louderville—Oxslips and cowslips—Wild narcissus—Col de Peyresourde—The view—Garin—Cazaux—St. Aventin—Lovely avenues—Our destination.

WITH a morning as lovely as the day of our arrival had been dreary, we left at 9.15 for Bagnères de Bigorre, the first part of our long drive. The valley, more fully clothed than it was a week ago, looked so fresh in the warm sunlight, with the river winding along, that we felt very loath to leave. The gorge below, all the way to Pierrefitte, added its share of beauty, and the graceful white heath growing up its sides loaded the air with a sweet scent. The wide expanse of the Argelès valley, with the busy farmers ploughing, sowing, or cutting the heavy clover crop; the lazy oxen ever patiently plodding beneath their heavy burdens; the Château de Beaucens—where the orchids grow—perched up on the hillside; the surrounding peaks throwing off their snowy garb; and the beautiful young leaves and tints, everywhere mingling with the brightness of the flowers blooming on the slopes or amid the waving grasses, made a scene as picturesque as it was charming.

Compared with the scenery so far, the remainder of the drive to Lourdes, which we reached in three hours from the time of starting, though full of many pleasant corners in which the river heightened the effect, was nevertheless not so fine; but Lourdes itself looked more attractive than on our former visit. After lunch, while the horses were resting, we drove in a local milord * to the church, as we had omitted before to visit the chapel built in the crypt underneath. In the entrance is the fine bronze statue of St Peter clasping the key, similar to the one in Rome both in size and in the highly-burnished appearance of the toes of the right foot, for which latter the affectionate pilgrims are answerable. On either side of the statue a corridor lined with marble tablets—presented by "grateful" individuals in acknowledgment of cures and cleansings—and dotted with confessional boxes, leads down to the chapel. The repulsive gaudiness of the tinsel display in the church above it is almost absent here, and though the same exaltation of the Virgin over our Saviour is manifest, yet otherwise this chapel, with its vaulted roof and its quietude, seems far more fitted for meditation and prayer.

Taking the easy gradient at the west end of the church, between the grassy slopes planted with lilacs and other shrubs and trees, we arrived at the grotto. A huge platform was in course of erection, for the

* A kind of victoria.

great pilgrimage expected from England in about a week, and the noise of the workmen combined with the sparse gathering of "worshippers" detracted greatly from the former pitiable solemnity of the scene, though the stand of candles was flaring with light, and the crutches, in their horrid rows, were still there.

We left Lourdes again at three o'clock, the sun still very warm, as the lazy attitudes of the peasants working in the fields attested; and, passing several crosses at the roadside—"ornamented" with pincers, hammer, nails, and sword, with a bantam cock on the top—reached the base of the col (600 feet high) which separates the respective basins of the Adour and the Echez. Half-way up the hill we discovered Mr. Sydney, who had walked on ahead, very busy with a team of oxen, towards which, having encountered them without a driver, he had taken upon himself to act as "guide, philosopher, and friend"; and by dint of great application of his umbrella, open and shut, in the last-mentioned capacity, he brought them to, and kept them at, a standstill by the side of the road till the carriage passed.

From the top of the hill we enjoyed an extensive view, the Pic du Midi de Bigorre standing out wonderfully clear. Descending again, we joined the Tarbes road crowded with market carts, and leaving the village of Montgaillard on the left, duly arrived at Bagnères de Bigorre, where we were received with open arms by Monsieur and Madame Bourdette.

The morrow being Sunday, was spent in resting, the magnificent weather still continuing. The trees on the Coustous and the different hills around were at length well covered with foliage, and gave a

FROM LUZ TO BAGNÈRES DE LUCHON.

prettier appearance to the town, which the ever-flowing streams by the roadsides greatly added to. In the evening the Orphéon (or local Choral Society) gave an open-air concert from the roof of one of the Coustous cafés. A tremendous crowd of some 2000 persons had gathered under the trees to listen, and kept perfectly still while the songs proceeded. The solos were not particularly wonderful, but the beautiful blending of the voices in the Pyrenean

part-songs was a very great treat, and the sounds, floating deliciously away on the soft evening air, could be heard like some whispering echo for a long distance.

We had some difficulty in arranging for a carriage, on the following day, for Luchon, as a great number had been engaged for the fête at Payole, and for those not yet taken high prices—considering the time of year—were asked. Not wishing, however, to lose a day, we settled for a landau and three horses to do the journey in two days—for 110 francs, including *pourboire*—stopping the night at Arreau. The day broke, like its predecessors, perfectly fine, and at 10.30 we made our adieus to Bigorre, and were on our way.

The scenery all the way to Payole was more charming than when we drove there* previously, and on our arrival at the Hôtel de la Poste there was a considerable difference visible there. The courtyard was filled with carriages, and a busy throng buzzed about the doors, while the windows were occupied by a variety of forms. Having with great difficulty secured utensils, we unearthed the lunch, and proceeded with our meal at a side-table. The participators in the fête, who were all men, occupied the centre table, and others were at the side. The noise they made was not appetising, and though they mixed wines considerably, their jokes did not improve; yet the scene was a very typical one of "Frenchmen out for a holiday." After our repast, we adjourned to see the fête, and a wonderful treat it was! Tame rabbits and fowls, fastened to a stake driven into the hillside, some 90 to 100 yards from the road, were the targets, at which a perpetual round of shots soon commenced. Double-barrelled guns loaded with ball were the usual weapons; one or two single-barrelled pieces and a rifle or two being occasionally seen.

The marksmen seemed peculiarly poor ones, from the country lad, or the genuine 'Arry, with huge check clothes, to the moustached "masher," with tight trousers and rounded jacket. About one "poulet" in fifty shots succumbed, and a white rabbit's dismissal was received with loud acclamations.

At 2.30, exactly two hours after our arrival, we

* See pages 40–44.

were off again, and soon entered the pine forest. It looked very bonny in the bright sunlight, while the view from the Col d'Aspin was singularly felicitous. Not a cloud anywhere. The mighty Posets, the Pic d'Arbizon, and the other snow-crowned heights, softened by distance and beautified by the tints in the foreground, stood out against the azure sky in all their splendour.

The Aure valley, as we descended, and the tiny hamlet of Aspin, looked very peaceful and lovely; in fact, the whole of the extensive scene—considered one of the finest to be enjoyed by driving in the Pyrenees—seemed to spread out its charms before us.

Winding down the splendid road, Arreau was soon in view, and at 4.30 we drove under the portico of the Hôtel de France, somewhat dusty, but wholly pleased. With some time to spare before dinner, we set out to explore this wonderfully quaint, and—though dirty —strikingly picturesque old town. A road leads from the courtyard of the hotel straight to the very ancient-looking market-place and the river, at which point the latter is crossed by a very old wooden bridge. Traversing this, and passing several curious houses with verandahs reaching over the street, we found ourselves at the ancient Chapelle de St. Exupère, built during the 9th and 10th centuries, but now restored. The windows are of fine stained glass, and the view from the belfry tower, over the peculiar old town—with its curious turrets and roofs, whose best days have long passed—is worth the somewhat arduous mount to get to it. The peasant girl who stands inside the door, and in a sing-song voice that never varies mixes up saints, fathers, towns, corn, potatoes, bells, and "quelque chose pour le gardien," in her rigmarole, was the least attractive adjunct of the venerable pile!

Down a little alley, across the river, directly opposite the church, Miss Blunt discovered a suitable spot for a sketch,* and on the production of materials and a chair from a neighbouring grocer's she set to work, and in spite of the nearness—we might say the "too odoriferous nearness"—of a dust-heap, a drain, and a swarm of midges, she gallantly pursued her task till it reached a highly satisfactory termination.

Leaving the "ambrosial spot" (Jupiter save us!) we followed the road leading past the old market-place at right angles to the wooden bridge, and reached the church of Notre Dame. Though more modern than the "Chapelle," it is at least three centuries old, having been built on the ruins of the one originally erected in the 12th century. The wooden reredos behind the altar, and other wooden carvings, seemed especially good, but the curé, jingling a bunch of keys, preceded by an abbé, seemed anxious to see us depart; so we prematurely left. Strolling back through the town, and over the stone bridge that spans the Neste, we walked for a short distance on the other side, and then past the post-office and the Hôtel du Midi, to our own quarters for dinner. The Hôtel de France, as it is called, is the best in Arreau, but is nevertheless not much more than a fairly large country inn. The rooms are very clean, and the food good, but the arrangements are somewhat primitive; yet for all this we were very well satisfied on the whole, though the necessity of starting at nine o'clock next morning prevented us indulging in rhapsodies.

* Unhappily this sketch was afterwards lost, so cannot be reproduced.

When we left the courtyard and passed through the back part of the town by the old church, the sky was still of the same lovely hue, though unhappily there was hardly a breath of wind. Notwithstanding that Arreau is charmingly placed, and that the trees were fairly forward there, we soon found at a very slight increase of altitude that this was not to last; in fact, almost at once after passing Bordères (2¼ miles)—an old village with a castle of Jean V., a change was apparent. Two miles further brought us to the insignificant hamlet of Avajan, and another three of continual ascent to the outskirts of Louderville (3280 ft.), with its old watch-tower (14th cent.) and cool cascade. Here we had a fine view of the valley below, and passed fields covered with oxslips, cowslips, and other flowers; while lower down, meadow after meadow was whitened by the lovely wild narcissus. Following at a very easy pace the long zigzags (two hours and a half from Arreau), we reached the highest point of the road at the Port or Col de Peyresourde * (5070 ft.), whence the view, though much more limited than that from the Col d'Aspin, extends over the valleys of Louron and Arboust, and many snow-peaks as well.

As we descended the splendid winding road at a rattling pace, with the slipper on the wheel, we quickly left barren trees and slopes behind, and even at Garin, that curious village built among the rocks, the silver birches were opening their leaves. Passing in turn the villages of Cazaux, with its 12th century church, and St. Aventin, with its double-towered church of a similar date, also, we sped under most splendid avenues of sycamore, elm, lime, and ash, past dashing streams and bright flower-clothed slopes—

* 35 miles from Bigorre, 11¼ from Arreau.

always descending—till we entered Luchon : Luchon surrounded by magnificent hills, Luchon guarded by the distant but ever-majestic snow summits, Luchon bathed in the scent of lilac and other sweets, Luchon cooled and beautified by avenues and squares of bright trees, and by gardens filled with the loveliest of shrubs and flowers. Such was the Luchon presented to us as we drove through the splendid streets and reached our hotel.

CHAPTER X.

BAGNÈRES DE LUCHON.

The bathing establishment and its surroundings—The lovely *Allées*—Montauban church and cascade—The Villa Russe and its genial host—Various excursions—Orphanage of Notre Dame de Rocher—The Vallée du Lys—The Rue d'Enfer and cascades—A lively scene—The view from Superbagnères—Loading wood—" The Oxen's Appeal "—Visit to the Orphanage—A " holy " relic—To Bosost—St. Mamet—" A Stumblingblock "—Cascade of Sidonie—Horse tricks and jockey dodges—Lizards in flight—Fashion on a donkey—On the Portillon 'twixt France and Spain—The Valley of Aran—Snug Bosost—A curious inn—Children with artistic bent—A bright pathway—Missing much, but thankful still.

THE most delightful of weather throughout our stay doubtless added greatly to our enjoyment of Luchon, and our willingness to agree with its title as "The Pearl of the Pyrenees"; and, in fact, to all people but those who love dust, noise, and fashion, this month of May is the pleasantest time of the year to go, see, and be happy.

The great bathing establishment, situated as it is in a lovely garden (Quinconces) with a charming lake overhung with the graceful weeping willows, and under the wooded sides of Superbagnères, seems to invite one to enter and bathe. When we looked in, very little business was going on, and one of the attendants, in the hope of receiving a small coin, was nothing loath to show us round.

It is the largest and most efficiently arranged of all the Pyrenean establishments, and can accommodate over 200 people at the same time; "douche" baths, swimming baths, ordinary baths, rooms for inhaling, rooms for "pulverisation," seemed to succeed one another with unending rapidity, as we followed our guide down long corridors or up flights of stairs; and when at last it was all over, and he had quietly and contentedly pocketed his coin, we felt as though we had been taking quite a long walk.

"THE 'PEARL' IN THE PEERLESS VALLEY."

The Allée d'Etigny—the principal street—and all the other *allées*, notably the Allée des Bains, make most delightful promenades, even in the heat of the day, so delightful is the shade afforded by the trees that line the way on either side. To walk from the "Thermes" along the Allée des Bains, turning into the Casino gardens, or continuing further—leaving the "Chute de la Pique" on the right—along the riverside till the road to Montauban cuts it at right angles, is a most delicious evening stroll. We prolonged this, by taking the road in question between the poplars up to the village of Montauban itself; but found more interest in the beautiful new church than in the waterfall at the back of the village, which is gained by passing through the good curé's garden, and for which privilege half a franc is charged. The church, of white

THE CHURCH OF MONTAUBAN.

stone, very symmetrically built and of quite a different architecture from the usual French types, stands out imposingly at the entrance to the village, backed up by the tree-clad hills and the cottages beyond. The interior is most chaste and tasteful, as different from the usual Roman Catholic interior as is the outside from the general exterior, the texts on the pillars near the entrance being quite an unusual feature. Whether the decoration was not yet finished, and the tinsel therefore not yet arrived, we could not learn ; but are afraid it is only too probable, as the church, as it stood, might have been one of our own; for even the gilt pulpit harmonised so well with the rest, that it did not detract from the religious and solemn effect, while the light through the finely-coloured windows threw a softening glimmer over all.

We returned by a short cut through the fields on the left and the garden of the Villa Russe, whose owner, "charmant et gentil," not only showed us all over, but very kindly invited us to a strawberry feast a month hence—which sorrowfully we had to decline—as well as making us free of his garden and fields, the latter being filled with the sweet-scented narcissus.

The Hôtel Canton, in which we were staying, was very conveniently situated and comfortable. While standing in a quiet part of the Rue d'Espagne it was close to the post-office and casino on the one hand, and the bathing establishment and the Jardin des Quinconces on the other. Moreover, the stables of Jean Sanson—a most excellent guide for all excursions—were close at hand, and his horses would be difficult to beat ; while his son Luis is experienced in all trips and ascents, not only in the vicinity, but over a large part of the Pyrenees.

The new casino, barely three years old, is situated in as charming a quarter as could well be imagined, for besides possessing a finely laid-out garden with many fine shrubs and trees, it is bounded by three beautiful *allées* as well. As previously mentioned, it can be gained by the Allée des Bains, but the most direct way to the building itself, from our hotel, was by keeping to the right along the Rue d'Espagne and the narrow street beyond (the post-office being to the left), opposite which a side entrance leads to the imposing edifice.

The three most popular excursions from Luchon are those to the Port de Venasque, the mountain pass at the head of the Pique Valley; the Vallée du Lys and the Cascades; and thirdly, the ascent of Superbagnères.

The greatest of all, and in truth the greatest in the Pyrenees, is the ascension of the Pic de Nethou (11,170 ft.), the highest of the range, and its two great buttresses, the Pics Maladetta (10,867 ft.) and Milieu (11,044 ft.). None but experienced mountaineers, with the most experienced guides, attempt this ascent, which is attended with much danger; but there are many other delightful trips in the vicinity, including a visit to the Spanish village of Bosost; up the Aran valley to Viella; a drive to the picturesquely-placed St. Béat, or to the old Roman town of St. Bertrand de Comminges.

Pleasant walks and drives are probably more numerous from Luchon than from any other Pyrenean resort, and though we were rather too early in the year for mountain climbing, the fine weather enabled us to enjoy several other outings, which we will describe in turn.

The Vallée du Lys and the Rue d'Enfer make an agreeable picnic, either in a carriage as far as the "Cabanes du Lys" ($6\frac{1}{4}$ miles), and then horses for the other $3\frac{3}{4}$ miles up to the abyss, the cascades, and the Rue d'Enfer, or on horseback all the way. We preferred the latter, and taking a good lunch in the saddle-bags, made a start at the favoured hour of

L

ten. Under the lee of the Quinconces, past the Hôtel Richelieu, Villa Richelieu, and the elevated Villa Marguerite, and we were fairly on our way, the air sweetly laden with the scent from the flower-decked fields and the lilac-trees in the gardens.

When we passed the little road on the left leading to the Orphanage of Notre Dame du Rocher, the lilac-scent was very strong; and the position of the various buildings in connection with the institution seemed so attractive that we determined to take a stroll there later on. Pursuing our way, with the restored ruin of the Castelvieil above us on its "monticule" overlooking the Orphanage, we were soon in a narrower part of the valley, with the wooded slopes on either side. Then we crossed the river to the left bank, which we followed until reaching the point where the road to the Hospice and the Port de Venasque led to the left, and ours crossed the river by a neat bridge (the Pont de Ravi) to the right bank again. A little beyond this, the route for Superbagnères—which we hoped to take another day—struck off among the trees on the right of the road, which in turn gradually bent in the same direction all up the beautiful Lys valley, till it again curved in the opposite direction and arrived at the base of the Cascades, where there is a fair inn (Auberge du Lys).* From thence the road forks, but the track to the left is the better of the two, at any rate if on foot, and by it—after fifteen minutes' labour—the foot of the Cascade d'Enfer is reached; and the Pont d'Arrougé in another quarter of an hour. A similar length of time is still necessary to reach a small tower whence a good view of the Gouffre d'Enfer and the Pont de

* Only in summer.

Nadie, above it, can be enjoyed. This tower is about a mile distant from the foot of the lowest fall. The other cascade (the Cascade du Cœur) is not a very difficult twenty minutes' walk by a path that leads through the trees to Lac Vert, and as there is a capital inn there (later in the season), we think that this would be a good spot for lunch. Even as it was, we managed to enjoy ours pretty well, for fresh air and sunshine are good appetisers, and the ride had added its effect besides. The return ride in the afternoon, when the sun was commencing to decline

THE RUE D'ENFER AND CASCADES.

a little, was very pleasant, and the snow-covered Port de Venasque, so beautiful in its whiteness, and yet for the same reason quite inaccessible, looked very lovely when tinged with the crimson hue that the setting sun shot o'er it, as we arrived in Luchon again.

The following morning broke beautifully fine, and Luis Sanson was at the door punctually at seven, with the horses for our trip up to Superbagnères.

The saddle-bags were again filled, and away we went, the horses—still so fresh—being eager for a canter in the fresh morning air. In summer the ascent is usually made by St. Aventin and the Granges de Gouron, in which case the road towards the Col de Peyresourde is followed as far as St. Aventin, and thence a way leading to the left; but we were too early for that route, as an avalanche had only lately fallen, so were obliged to go and return by the route used in the season for the return only, viz., by the "Pont de Ravi" up the Vallée de la Pique. Having reached the bridge and taken the path indicated by the sign-board on the right, we were soon among the trees, which lent a very welcome shade from the increasing heat, which even at this early hour (7.40 A.M.) the glorious Sol was not ashamed to diffuse.

At every fresh turn the strokes of the axe rang through the wood, mingled with the sound of voices, and after making considerable progress—during which our guide narrated incidents in his career as hunter, guide, and jockey—we arrived in view of a very lively scene. Workmen busy with the hatchet, the saw, and the plane, in the foreground; others in the rear occupied with mortar and stones, building a small but substantial house; a cart with oxen lazily waiting, like Mr. Micawber, for "something to turn up"; a few superior individuals in deep consultation, and the irrepressible sun struggling through the beeches and pines to have "his finger in the pie"—such was the scene we saw, but soon left behind. After this the

ON THE ROAD TO SUPERBAGNÈRES.

good broad carriage-road soon came to an end, and the easy gradient changed to a steep path among a grove of nothing but beeches, which emerged later on the slope of a somewhat bare and stony hill dotted with a few gentians. The view improved with nearly every step, growing magnificently vast ; and when at length we reached the summit, or rather a mound a few feet lower, but equally good as a point of sight (for the summit was covered with snow), we gazed on as grand an expanse of mountains and tree-clothed valleys as imagination could picture in the most lofty of its lofty flights.

Probably but few people will be disposed to deny that, considering the comparatively small amount of labour necessary to attain the summit, it is more than amply compensated for ; and, when the height of Superbagnères—which is only 5,900 ft.—is taken into account, such a grand sight is almost unique. For over two-thirds of a circle the chain of peaks continues, extending from the Céciré of Superbagnères to the Céciré* above Bosost, and even beyond. Beginning with the nearest, the Céciré (8,025 ft.) of Superbagnères, then come the Pêne de Montarqué (9685 ft.), and the cone-shaped Quairat (10,037 ft.), followed by the huge glacier of Crabioules, which, in spite of its eternal snow, supplies the various cascades in the Rue d'Enfer that flow into the Lys valley. Above rise up the Pic de Crabioules (10,233 ft.), the Pic de Boum (9,875 ft.), and the peculiar Tuc de Maupas (10,204 ft.) ; after which the Trous d'Enfer and the Pic de Sacroux (8,786 ft.) appear. The next of the near peaks is the Pic de Sauvegarde 9,145 ft.), but between the Sacroux and this, calm and clear, the highest peaks of the range, the Milieu, the Maladetta, and the Nethou, with the dead white glacier below them, rise in view. After the Sauvegarde, the Pic de la Mine (9,048 ft.), the Port de

* We have only the guide's authority for this name here.

Venasque (7,930 ft.), and the very pointed Pic de la Pique (7,854 ft.) appear, followed by the Pas de l'Escalette (7,877 ft.) and the Port de la Picade (8,219 ft.), towards which group the Vallée de l'Hospice leads.

To the left of the Picade, the cone of the lofty "Posets" may be seen in the distance, while more to the left, and more distant too, the Peña Blanca (9222 ft.) is also visible. Further round, over the wooded "cols" that guard the "Pique" valley, the Mont Ségu * and Céciré near Bosost, and the *Pyrénées Orientales* beyond, finished the magnificent chain. From another situation we could look down on Luchon and from this point were endeavouring to reach the little hut, where fodder and a few provisions can be found in the season, when an ancient shepherd bawled out in *patois* that the place was as yet tenantless, for which we felt thankful to that peasant, as it saved us a long tramp through rather deep snow, though for that same reason we were unable to reward his forethought as it deserved. Leaving him to pursue his guileless way, we descended into the beech grove for our lunch, and finding grateful shade at the foot of a fine fir, we opened the saddle-bags and proceeded to regale ourselves, finding some snow that we brought from the top very useful to cool the rather heated claret. After nature was satisfied we quickly descended past the previously busy scene, and when near the high road again came in view of some woodmen loading a cart with logs. To do this the logs had to be brought to an eminence above the cart, and bullocks were employed to drag up the wood. The men were treating them most cruelly, and

* We have only the guide's authority for the name.

once or twice they lowed so piteously, that we have translated it into

"THE OXEN'S APPEAL."

Working and toiling the whole of the day,
Working and toiling without any pay,
Only perchance a few mouthfuls of hay,
    From earliest dawn till late.
Held by the horns 'neath this cumbersome yoke,
Firmer fixed thus than a "pig in a poke,"
Feeling the "prong" and the lengthy stick's stroke,
    Ours, alas, is a terrible fate.

When straining our utmost, you bring the stick down
On our miserable backs; and you swear, and you frown,
Never thinking the sun is just "doing us brown,"
    As the furnace will do when we're slain.
We cannot pull more than we can, you must know,
And we cannot pull fast if we can but pull slow,
So why should you spike us, and ill-use us so,
    And make our hides tingle with pain?

We serve you well always, draw heaviest loads,
And never complain of the worst of bad roads;
While you in return use those blood-drawing goads
    At ev'ry conceivable time.
Be sure that no quicker or wiser are we,
But we *do* sometimes think if we got our horns free,
The position in which you would probably be,
    And you would not pronounce it sublime.

So listen, we pray, to our modest appeal:
With kindness more proud of our work we should feel;
And if those fierce blows you still ruthlessly deal,
    You'll make our flesh horrible stuff;
For though steaks are good beaten, that's done when they're cold,
And we're certainly not, nor as yet very old;
But as some day we'll have to be butchered and sold,
    We had better be tender than tough.
    If you'll try our plan—that is enough!

At twenty minutes past one we had repassed the graceful Jardin des Quinconces, with the weeping willows overhanging the lakelet, and were within the cool precincts of the hotel.

Having a couple of hours to spare another morning, we wended our way towards the Orphanage, "deep in the lilac grove." Turning off from the road, we followed the narrow track over the rustic bridge, and were received anything but hospitably by a huge white dog. We calmed him in time, however, and proceeded to inspect the buildings, but found nearly everyone shut up, though the little church—elevated above the rest—was, unlike them, thrown open. Its very rusticity and simplicity gave it a religious air which to us so few Roman Catholic edifices seem to possess. The badly-spelt and feebly-worded address to the Pope, to which he has affixed his signature, that hangs in a frame near the door, we did not consider much of an attraction, though to the members of the little congregation it would doubtless be a very holy relic. Forsaking this peaceful retreat, we climbed up the ascent behind, within view of the statue of the Virgin, but soon descended again, as the sun was at that time particularly "baking," and we were not doughty enough to pretend to resist it. After a cool spell near the chapel-door, watching the "painted ladies"* playing with the lilac blossoms, we trudged slowly back again.

One of the pleasantest as well as most interesting of our trips in the Pyrenees was from Luchon to the little Spanish village of Bosost, and as it is one of the principal pillars that uphold the chief title of this volume, it deserves a detailed mention.

This time the favourite hour of ten was not early enough for starting, so we were on horseback by 9.15, going very leisurely, being quite undesirous to force the pace, as the day was warm even at that hour.

* Butterflies, of course!

Up the Rue d'Espagne for a short distance beyond the Hôtel Richelieu (which hotel, from all we have heard, though large, is not too moderate nor owned by too polite a proprietor), and then we took the turning to the left, which (as the signboard tells) leads to St. Mamet. Without waiting to enter the old church to see its frescoes, we pursued the road branching off to the right, which presently left the Orphanage behind in the same direction. A few minutes later we had passed the frontier (French) custom station, and leaving the isolated Castelvieil (2514 ft.) for a short time on our right, and later in our rear, we bore up the Vallée de Burbe. We had only progressed a short distance when a huge rock was visible in the centre of the road, evidently a very recent gift from the adjacent height. Our horses having been so little used, were very fresh and rather fond of shying, and our guide's, which was an Arab, not only shied at the impediment, but wheeled round with the intention of going homewards. As we managed to make our own, however, pass quietly, the obstreperous one, after a brief struggle, was induced to follow their example. A little further on, we met a fine team of Spanish mules in their full picturesque trappings and bells. The two men in charge of them were dressed a little untidily, but their attire was equally picturesque, the coloured waistband, turban, and knee-breeches producing a very bright effect.

The bright yellow-green of the beeches, mingling with the dark and gloomy olive shade of the firs; here and there fields laden with the blue columbine and the "overrated" asphodel; the boulder-strewn slopes on our left, and the snow-ridges on the right; and the strong, fresh, and foaming cascade of Sidonie tumbling down beside us, made a very delicious contemplation as we went on our way.

Our guide in a most "gallant" manner got off his steed to gather Miss Blunt a few flowers, but when he endeavoured to assume his former elevated position, the "Arab" didn't see it. In fact he *would not be* mounted, and the unevenness of the track added not a little to the success of his manœuvrings. "Luis" had not been six months a "jockey" for nothing, however; so he lulled his steed into a sense of security by walking beside it for some time in circus fashion, with his right hand grasping the off side of the saddle, until a large stone showed its head at the side of the road. As they passed, he ran up the stone and was in the saddle before the animal realised that he was beaten, and when he did, it seemed to humble him to that degree that he never attempted even a curvet.

The number of lizards we disturbed was something wonderful. None of them were very large or very striking in colour, but they made up for this in animation; and their fearful trepidity and hurry to get anywhere out of sight was wonderful.

Just before entering the sunlit beech glades we overtook a noble cavalcade, consisting of three ladies on three donkeys, with a fat old woman leading the way on foot. They had their lunch with them, and apparently intended—judging by a certain hungry look they had—to make their repast at the earliest opportunity. The young and beautiful lady bringing up the rear was probably ignorant of the ludicrous figure she made with her "ultra" fashionable arrangement of steels, that gave her the appearance of having a large clothes-bag under her dress, or we don't think she would have started on the excursion in such a garment. If a member of the " Rational Dress Society" had seen her, there would probably have been an "exhibition" on the spot, and a general one —with all the latest "improvements" (?)—at Luchon a few weeks later.

After traversing a number of beautiful glades we entered the Firs—the Black Forest as it is called,— where bears are hunted in the winter, and through which the road ascends by a series of zigzags to the summit of the Col de Portillon (4275 ft.), and then descends for a short distance to the frontier, marked by a huge boulder, with the French flag on one side and the Spanish on the other. As we reined in the horses opposite to it for a moment, no one could dispute that we were indeed " 'twixt France and Spain." But we did not stay to enjoy this enviable position long ; and passing on, endeavoured to realise that we were no longer in France by fixing our eyes on the *Pyrénées Orientales ;* we could also see the Poujastou (6332 ft.) on our left, the Couradilles (6513 ft.), the Mont Ségu,* the Céciré,* and further forward the Entécade on our right. A short distance down the road there lay the Casino du Portillon, not yet opened for the summer gambling, and not very much further (viz., about a mile from the frontier), the Spanish custom-house, and the Casino de Roulette. Here the road divides, the branch to the Vallée d'Aran and Bosost bearing to the left, and the other, to Viella and the Artiques-Tellin, in the opposite direction.

Passing some ruined houses and fertile slopes in our descent, we soon obtained a fine view up both ends of the Aran valley, with the diminutive Garonne

---

* We had only our guide's authority for these names.

winding through, and Bosost snugly situated on the slopes of a hill round a bend in the road. The sun was pouring down in all his midday strength as we passed the roadside chapel of St. Antoine and entered the antiquated little village of Bosost, stopping at the Fonda de España for lunch.

This inn, from the road, was as much unlike an inn as anything we ever saw, and its ways and passages were somewhat unique; but upstairs there was a large room with a wide terrace facing the river, which only wanted an awning over to be rendered delicious. We were unfortunately too early in the season for this luxury, so had to content ourselves with lunching in the room, with wide-opened doors. When the provisions were spread out, in rushed the guide with an official document, and a franc to pay for having invaded Spain. We gave him the money, and asked to taste some honest country wine, which resulted in the domestic bringing us something rather strong, like new port, which did not go badly with water.

After the repast had passed pleasantly, we strolled out into the village, Miss Blunt being equipped with the requisites for a brilliant sketch. Unhappily, the subject was not easy to find, though we marched through most of the streets; but having visited the ancient church—with its chime of bells, like many others in Spain, arranged on a wheel—we found a spot by the side of a huge elm from which there was a good view of the sacred edifice. But it was a case of sketching under difficulties, as the whole or at least the greater part of the village children crowded round us, some carrying smaller children in their arms, some playing with flowers, others cutting bits of wood, and one and all managing to do their utmost to bother poor Miss Blunt. She accordingly finished the sketch as quickly as possible, and we all returned to the hotel to keep out of the oppressive heat.

At three o'clock we started homewards, going rather faster than when we came. Alternate clouds and sunshine overhead, the lights and shadows over the trees, the fields—radiant with gentians, oxslips, columbine, *polygalæ*, and asphodel—losing none of their charm.

At the Spanish custom-house we delivered up our passport, for which we had paid the franc, and then wound over the Portillon and gently back to our hotel, not arriving too late for the cup that soothes and cheers, but never cheers too loudly.

The morrow was to see us leaving Luchon—the charming, the beautiful—and all of us had a similar feeling, viz., that we might soon come and see the "Pearl of the Pyrenees" again.

It was true that we had missed all the noise and excitement which comes with the summer; that we had missed the troops of Pau-ites wearing out such of their "robes" as the heat would allow, and the throngs of gay Spaniards; that we had missed the crowds of invalids, the bands of music, and the worst specimens of the travelling world, "French tourists." But it was a truth for which we were very grateful, and we would certainly advise future visitors to take Luchon in the spring, and leave it before the heat and bustle of the season mar its peace, and the summer's sun melts the snowy splendour of the surrounding heights.

CHAPTER XI.

ST. BERTRAND DE COMMINGES.

Keeping to old friends—Valley history—Entering the Garonne valley — The picturesque St. Béat — St. Béat to Viella — Memories of the lovely Thames—Baths of Ste. Marie—Loures—The cross-roads—Weak walls—Entering St. Bertrand—An ancient house—The inn—A charming garden—The cathedral—A national disgrace—" The Crocodile of St. Bertrand "—The tomb of Hugues de Chatillon—Travelling desecraters—St. Bertrand's rod—The ruined cloisters—Desolation—Swine feeding—Montrejeau—The buffet—No milk!—French railway officials—Trying experiences.

It was not many years ago that travellers with heavy luggage were forced to travel in the clumsy diligence between Luchon and Montrejeau; and, especially in the summer when the press for places was great, very little comfort could be enjoyed during the journey, except perhaps on a fine day, when for a short space the vehicle stopped at St. Bertrand de Comminges. Now, the railway in an hour performs the whole distance; but we preferred to keep to our old friends, a "landau and four horses," and with the weather still propitious, left the comfortable Hôtel Canton at our favourite time, and were soon bowling down the Allée d'Etigny. In a short time the Allée Barcugna and the station were left behind, and we entered the broader part of the valley of Luchon. This valley was originally—*on dit*—a huge lake, and afterwards

—presumably when it had ceased to be such—became peopled by a Gallic race, whose "divinity," Ilixo,* has given his name to the surroundings. We presume in this derivation "consonants are interchangeable and vowels don't count."

Cier de Luchon (four and a quarter miles), above which to the west stands the Pic d'Antenac (6470 ft.), was soon passed through, as we crossd and recrossed the railway line, now following the River Pique, and now, for a short space, keeping along the line. Five miles further, and we left the Pique valley for that of the Garonne, passing through the village of Cierp, which lies to the right of Marignac, the station where passengers alight for St. Béat. This is a very picturesque village, about three miles east, perched above the Garonne in a narrow defile, possessing an ancient church and a good inn. The Pic de Gar (5860 ft.), which rears up to the north of the village, is very rich in flora; and the road passing through it (St Béat) afterwards leads by the villages of Arlos, Fos, and Lès to Bosost (twelve miles), whence it continues to Viella.

The valley at this point is particularly fertile and lovely, and as we progressed, frequently following the windings of the Garonne, memories of pleasant hours, both lively and dreamy, spent on some of the quiet reaches on the dear old Thames, seemed naturally to recall themselves; the similarity of the surroundings being in some parts so great.

At Saléchan (thirteen miles) the beautiful valleys of Siradan and Barousse branch off, and the scenery in the vicinity is deliciously bright and peaceful-looking. The bathing resort of Ste. Marie lies a mile

* Ilixo has now become Luchon.

northwards, and barely a mile to the west of it, on the road to Mauléon, the baths of Siradan are situated. Mauléon (1960 ft.) is three and a quarter miles west from Siradan by the village of Cazaril, standing at the head of the Barousse valley.

Still passing through charming country, we reached Loures (not to be confounded with Lourdes), at which place—being the railway station for St. Bertrand—carriages can be hired for the drive, a distance of six miles there and back. Traversing the village and crossing the bridge, we issued again on a vista of fields bright with trefoil and waving flowers, and backed up by finely-wooded hills. Away to the right, nestling among the trees, stands a pretty little village and castle, and as we passed on, St. Bertrand came in view over the crest of a wooded hill; and, arriving at the junction where the roads from Auch, Toulouse, and Ax join in, we ascended the hill on which this ancient town is situated.

Founded by Pompey the Great, B.C. 69, Lugdunum Convenarum, or Lyon, or—as it is now called—St. Bertrand de Comminges, though standing only 1690 ft. above the sea, seems from its isolated position, to be much higher; as the accompanying sketch by M. Doré testifies, though the latter exaggerates the proportions of the cathedral.

Though in a ruinous state, much of the old ramparts and fortifications remain, while in some parts many of the old stones seemed to us to have been used for ornamental walls, such as no one would consider fit to resist even a very modest cannon-ball.

Bearing to the left, we passed beneath the " Porte Cabirole," opposite to which stands a small kiosque, built, on account of the beauty of the view, at that point. The road continues between high walls underneath another archway, past the ruins of a curious house, with a winding staircased tower of the 13th century, which alas! before this appears in print, will probably have disappeared altogether; then bending to the left, and again to the right after a few yards, we

ST. BERTRAND DE COMMINGES.

drew up at the Café (called by courtesy Hôtel) de Comminges, with the ancient cathedral in full view. Having sent a telegram early in the morning, we found lunch ready for us, and though we had fared better elsewhere, we did not consider that for a "primitive Roman town" the meal was to be found fault with;

while as to the garden belonging to the inn, it was indeed a charming little spot. Although in truth but little more than a " spot," the bright and varied hues of its stocks, columbines, pansies, and sweet peas, with here and there a particularly fine iris, contrasting so effectively with the dark green of the ivy leaves and the blackness of the berries clustering over the old wall, gave it a charm which we could not fail to feel; and the view from the creeper-grown arbour over the richly-wooded hills and brilliant fields, with the bright garden as a background, made a scene to remember and enjoy.

Notre Dame, or Sainte Marie, as the cathedral is called, attracted our attention most, and though the front view is perfectly spoilt by the lofty scaffolding erected before it, the inside fully compensates for this defect, although it is impossible to view the ruinous state of some portions without great regret.

The English are supposed to be a very lucky people, and at any rate we have reason to be thankful that we are not a republic, nor as a rule neglectful of old historical buildings; and the sight of this magnificent old place, mouldering away with no apparent aid forthcoming—except such as the liberality of occasional visitors provides, and that, for such a work, is practically *nil*—did not provoke any wish to change our nationality. It is not as if the French said, "We are becoming a Protestant people, and therefore wish to destroy all signs of our having once followed the faith of Rome;" for in that case censure would be utterly misplaced; but surely if the national religion remains Roman Catholic, an ancient and wonderfully interesting old cathedral like this ought to be suitably preserved.

Having been built at two different periods (viz. the close of the 11th and the middle of the 14th centuries), the architecture presents two distinct styles, which in parts are particularly incongruous. The organ and pulpit combined, which are on the left of the entrance, constitute a very handsome work of the " Renaissance " period, and are most unique. On the opposite side of the building a crocodile—or the remains of one—hangs from the wall, doubtless brought, as M. Joanne suggests, from some Egyptian crusade ; but the " church " puts a very different complexion on the subject, as will be seen from the following, which —with all its faults—will be, we trust, pardoned, since it issues from the mouth of so badly-treated a reptile as

"THE CROCODILE OF ST. BERTRAND."

A crocodile truly, there's no one could doubt,
  On taking a look at my skin :
It's as dry and as tough as a petrified clout,*
  Though, alas ! there is nothing within.

I've been here on this wall for a jolly long time,
  And the " cronies " a legend will tell
Of the wonderful things, void of reason and rhyme,
  That during my lifetime befell.

They'll tell you I lived in " this " beautiful vale,
  And found in the river a home ;
While even the bravest would start and turn pale,
  If they chanced in my pathway to roam.

They'll tell how I swallow'd the babies and lambs,
  And harassed the cows in the mead ;
And such slander completely my character damns,
  While I've no one to help *me* to plead.

And they'll whine how I met the great Bertrand himself,
  The miracle-worker and saint.
But those women will tell any " walkers " for pelf,
  And swear I'm all black—when I ain't.

---

* This is a Yorkshire word, meaning " cloth."

ST. BERTRAND DE COMMINGES.

Yes! they actually say that St. Bertrand came by,
  And lifted his ivory stick,
Then dealt me a terrible blow in the eye,
  Which levell'd me flat as a brick.

But it's false! Just as false
    as that "here" I was
    brought
  On the back of that
    wonderful man.
But the crones just repeat
    what the "priest-
    hood" have taught,
  And it's part of a regular
    plan.

Why, believe me, they
    caught me afloat on
    the Nile
  As my dinner I just had
    begun;
I was chased by a host of
    the picked "rank
    and file,"
  And to them my de-
    struction seem'd fun.

And when I was dead they
    anointed my bones,
  And placed me up here
    on the wall;
But that organ at first was
    so loud in its tones,
  Of rest I found nothing
    at all.

A crocodile truly. You've
    heard my sad tale,
  And I say that such lies
    are a sin;
While the protests I make,
    seeming nought to
    avail,
  Are enough to make any
    one thin!

THE CROCODILE OF ST. BERTRAND.

Turning away from this "priestly" monument to St. Bertrand's miraculous powers, we passed along the side of the remarkable choir stalls—which take up the greater part of the edifice—and turned inside at an opening, near the high altar. The latter, decorated with the ordinary display of 19th century tinsel, does not call for much comment, but in a passage close behind it stands the mausoleum of St. Bertrand, built in 1432. The stalls were erected in the 16th century, and are worthy of much attention.

The rood loft, which is nearest the entrance to the cathedral, is ornamented with figures of the Apostles and Saints, and the exterior panels running along both sides, and divided by small choicely-carved columns, represent a diversity of figures; none, however, seeming to bear much, if at all, on religion. In the interior, besides the throne, there is a remarkable " tree of Jesse "—near the first stall on the right hand—which we thought was well done; but what with the different figures above each stall, the arabesques uniting them, and the less minute work under each seat, there was no lack of carving to be seen; and even if it was not all of the highest order, the general effect was strikingly good. It is worth noting that the cathedral, owing to some great error, was built facing north instead of west, and that consequently the east side is on the left of the entrance. Half-way up this side is the small chapel of Notre Dame de Pitié, in which the fine marble tomb of Hugues de Chatillon lies. The sculpture is especially fine, though the beauty is somewhat marred by names scratched with a pin or written in pencil, wherever sufficient level space is afforded. Since English people as a rule are credited with being by far the most numerous of this class of travelling desecraters, it was at least a satisfaction to notice that most of the individuals, who had chosen this objectionable—though probably the only—method of handing their names down to posterity, were French. This tomb was only erected in the 15th century, although the good bishop died in 1352, the same year in which the edifice was finished.

Several relics may be seen in the sacristy, and amongst them is the wonderful ivory rod with which the great St. Bertrand is supposed to have slain the much-maligned crocodile.

Close to the entrance to the sacristy a door leads into the cloisters, where the scene of ruin and desolation is painfully evident. In the portion nearest the church, which is roofed over, several curious *sarcophagi* may be seen; the rest is a series of pillars and arches from which the roof has long vanished. In the photographs (which may be bought at the inn) there is some appearance of order even in the midst of the decay, but this was probably carefully effected prior to the artist's visit; for when we were there the whole space was overgrown completely with weeds, among which a rose-bush and a few other flowers struggled to bloom, untended and apparently unthought of.

Passing again through the cathedral, whose windows are well worthy of mention, we made a detour round the town, and then started for Montrejeau.

The road does not pass through such charming country as we had seen in the morning, but at times there are some pleasing little bits. At one spot, where a grove of trees skirted the way, we noticed a large herd of swine, watched over by a solitary and silent female, to whom they appeared to give no trouble, never seeming to stray far.

Going at a fairly fast pace, we only took forty-five minutes to reach the ancient town of Mons Regalis, now completely modernised into Montrejeau. The advancing years have not only altered it in name, for, with the exception of the ruins of a twelfth-century castle, there is nothing to indicate its mediæval origin ; and as to the old-world look that is so pleasant to meet with, but now so rare, this town of the "Royal Mount" has no trace of it. The "buffet" at the station, however, can be recommended, although the "lacteal fluid," either in its pure or watered form, is decidedly scarce there. The dinner and coffee are good, and, like most dinners at the stations (always excepting such places as Amiens and Tours), moderate, when taken at the table d'hôte.

We had plenty of time for a meal before the train destined to carry us on to Pau was due, but in spite of that, through the boorishness of the station porters and staff generally, we did not depart without a lively experience.

It is well known that ladies as a rule are wont to travel with numerous small parcels, and there was no exception in our party to this rule, while Mr. Sydney and myself were not without *impedimenta* as well. In all, there were about a dozen—to put a familiar figure —too small or too fragile to share the dangers of the luggage-van. These, three respective porters promised to bring to the train, but as every porter broke his word, they remained *in statu quo*. And we may here remark how noticeable it is, that whereas English porters are always on the alert to earn a few coppers, their French representatives will rarely if ever help with anything but the registered luggage (which of course is in the company's charge), while a higher official, such as you would never ask in England, will occasionally assist—if desired to do so with politeness—but only occasionally. It is evident that the French Government reduce the staff to the narrowest limits, and do not intend porters to help in transporting any luggage but that which has been paid for in registration; and on the same principle as armies are organised in South America, for every "porter" there will be two or three superintendents.

To resume.—This perfidy of the porters placed us in a very unenviable position; the train was due to start, the ladies were in the carriage, but the luggage was in a pile at the other side of the station, and Mr. Sydney, thinking all was well, had followed the ladies. I was requested to do likewise, as the train was off; but instead of so doing, launched such a tirade at the head of every official within reach, that they kept the train waiting to return it; at last, seeing I was obdurate, at least half a dozen rushed to the offending pile, collared the various items, and bore them towards our compartment. As the first instalment arrived I got up, and the train started. The rest of the laden officials were ranged a few yards apart, and as our carriage passed, the packages and cloaks were thrown in. The scene they presented when the door was first shut was unique, but very deplorable, and it required the whole of the journey of four and a half *hours* to Pau, to calm our troubled minds, cool our heated frames, and make us look with equanimity on our experience. It would require *years* to efface the opinion formed on "French railway station" management; so in that we followed a method often pursued by schoolboys in early life, over the "Pons asinorum," and gave it up.

CHAPTER XII.

EAUX BONNES AND EAUX CHAUDES.

Carriage *v.* diligence—Early birds—Height of absurdity—Diminutive donkeys—A whitened region—" Crystal clear "—Washerwomen and their gamps—A useful town-hall—A halfway house—Moralising—A much-loved pipe—An historic ruin—A noteworthy strong box—" Ici on rase "—Where are the bears?—Women in gaiters—Picturesque costumes—A lovely road—A " perfect " cure—A spring scene—A billiard-playing priest—A well-placed pavilion—The Valentin and its cascades—Through solid rock—Gaps in the road—A grand scene—Wanted, an artist—A fine torrent—Professional fishers—Lucky guests—Musings—Poor Mr. Tubbins—Bonnes *v.* Chaudes—Over the Col de Gourzy—Peculiar teams—Guelder roses—Spinning.

NEXT year, travellers with luggage will probably be able to reach Eaux Bonnes in a much shorter time than now, since the railway ought then to be in working order as far as Laruns; but at the period when this was written, the only choice of conveyances lay between a clumsy diligence and a comfortable carriage.

Very few people would be likely to hesitate between the two, provided they were not travelling alone, and in that case even, they would probably only take the former as an " experience."

The " diligence " which starts from the Hôtel de la Poste at Pau has three compartments, for a seat in any of which the respective charges are 8 frs. 80 cents,

7 frs. 70 cents, and 6 frs. 60 cents. The "first-class" seats—which are of course the best—are placed behind the driver, and a large dusty-looking hood shields the passengers from the rain, but not from the dust, nor, since it is black and low, from the heat of the sun. The position therefore, even with ample accommodation, is a trying one, but when tightly packed, and wedged in with luggage to boot, on a warm summer or even spring day, the lot of an individual during the $5\frac{1}{2}$ hours' journey, with only a half-hour's break between, would, like the policeman's, be certainly not "a happy one."

When a party are going it is of course cheaper to take a carriage, which may be had for from 35 to 50 francs to do the trip in one day, or at the rate of 25 francs per diem, taking it for two days or more. As the distance between Pau and either Eaux Bonnes or Eaux Chaudes is $27\frac{1}{2}$ miles, and the distance of the one watering-place from the other $6\frac{1}{4}$ miles, the actual mileage from Pau and back again is $61\frac{1}{4}$ miles, to perform which in one day, and see the two towns as well, is a feat—though often done—hardly to be recommended. At least two days should be given to the task, and we do not think they would be regretted.

The heat in Val d'Ossau during the summer months is very great, and the lumbering old diligence usually runs during the hottest part of the day; we preferred an early start, and by half-past six were on the road, meeting a few people apparently wending their way towards the market, with flowers and vegetables for sale. Crossing the bridge and through Jurançon, where hardly a soul was astir, we sped along the dusty road to Gan (5 miles), at which town—one of the chief centres of the wine district—a road to Oloron branches off to the right. Here the inhabitants were really beginning to bustle; and as it was getting on towards eight o'clock, they were nothing too early, although they may have held a different opinion. At the corner of one of the streets we came upon a team drawing a long cart, which we unanimously christened the "height of absurdity." A pair of 17-hand horses were in the shafts, and in front, attached as a leader, was the smallest of donkeys. Miss Blunt thought it the *smallest donkey in the world;* but we have met with so many lately in the Pyrenees which were in turn, in her opinion, the smallest she had ever seen, that by this time the smallest donkey might be but little bigger than a rat; this, however, was not the case, as Mr. Sydney will attest.

The valley grew more lovely as we progressed, with the winding Néez stream running with merry music beside the road, and although Mrs. Blunt did not indulge—as on the way to Cauterets—in any raptures of her own, she was quite willing to agree with the rest that the frequent resemblance of the scenery to many of the lovely bits we have in Wales was most pleasantly apparent.

Shortly before reaching the blanched region of the lime-works ($7\frac{1}{2}$ miles), we caught a momentary glimpse of the Pic du Midi d'Ossau (9466 ft.), on which the summer sun had of late so relentlessly played, that the snowy crown had quite disappeared. Rebénac ($9\frac{3}{4}$ miles) was reached at 8.40, and there we crossed the Néez by a stone bridge, the stream then running on our right, and continuing thus for three kilomètres farther (11 miles from Pau), when it issues from the Grotto du Néez—only a few yards from the road. From this grotto a great part of the torrent is diverted, being utilised to supply Pau with its pure and sparkling fluid. Half-an-hour after leaving Rebénac we passed through the village of Sévignac, (12¾ miles), and had a splendid view of the Val d'Ossau from the bridge which overlooks Arudy, and which is overlooked in turn by a fine and well-situated house.

We had barely time to appreciate the curious rocks which abound near Arudy, when we passed the road leading off through that town to Oloron, and came in sight of a merry group of washerwomen, whose enormous umbrellas—being unnecessary, since it was perfectly fine—were open in a row, and with their shades of magenta, green, and blue, without mentioning sundry patches of other shades, made a wonderful contrast to the green bushes fringing the river.

At 9.40 we entered Louvie Juzon (16 miles), with its old church and curious belfry-tower, and its " mairie " turned into a school—for the nonce at least ; and passing the latter, we crossed the fine bridge over the Gave d'Ossau, on the other side of which the Oloron road leads off through Izeste to the right, and the courtyard of the Hôtel des Pyrénées bids us enter and rest.

How gladly the occupants of the diligences descend, for the short while adjudged sufficient, at this customary half-way house, who but themselves can tell ? Even we were glad to let the horses have an hour's rest, and to enjoy meanwhile some good hot coffee and chicken. The inn itself was certainly not a paradise ; but there were some lovely fields behind it, and in front, across the road, there was an old table and an older seat among the trees, down by the swift-flowing river. A charming place for moralising indeed ! None of us, however, were much in the style of the " melancholy Jacques," or, with our eyes on some vigorous fisherman higher up the river, we might have begun :

> "And yet it irks us, these bright speckled trout,
> Being native swimmers in this river, should
> From their own limpid pools, by gay, false flies
> Be cruelly decoyed."

Instead of this, however, we returned to the inn, where we saw a worthy count endeavouring to clean a huge meerschaum pipe that he handled with evident fondness, and finding our carriage ready—it being then nearly eleven o'clock—we continued our journey.

It was now that the real Val d'Ossau commenced, and though the drive so far had been much enjoyed, we soon passed into scenery both more fine and more wild. One kilomètre from Louvie on the left stands the ancient Château de Géloz ($16\frac{1}{2}$ miles) on a small hill, and on another hill beside it—of corresponding size —stands a church. The view here, with the village of Castets behind, the beautiful river below, and the wooded slopes and massive rocks above, was especially charming.

With many lovely fields on either side of us we drove at a smart pace towards Bielle ($18\frac{1}{4}$ miles), and at a quarter-past eleven entered the town, which in bygone days was the capital of Ossau. Here the celebrated Coffre d'Ossau, that contained archives dating from the year 1227, was kept ; and it is a noteworthy fact that the presence of the mayors of three towns, besides that of the President of the Valley Council, was necessary before this "strong box" could be opened.

There are many old houses and objects of interest, including some mosaics, to be seen in the town, and among other things that attracted our attention was a large board, painted in the most modern style, with a pair of scissors at one side and an open razor at the other, and the " welcome " information—" Ici on rase " underneath.

The village of Bilhères, situated above Bielle on the slopes of the hill, is not without interest on account of the richness of its copper mines, while during the dry season a track leads from it over the Col de Marie Blanque to the Vallée d'Aspe.

As we continued our journey the frequent puffs of dust alone gave us any trouble, but they caused us at times to screen our eyes and miss the view. The valley, now at its widest, with pastures high up on the hills seemingly as fertile as those beside the river, all bright with flowers or studded with well-leaved trees, spoke of peace and prosperity. It would have been hard indeed to imagine a huge and ferocious bear appearing among such cultivation, although the valley still retains its ancient name, signifying that it was once the resort of these animals; but a "dancing bear" is the only specimen of the race seen about there now.

At half-past eleven we passed through the village of Bélesten (20 miles), and a little beyond, when once more among the fields, came in view of a curious sight. Among the many fields, variously cultivated, was a square one dotted over with small manure heaps in rows. On the top of several of the heaps, native aprons (belonging, we presumed, to girls at work in the vicinity) were neatly placed. Was this a new fashion of rearing mushrooms, or a native invention for the propagation of aprons? No one could say, so we have given it up!

Further on we noticed a lovely little village among

the trees on the hillside to the left; our coachman called it Louvie la Haute, and we have heard no other name, as it is too insignificant to be mentioned in a guide-book.

One peculiarity of this valley seemed to be the wearing of frilled gaiters or leggings by the women. They seem to supply the place of stockings and shoes, being visible from just below the knee, and descending well over the instep, so as to hide everything but the toes.

It must have been market-day at Laruns (23¾ miles), for when we arrived there at noon the streets were so full of carts and people that it was a matter of difficulty to get past. If the extra bustle had betokened one of the fêtes, of which the chief is held on August 15th annually, we should have been far from disposed to grumble, since it is at these Laruns fêtes alone now that the old picturesque Ossalois costumes can be seen. M. Doré has depicted a few natives in these costumes at their devotions in the ancient church that stood beside the route; but no one is likely to do so again, as the edifice—when we passed it—was falling into ruins and looked in a deplorable condition, the finely-sculptured doorway being partly hidden by the fallen débris. But not only the church, but more or less the whole village, seemed in a tumble-down condition, and this appeared to us especially strange, as everywhere around prosperity seemed to reign; and further, since the railway from Pau, which was to be opened this year, appeared nearly completed, the fact of Laruns being the terminus at this end of the valley ought to render it yet more prosperous.

Just inside the village we crossed the bridge over the almost dry bed of the Arrieuzé (beyond which the old road to Eaux Chaudes branches off to the right), and then traversing the Gave d'Ossau, we continued under the trees along the ancient route to Eaux Bonnes. But not for many minutes, for, where the old road which leads to the Bear Grotto also begins

to ascend, the new route strikes up to the right, and continues with an easy gradient to the point where it forks (2¼ miles), the continuation to the right leading to Eaux Chaudes, and the branch to the left—which we followed—to Eaux Bonnes.

No pains have been spared to render the remainder of the journey attractive to either the rider or the pedestrian, and to us the drive up the broad zigzags, planted with plane trees, silver beech, ash, polonia, aspen, arbutus, burberis, and innumerable other handsome trees and shrubs, was a pleasant one indeed. One rocky bit on the right of the way, completely overhung with beautiful ivy, seemed to us especially picturesque. Admiring thus all the poetic touches in form or colouring as we passed, we suddenly, and almost without warning, found ourselves entering Eaux Bonnes ($27\frac{1}{2}$ miles), and but a very few moments more sufficed for our conveyance to the excellent Hôtel de France, where the hostess was ready to receive us.

It would, indeed, be hard to find a more charmingly compact little town than Eaux Bonnes, anywhere: a perfect little miniature, very happily situated and beautifully clean and neat. What more could an invalid desire? Why, the very beauty of the surroundings ought to act perceptibly on the constitution, and when baths and perpetual tumblers of the rotten-egg fluid are indulged in besides, a perfect cure *must* be guaranteed.

It requires but few words to describe the shape and appearance of the place, but to convey an *accurate* idea to the reader is, we are afraid, a very difficult matter. The town is triangular in shape—almost an isosceles triangle, in fact—and this triangle is formed by the shape of the gorge, whose rocky, tree-clothed sides overlook it. Fine rows of hotels and restaurants, and other buildings—mostly let as furnished apartments—form the outer edge of the triangle. A good road separates these from the Jardin Darralde, which is likewise triangular, and planted with trees and shrubs in the most agreeable manner, both for neatness and shade. In the centre is the band-stand, and a bed of roses surrounds it. This is a general description, but it does not speak of beauty, and we thought that Eaux Bonnes was undoubtedly a beautiful place.

Suppose a triangular slice were cut out of Hyde Park, combining some leafy trees and a pleasant flower-bed with a band-stand added, and hotels and restaurants were erected around it; then, that it were transported to a narrow part of the Llanberis Pass under the very frown of Snowdon; and snow should fall on the surrounding summits; and magnificent beech groves and cascades appear down the wild slopes below, some idea of what Eaux Bonnes is like might be gained; but even then it would be little more than an idea.

It certainly has not the grandeur of Cauterets, the freedom of St. Sauveur, or the expansive loveliness of Luchon. It is hemmed in by the surrounding heights, of which, at the head of the Sourde (or Soude) valley (in which it lies) the magnificent Pic de Ger is most conspicuous, and doubtless this renders it a "warm retreat" in summer; but to see it as we saw it, with the sun shining on the rain-spangled leaves of the trees in the Jardin Darralde, on the lighter green of the beeches above, and glinting through the foam of the "Valentin" cascades; with no invalids, no gallant French horsemen, no gaily-dressed women, but only a few peasants dotted here and there, at work, to give life to the scene—to see it, in short, as it is in spring, can only give rise to pleasant feelings, which would mellow into pleasanter and more appreciative memories!

The amount of rain we had during our stay was only sufficient to cool the heated atmosphere and lay the dust; but Eaux Bonnes has rather a watery reputation, and many are the times that the visitors become victims to a shower, returning from their "constitutional" or their visit to the baths.

When we arrived the hotel had only been open a very short time, as the "season" was far from beginning, and the only other occupants, as visitors, were a rather stout man and a fat, jovial-visaged priest. We discovered them in the billiard-room as the priest was just in the throes of a most simple cannon, and our entrance appeared to damage his play, while his face rather lengthened, as though he felt ashamed at having been surprised at a worldly game. This may have been our fancy, as he was certainly the first R. C. priest we had seen with a cue in his hand; perhaps, however, he will not be the last.

After this we lunched, and after that, left the hotel and walked up the main road towards the Sourde Gorge, passing a choice marble shop, the bathing establishment, the church, and the town-hall. Beyond this last-named building the gorge narrows and extends to the base of the Pic de Ger (8571 ft.). Leaving this on our right, we followed the Promenade de l'Imperatrice, that ascends above the town-hall, till the path leading to the little kiosque—built on the summit of a rocky eminence called the "Butte du Trésor"—branched off to the right.

The view from the little pavilion is indeed a gratifying one, for though not extended, it is so entirely choice and picturesque; while the name of the eminence on which it stands, and from which some of the healing springs are said to rise, is decidedly appropriate, since there can be no doubt that they have proved a "mine of wealth" to several, although, as M. Taine remarks, it is "grotesque that a little hot water should have caused the introduction of civilised cooking in its very cauldrons."

Descending from the kiosque, we continued along the Route de l'Imperatrice, over which the beeches and other trees made a pleasant shade. This is a

CASCADE DU VALENTIN.

special walk for invalids, as it is constructed in zigzags of the easiest gradient, and while being both sheltered from west winds and open to the sun, it also commands at various points a good view of the River Valentin, the lower or Discoo Cascade, and the bridge which spans it; as well as the Route Thermale to Argelès, which follows the right bank of the river.

Most of the numerous cascades in the neighbourhood—thanks to the engineering of the "Empress's Walk" and the road to Argelès—are in easy walking distance for most people, even invalids; those usually visited being the Cascade des Eaux Bonnes, de Discoo, du Gros-Hêtre and du Serpent; the Cascade de Larsessec (3¾ miles) requires some fatigue to reach.

The road leading from the river back to the Hôtel de France passes between two walls of rock against which the houses are built. This passage has been made by blasting the solid rock, and it seemed that the work had been one of no small difficulty.

All great excursions were denied us, as neither the Pic de Ger nor the fatiguing Pic de Gabizos were sufficiently free from snow; while the road to Argelès still remained broken down in three places, and it seemed as though July would disappear ere the terrible gaps made by the avalanches could be built up anew.

We started for Eaux Chaudes in the cool of the afternoon, anticipating a pleasant drive, and were very far from being disappointed. After retraversing the road to the branching point above Laruns—near which the fields and banks were rich in gentians, violets, scabii, *linariæ*, and columbines—we seemed suddenly to plunge into the Gorge de Hourat. There can be little doubt that there is no truer specimen of a gorge in the Pyrenees than this. The piled-up crags overgrown with heather, and the splendid pastures above on the hill-tops, seen in the Cauterets Gorge, were missing; so, too, the varied tints and softer landscape bits of the St. Sauveur defile were absent; but here the masses of rock rose straight up on either side, at times seemingly ambitious to hide their summits in the clouds; while the roar of the torrent issuing from the Hourat (or Trou, *i.e.* hole) above which the road passes, only served to heighten the grand effect of the scene.

Just after the narrowest part is passed, a small chapel may be noticed high above the river on the right. It marks the scene of a frightful accident. The old road, which was in use till 1849, passed by the spot, and a heavily-laden diligence full of passengers overturned—through the horses taking fright, it is said—and the whole complement were dashed over the rocks into the torrent below. The chapel has since been erected, but though the old road still exists, and, in fact, joins the new one at the Pont Crabé—which beautiful place is admirably depicted in the sketch—there is little danger of such an accident occurring again.

A little further on—viz. about two miles from Eaux Chaudes—we noticed below us as charming a subject as any painter could wish for. A small plot of velvet-like green-sward beside the rushing river; some trees, leafy almost to extravagance, gracefully arched above; a few sheep descending a narrow track on the hillside; and above all, the immense rocky heights, around the base of which beeches and other trees luxuriantly grew, and many beautiful flowers bloomed; and, thus garlanded at their base, their stern and massive summits looked grander still, and completed such a picture of majestic beauty as no lover of nature could fail to enthusiastically admire.

One mile further there is another fine sight, though not of the comprehensive beauty of that just mentioned. This one doubtless is not worth seeing in mid-summer, when the sun has dried up the mountain streams, but when *we* passed that way we could see

CRABÉ BRIDGE, IN THE EAUX CHAUDES GORGE.

from the very summit of the hill—above which the pointed Pic de Laruns reared its crest—a mass of foam issuing from between two rocks, no puny meandering streamlet, but a strong torrent, which, as it dashed from rock to rock, gathered strength and velocity till it rushed amid a cloud of spray into the river below.

We saw one or two gentlemen—evidently early visitors like ourselves—anxiously whipping the river for fish, but they caught nothing; in fact, they told us afterwards that it was done with hardly any hopes of catching, since the "professional"—save the name—element came out with rods and nets, so that if the rods didn't answer they could net the pools instead. It seemed to us a remarkably good thing that "professionals" can't do the same in England!

There is another lovely scene not half a mile away from the town, where a path leads from the road to the riverside. There is a plot of green-sward here, and a grove of trees; and the river passes under a bridge, that vibrates with the force of the torrent surging against its rocky base. The path over the bridge leads through the leafy glades on the heights that overlook the river, and the town may be regained by crossing another bridge higher up.

Soon after, we were entering Eaux Chaudes (27½ miles), and having passed the Hôtel de France on the left, and the gardens and bathing establishment on the right, we drove up to the Hôtel Baudot and were courteously received by Madame.

It appeared that we had arrived a day too late, as the marriage of Madame's niece with the hotel *chef* had been celebrated the day before, and wonderful festivities had taken place in their honour; while the guests in the hotel (fortunately not more than eight in number) had been regaled with champagne and many choice dishes.

While waiting for dinner we strolled about on the terrace, opening out of the dining-room and overlooking the river. It did not need the boxes of bright flowers that lined the terrace sides to entice us there, but they certainly added to the delightful picture of river and trees; and as one face reminds us of another, so this scene carried our memory back to another, but a more lovely one even, because the beauty of the trees was heightened by large bushes of azaleas—bright with various-coloured blooms—growing between. But beauty and comfort do not always go together, and for calm enjoyment this Pyrenean scene had the preference; for the other was in the heart of Japan, at the tiny village of Sakurazawa, and we gazed on the picture through the open *shoji*,* lying on the neat but hard—very hard—mats, that were our tables, chairs, and beds in one; which our host's assurance, that the Mikado himself had slept upon them the year previous, didn't make any softer. The announcement of dinner cut short further musings, and we took our places at the table, profusely adorned with evidences of the previous day's ceremony.

At a table-d'hôte of eight or ten people conversation is as a rule easy and general. It requires a so-called "typical Englishman" to keep himself within himself, in a shroud of pride and reserve, and the "typical Englishman" is, thank goodness, nearly out of date. We were very anxious to learn about the plateau above Gabas. Was this plateau really worth seeing; and if so, when was it best to start? Every-

* Sliding screens, being frames of wood pasted over with paper, acting as doors and windows.

body was ready to give their version of the trip, but Mr. and Mrs Tubbins (if we recollect rightly) seemed the most anxious to speak. Mrs. T. was simply a combination of bolsters which shook with the exertion of speech, while poor Mr. T., a meek, thin, haggard-looking man—and no wonder—seemed to be ready to put in a word if required, but looked in momentary terror of getting a snub instead.

This look was not an unnecessary one; for Mrs. T., with all her anxiety to give information, did not get on very fast, and made many mistakes in names, &c., which her worse-half tried to rectify, with the result that she turned on him with "Frank, I wish you wouldn't interrupt; you are quite wrong, you know!

However, from the general company we managed to gather a good deal of information, which, as a cloudy day spoilt our own trip thither on the morrow, it may be expedient to repeat. Gabas is only a hamlet of a few houses, and is in itself uninteresting. Situated five miles from Eaux Chaudes, it is reached by a good carriage road, which, crossing the Pont d'Enfer, continues along the left bank of the river the rest of the way, the views being chiefly of granite summits and thick pine forests. But though Gabas makes an excellent resting-place or starting-point for several excursions, no one stays there for any other reason, and tourists from Eaux Chaudes usually pass it on the way to the Plateau des Bious-Artigues or to Panticosa. The road forks at Gabas, and becomes no longer anything but a bridle path, the right branch leading to the plateau, the other passing by the Broussette valley, across the Spanish frontier, to Panticosa. The plateau is reached in one hour and a half, not without exertion, and the view over the

Pic du Midi d'Ossau is considered wonderfully fine. Several of our informants, however, had chosen bad days, and after all their labour, found a thick mist over everything that was worth seeing. Among these Mrs. Tubbins had figured, and her goodman had suffered in consequence. "The idea," she said, "of bringing me all this way, and at my time of life too, simply to see a mist, as if I hadn't seen plenty of them at home!" Of course she had come of her own

THE BIOUS-ARTIGUES.

accord, and the meek and injured one had followed as a matter of course.

The journey from Gabas to Panticosa requires a good twelve hours, and generally more; consequently an early start is advisable. It is a favourite way of entering Spain, and much more practicable than the route from Cauterets to the same spot.

Of Eaux Chaudes itself there is but little to say, for with the exception of the hotels, the bathing establishment, and a few shops, there is nothing to form a town. Like Eaux Bonnes it is shut in by the mountains on either side, but it is more oblong in shape, with two parallel streets. The Promenade du Henri IV., which leads southwards from the Hôtel Baudot along the side of the river, is a cool and pleasant walk, especially of an evening.

Various opinions exist as to which place is most suitable for a residence, the "Bonnes" or the "Chaudes." In spring probably the former, but the latter certainly in summer ; for not only is it free from the bustling, gaily-dressed crowd which throngs its rival, but there is a fresh breeze that blows up the valley which renders it always cool and pleasant ; while the scenery is as fine as the most fastidious could wish for.

The Col de Gourzy and the lofty Pic of the same name tower above Eaux Chaudes, and a route to Eaux Bonnes—which to good pedestrians is well worth the exertion—passes over the former. The path strikes off from the Gabas road to the left, while yet in the town, and passes by the Minvieille "buvette." For the first half-hour the route is the same as that to the Eaux Chaudes grotto ; this is an excursion, of two hours there and back, that is in great favour with tourists. Where the path forks, the one to the grotto is left on the right, and after some fatiguing work the Plateau de Gourzy is reached, from which the view on a fine day is splendid. The track then leads through beech glades and box thickets to the "Fontaine de Lagas" (near which a wild and beautiful valley branches off to the right), and finally joins the Promenade Jacqueminot at Eaux Bonnes. Horses may be taken the whole distance, but it is easier for them

—if tourists choose this highly-recommended route—when the start is made from Eaux Bonnes.

It rained severely early on the morning of our departure, but later, cleared up into a lovely day, enabling us to start at 8.30. The river and the cascades were full, and the sun glinting on the wet leaves gave a fairy-like appearance to this magnificent gorge. As we looked back from the cascade, which seemed to tumble from the summit of the Pic de Laruns, the clouds gradually rising over the head of the valley disclosed a huge snow mountain * to view, that appeared to form an impassable barrier 'twixt France and Spain.

When we reached Laruns we had a fine view of its pointed peak, and through the morning haze the lofty Pic de Ger over Eaux Bonnes looked imposing indeed. Travelling we found very pleasant. There was no dust, the air was cool, the roads just soft enough for comfort, and the whole valley refreshed with the morning's rain. The people in the fields worked with greater energy, and the bright scarlet hoods of the damsels, many of whom followed the plough, gave a pleasant colouring to an animated scene. We passed several flocks of geese, apparently unwilling to proceed at as rapid a pace as the good woman—with her frilled gaiters—who was in charge of them wished; but with those exceptions we hardly met anybody or anything on the road till we had passed Louvie.

What we then met were a couple of carts filled with coal, and as we never recollected having seen any such peculiar teams as they were drawn by, we con-

* The "cocher" called it the Pic d'Estremère, but we had no confirmation of this.

cluded they were "Ossalois," and "peculiar" to the valley. There were eight animals to each cart, four bulls and four horses. The bulls were harnessed in pairs (as in a four-in-hand coach), and acted as

THE PIC DE GER.

wheelers, while the horses, acting as leaders, were harnessed in line, one in front of another. Curious as this arrangement seemed, they made good progress with a very heavy load!

At Sévignac a splended Guelder rose-tree grew in a small garden over a mill stream, and a very ancient dame very willingly sold us some clusters which were peculiarly fine; in another garden a very fine bush of white *cistus* was completely covered with blooms. The hedgerows, too, were bright with flowers; the wild Guelder roses and medlars * preponderating, but elder bushes were also plentiful, and covered with blossoms.

At Rébenac we stopped at the Hôtel du Périgord for coffee and a fifteen minutes' rest, the horses not requiring any more, as the day was so cool. While drinking the "welcome liquid" we watched an old woman out of the window, spinning. Her distaff was apparently very old and dirty, and as she span she seemed to be crooning some ancient ditty to herself, thinking, maybe, of her children and grandchildren, or even of the days when she was herself a child.

We started again when the quarter of an hour was up, and bowled along towards Gan, meeting on the way several natives (men) with their hair in long pigtails, like Chinamen; they looked otherwise decidedly *Béarnais*, but their appearance was peculiar, to say the least of it. Beyond Gan we passed into full view of the lovely Coteaux, which afford such pleasant rides and drives from Pau, and as we gradually neared the town, the heat seemed to intensify to anything but a pleasurable degree.

Four hours forty minutes after starting we were once more under the roof of Maison Colbert, with

---

* The "makilahs," or sticks peculiar to the Basque people, are made from the wild medlar. They are very heavy, tipped with iron, and unpleasant to carry.

such a luncheon before us as fully justified the hospitable repute that it has always borne.

But Pau was far too hot for us to remain for more than a few days, although the heat was unusually great for that time of the year, and we were very glad when once more on our journey towards the pleasant breezes and blue waters of the Biscay.

CHAPTER XIII.

BIARRITZ.

A warm ride—Bayonne—A " Noah's ark " landscape—Amusements—Bathing—Shells—Cavillers—A canine feat—The pier and rocks—A restless sea—"The Three Cormorants"—Dragon's-mouth Rock—To the lighthouse—Maiden-hair ferns—Mrs. Blunt's adventure—The drive round the lakes—*Osmunda regalis* ferns—The pine-woods near the bar—St. Etienne and the Guards' cemetery—Croix de Mouguère—Cambo and the Pas de Roland—Anemones—A fat couple—A French scholar—Hendaye—Fuenterabia—A quaint old-world town—The Bidassoa—Pasages—San Sebastien—The Citadol and graves—The "Silent Sisters"—Raised prices—Parasols and spectacles.

THE journey to Biarritz began comfortably enough, but after the first few miles the heat became very oppressive, and though we had no repetition of our Montrejeau experience at starting, we felt nevertheless almost as warm as if we had.

Our arrival at Bayonne was a great relief, for the sun had partially retired, and as we crossed in turn the Adour and the Nive, a scent of the "briny" was borne into our omnibus with revivifying effect. Passing up one of the narrow old streets to execute a few commissions, we regained the "Place," crossed the drawbridge, and entered the lovely avenues, from which, beyond the "fosse," the twin towers of the beautiful cathedral come into view. On the right is the station of the "steam tram-line," and some hundred yards beyond it the road to Biarritz curves in the same direction.

This road cannot be called beautiful! The never-ending line of poplars along each side turn the landscape into that Noah's ark style which even the soul that could be "contented with a tulip or lily" would hardly admire. Approaching Biarritz, however, the handsome villas and their gardens fully deserve the epithet which cannot in justice be applied to the road. They are indeed beautiful; and to pass them even in winter, with the camellia trees laden with blossoms and the roses scenting the air, makes comparison with our London gardens very odious indeed!

Under the small-gauge railway-bridge, and past the new "English Club," we soon entered the town,[*] and driving down the Rue Mazagran into the Place Sainte Eugenie, drew up at the familiar Hôtel de Paris, in time for dinner.

Although Biarritz is in the department of the Basses-Pyrénées, it is so far away from the mountains that many might consider its introduction into this volume as questionable; we do not therefore intend to say as much as could be said about it. At the same time, it is so greatly recommended by doctors as a beneficial spot for a final "brace up" before returning to England, after a mountain trip, and is, besides, such a favourite winter residence, that we consider it would be more "questionable" to omit it.

Unlike Pau, its amusements are not of a very varied character. In winter, lawn-tennis and balls are the chief, and concerts occur generally weekly or bi-weekly. As spring asserts herself, bathing commences and picnics become the fashion; and in the

[*] The distance between Bayonne and Biarritz is 5 miles.

early summer—as long as the English remain—tennis and bathing go almost hand-in-hand.

The tennis-ground—which is only a short distance from the English church of St. Andrew's—is well laid out and commodious, possessing an excellent reading-room for members' use, as well. Of bathing establishments there are three; the large building in the Moorish style on the Plage, the less pretentious but more picturesque one in the Port Vieux, and the least pretentious and least protected one, under the "falaises"* beyond.

The first and last are only used in the height of summer; that in the Port Vieux—from its sheltered position—opens its box-doors as soon as winter really gives place to spring. The scene, when the tide is high on a morning in June, is often an exceedingly pretty one, for to the pristine picturesqueness of the surroundings is added those touches of human nature enjoying itself, which, if it doesn't "make us kin," goes a long way towards it.

The "Port Vieux" is triangular in shape, with the apex inland, along the sides of which the boxes are erected, reaching to the water's edge at high tide. In the middle lies an expanse of deep sand, and the blue waters roll in between the rocks and gently break on a shingly beach, where the tiniest shells and pebbles mingle to make the one drop of bitterness in the bather's cup.

When the sandy expanse is crowded with merry children, the roads and seats above filled with spectators, and the water with members of both sexes in varied costumes and "headgears"—not forgetting the boatman in the tiny skiff who is here, there, and

* Blue chalk cliffs.

everywhere in case he is needed—the scene is a very pleasant one to look upon. Of course there are always some narrow-minded individuals to find fault, some "maiden" aunts "with spinster written on their brows," who will put up their gold-rimmed glasses with that peculiar sniff that invariably prefaces some *extra sweet* remarks, such as, "Dear me, how wicked! Men and women bathing together in that barefaced manner; and . . . I do believe there's that forward Miss Dimplechin actually taking hold of Captain Smith's hand, and he a married man too! Thank goodness, I never did such a thing—never!"*

Above the Port Vieux, on the left, stands Cape Atalaya, with the ruins of an ancient tower, and a flagstaff on its summit. A road leads round its base, passing between a circular mound overlooking the "old harbour," and the yard where the concrete blocks are fashioned for the strengthening of the pier.

There are seats on this mound, whence people can watch the bathing; and we often saw a remarkable feat performed from it as well. A race of wonderful water-dogs—said to be a cross between the Newfoundland and the French poodle—is bred at St. Jean de Luz, eight miles from Biarritz. One of their uses is to drive the fish into the nets, and for this purpose one is taken in every boat that puts to sea. The method is extremely simple. As soon as the net surrounds a shoal, the dog is put in the centre, and by beating the water with his paws he effectually drives the finny creatures into the meshes. It was one of this same species of dogs that attracted so much attention at the Port Vieux by leaping after a stick from the mound—a distance of some fifty feet—into

* Did she ever have the chance?

the sea. He would do it as often as his master would let him, and appeared to enjoy it immensely, though he always reached the water before the stick, and had then to turn round and hunt for it.

The road, after skirting one side of the yard, crosses the trackway that runs down the pier and doubles up the other side, through the tunnel and past the Port aux Pêcheurs, into the Place Ste. Eugénie; whence, continuing by the base of the Hôtel d'Angleterre and the casino, it extends to the bathing establishment on the Plage. In the other direction it rounds the Port Vieux, and leads under the cliffs to the other resort of summer bathers; consequently, it might be appropriately termed the "Chemin des Bains."

The pier is a very favourite resort, and many a fierce fight with the waves is enacted at its extremity, in which, alas! the sea has always proved the stronger. As a rule, visitors are not permitted to pass the "Cucurlon" rock, on which the Virgin's statue stands; but if the weather is very fine, the gate is opened to admit of any who are so minded going to the end. On a wild day, with a high wind blowing inland, the "battle of the waves" is a fine sight, especially from the platform erected below the flagstaff on Cape Atalaya. Thence the full beauty of the huge billows, dashing into clouds of spray against the pier, and, unallayed, pursuing their course with relentless energy till they boom amid the hollow caverns of the hill, may be admired and wondered at.

There are two rocks which (as one looks seaward) rise up to the left of the pier, and serve to break in some measure the force of the waves. The larger of these in calm weather is frequented by cormorants, and has gained the name of "Cormorant Rock." There were three of these birds on it one very rough day, and we saw a scene enacted which—with due apologies to the late Rev. Charles Kingsley for thus adapting his pathetic verses—we have commemorated in the following lines, under the title of

"THE THREE CORMORANTS."

Three cormorant dandies were perch'd on a rock,
    Were perch'd on a rock as the waves dash'd high;
Each thought himself equal to any black cock,
    And proudly determined the sea to defy.
For cormorants fish, and cormorants catch,
And they swallow their prey with the utmost despatch,
    Without all the trouble of boning!

Three cormorant damsels were waiting at home,
    Were waiting at home for the dandies so dear.
"Oh, say! are they fishing where fierce billows foam?"
    And the damsels sat chattering their bills with fear!
For cormorant maidens *can fish* and *can catch*,
And each one considered she'd made a good match.
    And now for her dandy was moaning.

Three cormorant dandies were washed off the rock,
    Were washed off the rock by a powerful wave;
And, quite unprepared for the terrible shock,
    They sank in the depths of a watery grave.
For cormorants fish, and cormorants catch,
But if waves dash high they should use despatch,
    Or their loved ones will always be groaning!

There are some curious rocks in front of the new harbour, notably the "Dragon's-mouth Rock," through which on a rough day the water continuously pours; more to the right, between this and the "Plage," is a curious group known as the "Chinaougue."* A bridge communicates with the largest, on which

---

* Have never found any one able to account for this title, which is more barbaric than pronounceable.

"petticoat daffodils" grow, and the couples that may occasionally be seen going over there *doubtless* do so to gather these. Beyond the Port Vieux and underneath the Villa Belzar other curious formations may be seen, to which an iron gate at the head of a few damaged steps gives access.

At Biarritz itself there is really nothing to be seen except the sea. And yet this sea is so beautiful in

THE ROCKS OF BIARRITZ.

its varied moods, that a lover of nature can watch it day after day for any reasonable period, without a feeling of *ennui* or a wish for anything more lovely!

There are many pleasant walks and drives around, but most of them require a whole day, and are more preferable as a drive than as a walk. The shortest is to the lighthouse and back, and this is only a very easy promenade, taking about an hour; so we will deal with it first, leaving the longer ones to await their turn.

We started one afternoon when the sky was cloudless and the coastline very clear, hoping to obtain a good view of the Spanish coast, and a few specimens of maiden-hair fern, if fortune were favourable. We traversed half the town, when Mrs. Blunt suddenly came to a halt opposite the Hôtel de France, and pointed to a three-wheeled vehicle of the bath-chair type, to which a weird and very ancient-looking steed was attached. "I think," said she, "that would be more comfortable for me than walking; please inquire if it is on hire." So we applied to a fat dame, who was busily knitting hard by, and having arranged terms, Mrs. Blunt got in and we continued our way.

Down past the bank and at an easy pace to what was once the Villa Eugénie,* and continuing up the hill at the same speed, we gradually drew near the lighthouse, and when once the Villa Noailles was left behind and the level road reached again, we were soon at our destination.† The view of the coast to St. Jean de Luz, San Sebastien, and almost to Santander, was peculiarly good, as well as that on the other side in the direction of Bayonne; and while Mrs. Blunt remained in contemplation from her vehicle, we descended to view the rocks and caves below.

As a rule it is unwise to disclose where botanical treasures grow, as they generally become extinct soon

---

* This building, where Emperor and Empress lived at different times, now belongs to a company under the title of the "Palais Biarritz," and is employed as a casino and restaurant. "Sic transit gloria imperatorum."

† At low tide there is a way to the lighthouse along the beach in front of the Palais Biarritz, and up a steep path over the rocks. The other is much the better way, however, at all times.

afterwards, from excess of admiration on the part of collectors; but the maiden-hair ferns, for which the lighthouse rocks are known, can take very fair care of themselves, as they grow in such awkward positions—we might say dangerous—that only a few real enthusiasts, or an anxious collector with a *steady head*, are likely to venture to attack their strongholds.

We saw many specimens in the interstices of the rocks surrounding a moss-grown pool, but they were quite unapproachable. One clump above we did

VILLA EUGÉNIE.

manage to reach and bear away a few roots of, in triumph; but at one time there was only two inches of stone for the foot to rest on, with sheer rocks below; and consequently, without a rope, the experiment would hardly be worth repetition. However, without mishap we started on our return journey, and all went smoothly till the Villa Noailles was again reached; but at this point we suddenly noticed that Mrs. Blunt was rapidly out-distancing us. Whether the ancient steed dreamt of its former youth and activity, and "grew young once more," or whether its long rest had made it anxious to reach its stable, we know not; but the unpleasant reality was forced upon us, that it was rapidly bearing Mrs. Blunt away. Miss Blunt had been walking near the vehicle, Mr. Sydney and I had been rather behind; but as Miss Blunt started to run, we rapidly followed, and soon overtook the fiery steed, which, having by that time pulled up at the bottom of the hill, appeared to be anxious to turn round and have a look at Mrs. Blunt. As it neighed at the same time, perhaps it was asking, " Who's my driver?" but this was mere conjecture on our part, although we were not sorry to restore the

SCENE 1.—BEFORE THE START.

SCENE 2.—THE ANCIENT STEED GREW YOUNG ONCE MORE.

SCENE 3.—WHO'S MY DRIVER?

animal to the fat old lady—still knitting—and escort Mrs. Blunt back to the hotel, none the worse for her little adventure!

The favourite of the short drives is known as the "Tour des Lacs." It embraces the prettiest country in the vicinity, and the whole distance is about six miles. We found it most pleasant to start, after lunch, from the Place de la Mairie, turning up the Rue Gambetta past the market and on to the "Falaises," where the sea-breeze blows fresh and free. Keeping to the right where the road forks, the "abattoir" was soon left behind and the Villa Marbella reached; we then curved round "Lac Chabiague," and ascending slightly between fields gay with the "fleur des frontières"* and the wild daphne, we dipped again slightly to the point where the road to St. Jean de Luz forks to the right. Bearing to the left between hedges overgrown with *sarsaparilla*, and entering a shady lane, a few minutes sufficed for us to reach the "Bois de Boulogne," where the road skirts the Lake Mouriscot, and passes beside many splendid clumps of the *Osmunda regalis* fern. The lake is very deep and full of fish; but bathing is certainly not advisable, as there is a great quantity of reeds and weeds all round the water's edge.

Leaving the pleasant woods, we emerged on to the Route Impériale—the direct road from the Negresse station (on the main line to Spain) to Biarritz—and following it as far as the metals, we turned to the left up the Irun-Bayonne route. This, however, was not our road for long, as we took the first turning on the left-hand side up a pretty lane, which brought Lake Marion into full view. The other end of the lane

* A lovely blue flower, something like a gentian.

joins the "Route Imperiale" again; which, leading in turn past the cemetery, the parish church, and the terminus of the "steam tram-line," enters the town near the International Bank.

It will be noticed that there are several ways of reaching Bayonne. The cheapest and most expeditious, for marketing or other business purposes, is by the narrow-gauge railway, with its curious double carriages, one above the other. By driving the two miles to the Negresse station, and catching the express from Spain, is another way, but one not recommended to anybody but travellers* going to stations on the line between Bayonne and Paris. Of the three routes for driving we have already mentioned the most frequented one—at the commencement of the chapter; from the Negresse station by the Bayonne-Irun road is another; and the last and prettiest passes behind the Villa Eugénie almost to the lighthouse, but there branches off to the right past the Chambre d'Amour inn, to the pine-woods near La Barre, and thence into Bayonne! This drive may be prolonged in two directions: firstly, by crossing the Nive and the Adour to the Guards' cemetery (where those who fell in the sortie from Bayonne 1813–14, are buried) at St. Etienne; and secondly, by following the bank of the river for some distance (past the market), and turning up into the country by way of St. Pierre to the Croix de Mouguère. This latter makes a splendid picnic, and the locality is a rich hunting-ground for entomologists.

There are four other excursions that we must not

* Travellers for the Pau line have to change at Bayonne, consequently it is simpler for them to drive the five miles from Biarritz direct to Bayonne, than drive two to the Negresse station, with the necessity of changing ten minutes after entering the train.

omit to mention, viz., Cambo and the Pas de Roland, St. Jean de Luz, Fuenterabia, and San Sebastien. All of these, with the exception of the first, can be reached by *rail*, and as far as St. Jean de Luz the *road* from Biarritz * is common to all; so that to save space we will only mention it on our way to Cambo.

Starting at an early hour with plenty of provisions, we bowled down to the Negresse station, crossed the line, and ascended the hill above Lake Mouriscot, at the top of which Bidart—the first of the Basque villages—comes into view.

Guétary (3 miles), standing on a hill to the southward, was next seen, and in due time we reached St. Jean de Luz (8 miles), a town of over 4000 inhabitants (possessing a very good hotel and baths, and some historical buildings), situated on a strip of sand between the River Nivelle and the sea. Here the road to Cambo branched off to the left, inland—the high road to Spain continuing near the seaboard—and frequently skirting the Nivelle as far as St. Pée, we passed on by Espelette to Cambo. The Hôtel St. Martin there, which generally attracts visitors for a few days at least, was not our destination; so we took a glimpse at Fagalde's celebrated chocolate factory and the old churchyard high above the river—while our horses were being changed—and then resumed our journey to the Pas de Roland.† The scenery now became very charming, the winding river (Nive) adding much to the general beauty, especially where it dashed out from between the rugged rocks of the gorge with which Roland's name is associated.

* There is a more direct route to Cambo from Bayonne.
† So-called from the fable that Roland, coming to the place and wishing to cross, found the rocks barring his passage, so kicked them, whereupon they parted for him to pass between.

After exploring this narrow pass we found a suitable place for luncheon and sat down.

In returning, we halted near the village of Itsatsou, to gather some of the lovely scarlet anemones* which grow near there, and cover the fields with such a blaze of colour as makes them conspicuous from a long distance. The rest of the journey in the cool of the afternoon was very pleasant, but our route was the same till reaching Bidart, where we curved to the left, and came by a branch road (previously mentioned), *viâ* the Villa Marbella and the Falaises, back to our hotel.

At dinner that night we noticed that there had evidently been some "goings and comings" among the guests; and doubtless the new arrivals were congratulating themselves on having succeeded in getting rooms in the hotel—for be it understood this good house is nearly always full, as it deserves to be. We missed with sorrow the familiar forms of Mr. and Mrs. Berecasque, who, with all their bigoted hatred for anything approaching to High Church notions, were as a rule exceedingly genial and good-natured, as fat people usually are.

The ladies certainly used to say that Madame had a perplexing way of putting leading questions as to why somebody's daughter went with somebody else's son, or what on earth could that nice gentlemanly young curate (Low Church of course) see in that fast young lady who was always working banners and such like enormities? But we never noticed this; though that which on this particular evening probably no one could fail to notice was, that their places were

---

* A fee of 1 franc for one person, or 2 francs for three, is expected for admission into the fields.

now occupied by a couple of beings as strikingly thin as Mr. and Mrs. Berecasque had been fat. We were told their name, but there was rather a buzz of conversation going on at the time, and we might not have caught it properly, but it certainly sounded like "Grouser." However, that does not matter much; what is far more to the point is the amusement that Mr. Grouser gave to those who had the privilege of sitting near him. Apparently a self-made man, without any children—who by better educations might have helped him to knowledge—his acquaintance with the French language was like a peasant child's with turtle-soup; perhaps "a lick and a promise" would best explain it. But though only knowing a few words, which he pronounced with the vilest of accents, and then only when he had inserted his glass in his eye, he brought them out with ludicrous frequency whenever he had the chance. Here are examples—"*Hi garsong!* bring me another plate!" "*Garsong poorquar* don't you fetch some bread when I've asked three times for it?" "*Hi garsong! sil voo plate*, where are those potatoes?" And so on all through dinner; while he appeared rather to enjoy the merriment he caused, thinking he must have said something really good, although of course he hadn't the slightest idea what it was!

To sketchers and lovers of contrasts a visit to Fuenterabia cannot fail to prove a treat, and a better specimen of an old Spanish town it would be difficult to find. The only convenient train in the morning thither leaves early, and although we preferred driving, we made an early start too, in order to spend a long day. Having accomplished the eight miles and arrived at St. Jean de Luz, we had still a distance of

8 miles more before reaching Hendaye, the frontier town. There were occasional pretty bits of country to be seen, especially in the vicinity of Urrugne (10½ miles), a village in which the Spanish element is noticeable, but the succession of poplars along the roadside all the way—more or less—to Béhobie, was very monotonous. At Béhobie (14½ miles) the road to Hendaye leaves the direct route to Spain and branches off to the right. Following this, we were soon at the frontier. Hendaye (16 miles) is celebrated for its cognac and a certain liquor called by its name, as well as for an excellent beach and bathing establishment, beyond which there is little worth mention. Having put up the horses at the Hôtel de France, we repaired to the jetty, where happily the tide was high enough to permit of our being ferried across, instead of carried on the back of some brawny (and garlicky) native. As we were half-rowed, half-poled, down the narrow winding channel of the Bidassoa, we were once again indubitably "'twixt France and Spain," though the vicinity of the ancient Spanish town, and the lazy sentinels on the river's bank, made the scene much more Spanish than French. Once landed, we strolled slowly across the "*Embarcadéro*," and entered the town by the ancient gateway. The principal street, which we then ascended, is indeed picturesque. The miniature verandahs and overhanging roofs of the houses, the latter approaching so close to one another as nearly to permit of shaking hands across; an occasional bright costume appearing at the window or on the verandah; the old church higher up the street, and the battered "Castilio" at the top, furnished ample materials for a very pleasant sketch. The church is well worth a

visit, being very old and of interesting appearance. Owing to its sheltered position it did not suffer nearly as much as most of the buildings from the missiles in the late Carlist war. We passed several groups of lazy soldiers, who leered at us offensively and made some uncomplimentary remarks, but otherwise—beyond the fact that the women stared a good deal when Miss Blunt attempted to sketch—we met with no discourtesy. The new casino proves an "extra" attraction in summer, but it is to be regretted that, for gambling purposes alone, many people should be drawn to this quaint old-world town, so worthy of a visit for its picturesqueness alone.

At the time when we wished to visit San Sebastien we learnt that the "Citadol" was closed to visitors, owing to some foreigner having foolishly lighted his cigar near a powder magazine. As the "Citadol" is the chief attraction, we penned a highly polite letter to his Excellency the Governor of the Province, asking for his permission to visit this otherwise forbidden ground.

We received a most gracious reply, to the effect that, whenever we liked to come, the place was at our disposal, and accordingly selected the first fine morning for our trip. On this occasion we formed a party large enough for a coach and four, but were very careful to avoid a repetition of our Bétharram experiences.

We discovered no new features of interest as far as Béhobie, but the day being very clear, we had a fine view of the distant Pyrenees and the Spanish coastline from various points along the road. Passing through Béhobie's narrow streets and crossing the Bidassoa by the strong stone bridge, we were only a minute "'twixt France and Spain," and entering Irun found ourselves in the hands of the Customs authorities. Having "nothing to declare" and nothing contraband undeclared, we were soon permitted to proceed, although our "cocher" almost immediately afterwards stopped to change horses. Accordingly, we walked on up a pretty lane with ivied walls, near which—in the background—stood an old church. Finding a comfortable place for lunching in the vicinity, we awaited the arrival of the coach, and discussed our hamper before again moving on. Not having too much time, however, we did not delay long, and remounting, bowled merrily along to "Pasages." This was once the safest port on the coast, and in fact is yet; but the accumulation of sand, &c., at the entrance, has made it practically useless for any ships but those of very light draught. It forms a tidal basin, and houses are built on its sides, along one of which the road for some time skirts, but afterwards assumes a straight course and descends into San Sebastien. From the highest point of the road, before we commenced descending, we had a splendid view of the town, which looked busy, imposing, and clean.

When once inside, we drove to the Hôtel de Londres; then crossed the street to the guard-house, presented our "permit" for the "Citadol," and after a little fuss and *red tapeism*—such as Spaniards, even more than Frenchmen, dearly love—under the guidance of a soldier, commenced the ascent. How many times we presented our "carta" we know not, but at every turn some official was ready to ask to see it, and this business took almost as long as the actual mounting, though in the end we did manage to reach the summit. The view from thence was very fine, extending for miles in all directions, but after enjoying it for a short time, we descended to visit the graves of the English who fell in defending the place in 1836 against the Carlists, which lie in a little cemetery on one side of the hill. Maiden-hair ferns grow among the rocks by the path, which from time to time discloses views of the town and the pretty rocky island—Santa Clara—in the bay. After descending, we had time for a glimpse at the interior of the church of Santa Maria and the bull-ring, as well as a stroll along the beautiful beach, before it was necessary to start homewards, and when at length we were deposited in safety at our hotel, we all acknowledged that the day had been a very pleasant one indeed! With such enjoyable drives, and the tennis, and the ever-changing sea, we never found time hang heavily on our hands; and if we had, there was the little railway to carry us into the bustle of Bayonne for shopping or listening to the band, where *ennui* would speedily have been driven away. Speaking of this railway reminds us that at Anglêt, one of the stations on the line, there is a very interesting convent of " Silent Sisters " within easy access from the train. Although it is a sad sight to see all these women deluded with the notion that their sins, however great, could not be pardoned without such a bitter expiation; yet the order and cleanliness that is patent everywhere, and the gardens and greenhouses, lend an attraction to the place in spite of its melancholy associations.*

When June has succeeded May, Biarritz begins to empty of its English and American visitors, to give

---

* Visitors are expected to purchase a specimen of the needlework exhibited to them, or at any rate to put a donation in the convent box.

place in July to the Spaniards and French. On the 15th of that month prices go up with a bound, often becoming double and even treble what they were during the winter season. This is the time to stroll on the "Plage" and watch the bathing; to note the varied costumes, see the merry faces, and listen to the children's laughter, mingled with the splash of the waves. But we are only treating of spring, so must not encroach upon summer; but—following our countrymen's example—bid "Au revoir" to Biarritz before the glare forces us to parade the streets with blue spectacles and double-lined parasols.

CHAPTER XIV.

CONCLUSION.

"Where duty leads"—Resorts in the Eastern Pyrenees—Caen—"Riou"—Our paths diverge—"The Lesson of the Mountains"—Farewell.

ALTHOUGH we have in reality come to the end of our tour, and have consequently no more places to discourse on, it may be suggested that our task is but badly ended if we omit to mention such resorts as Amélie, Vernet, Molitg, and other spots, which, if of less importance than those we have visited, are nevertheless *in* the Pyrenees. That they are *in* the Pyrenees cannot be disputed, but being in the eastern portion, the way of reaching them from the resorts among the western heights is so roundabout, that but few people would think of visiting both. However, for the information of any intending travellers, we have collected what reliable facts we could about the above-mentioned places—as well as Capvern, Preste-les-Bains, Panticosa, and a few others—which will be found in the general information* at the end of the volume, and will, we trust, be of service.

We have but little left us now to do but to take our leave, though we have one little incident to record,

* See Appendix A.

which, though it occurred far from the Pyrenees, resulted, nevertheless, from our visit.

Travelling slowly homeward by the route through Normandy to Cherbourg, we stopped a few days at the delightful town of Caen. While there—in consequence of negotiations that had been carried on for some time—Miss Blunt had her desires gratified by the arrival of a fine Pyrenean puppy—like a small white bear with brown points—from Cauterets, one of

"MY PAW IS ON MY NATIVE HEATH, AND MY NAME IS 'RIOU.'"

the identical pair about which we had such a lively scene with the old French fancier. He was christened "Riou," after the Col of that name, and his owner has very kindly drawn his portrait among his native hills, to adorn these pages.

Our party did not break up till we reached Weymouth, but after that our ways diverged. We were by no means glad to part, the memories of our trip being very pleasant ones, and we can hardly think of a more delightful way of spending a couple of months than in driving about these beautiful mountains. The people are so pleasant, and hotels so moderate (in the spring-time), and the country in the full beauty of spring is at its best; and yet, as a rule, the few English and Americans who do go, wait till the season begins, with its crowds, heat, and extra expense, and the fiery sun has effectually cleared the mountains of that snowy mantle which was their greatest charm.

We were once asked, "Are not the Pyrenees very bare mountains, without any trees or herbage?" We could only repeat, what we have so often asserted in this book, that the foliage on the mountain slopes is magnificent, and their fertility and wealth of flora are of the highest order.

They are indeed so beautiful in every way that they cannot fail to touch many a chord in the heart of any lover of nature. At one moment hid in mists, at another clear and stately under a cloudless sky; in winter, wrapped completely in their garb of snow, trees and grass and rocks and all, only to reappear under spring's influence, still retaining their snowy crown, but with their slopes bright with the contrasting tints of beech and fir, oak and maple, interspersed with banks of bright gentian and fields of golden daffodils; what could be more lovely than a scene such as this, with the morning sun gilding the snow summits, or the last rays of a roseate sunset lingeringly bidding them "Farewell"?

As we then follow their example, we do not think we could make a more fitting ending than these lines, written amid those lovely scenes, and entitled

"THE LESSON OF THE MOUNTAINS."

 Look on yon mountain peaks,
 Mark how each summit seeks
Upward to lift its crest, base earth to spurn.
 Tow'ring above the plain,
 Over the weak and vain,
Ever for realms of light seeming to yearn.

 Look at each snowy crown,
 Whiter than softest down,
Oh! in what majesty thus are they drest!
 See how the setting sun
 Kisses them one by one,
And slowly, solemnly, goes to his rest.

 Look to the brilliant sky;
 —Dark though the clouds be, nigh—
Wavelets of gold grandly float 'neath the blue.
 Mark where the shades of green
 Mingle with crimson's sheen,
Till evening's dread decree curtains the view.

 Hark to the drenching rain!
 Hark how it beats the pane!
While the fierce fitful blast sweeps on its course.
 Fiercer yet swells the gale,
 Hark to the long-drawn wail!
Tenfold more dire—in the darkness—its force.

* * * * * *

 See! morning's golden rays,
 Breaking night's gloomy haze,
Tinge with a burning glow every proud height;
 Storms beat on them in vain,
 Steadfast they will remain,
Till the eternal day swallows up night.

* * * * * *

 So may thy soul aspire
 Ever to climb up higher,
Spurning the world's delights, caring for none;
 Shunning vain pomps and shows,
 Seeking but calm repose
In the "Hereafter," when life is done.

"See! morning's golden rays,
 Breaking night's gloomy haze,
Tinge with a burning glow every proud height."

So may'st thou yearn to wear,
Like ev'ry angel there,
Vestment as pure as snow, spotlessly white;
And on thy face to shine
That radiancy divine,
God's own unquenchable, immortal light.

And, if life's courses seem
Pleasant, like some sweet dream,
Be thou beware of the evils around :
Paths seeming paved with gold
Oft mighty sins enfold,
Oft where the sea looks still, quicksands abound.

Or should the trials come,
Shatt'ring thy earthly home,

Dashing fond hopes and despoiling thy life :
  Meekly thy burden bear
  To Jesus' throne, and there
Thou wilt find rest and help—strength for the strife.

  Then, when Heav'n's morning breaks,
  And ev'ry soul forsakes
This baser earth, and flies to its last rest,
  Chastened by cold and heat,
  Wash'd by the storms that beat,
Oh, may thy spirit soar 'mid God's own blest!

THE END.

APPENDIX A.

GENERAL INFORMATION CONCERNING THE PRINCIPAL TOWNS AND VILLAGES IN THE PYRENEES, INCLUDING NOTES ON THE MEDICAL PROPERTIES OF THE BATHS AT THE CHIEF RESORTS, AND THE EXCURSIONS IN THE VICINITY.

N.B.—*The following sign (∥) attached to hotels, &c., in this portion of the book, signifies that the Author can personally give his recommendation.*

AMÉLIE-LES-BAINS* (678 ft.), on the River Tech, in the Eastern Pyrenees. A winter resort, with a dry, clear air, tonic and slightly irritant, and a mean temperature during the months of January, February, and March (taken collectively) of $48\frac{1}{3}°$ Fahr. The average number of fine days in the year is 210. The baths are naturally heated from $100°$ to $144°$, according to the distance from the source. They contain soda in combination with sulphur, carbon, and silica, with a very small proportion of the carbonates of iron and lime. They are recommended in skin diseases, affections of the throat and kidneys, and for chronic rheumatism. The **season** lasts throughout the year.

Bathing Establishments.—Thermes Pujade; Thermes Romains. With hotel accommodation at both.

Hotels.—Pujade, Romains; Du Kursal, Farret, and Martinet.

Post and **Telegraph Office, Cafés, Casino, Theatre,** &c.—Living is by no means expensive. In the first-named hotels the charge per diem ought not to exceed 7frs. 50c. for "pension"; in the others it is cheaper. The bathing establishments have excellent accomodation, twenty-seven baths, a large swimming bath, inhaling rooms, &c: There are **doctors**

---

* For routes thither see Appendix B.

in connection with the baths and others resident in the town. The scenery around is very pretty, and rich in groves of olive, cherry, cork, and fig trees, besides banks of heather and ferns, and clusters of honeysuckle.

The Chief Excursions are :—

Prats de Mollo (2618 ft.), 12½ miles by mule path—15 by road; carriage (23 francs with pourboire) 5¼ hours.

Inns.—Maillard ; Guin-Come.

Preste-les-Bains, 19 miles—8½ hours; carriage 33 francs with pourboire.

Roc de France (4698 ft.) : splendid view ; 6½ hours there and back. A stiff climb, fully compensated for by the expanse of scenery to be seen from the summit.

Gouffre de la Fou, 4 hours there and back—guide necessary to descend to the bottom of the "Gouffre," for which the "espadrilles" (cord sandals) must be worn.

Col de Faitg, Massanet, 6 hours there and back—a very charming and picturesque excursion.

La Junguera, 20 miles ; carriage 23 francs, i.p.* The first Spanish village over the frontier ; an interesting drive.

Le Pertus (958 ft.) 15¼ miles. There and back 6 hours. Carriage 23 francs, i.p.*

From Amélie to Perpignan, or vice versâ, 23½ miles ; a carriage with luggage costs 28 francs, i.p.*

Carriages and Horses may be hired at Labrunie's or Victor Olive's.

Guide.—Bertrand Oms at Arles.

ARCACHON *—Situated in the forest, and on the shores of the basin of the same name. The English season is in winter, the French in summer. A favourite resort on account of its mild and sedative climate. Most people live in villas in the forest during the winter, where the strong winds are not felt, and where the mean temperature is 50° Fahr. The calmness of the atmosphere, and the strong scent from the pines, has a beneficial tendency for those suffering from chest complaints.

To those who find it relaxing, Biarritz is recommended as a suitable change.

Hotels.—Grand (on the Plage), Continental, Grand du Forêt, &c.

Pensions.—Villa Riquet ‖ (Mons. Ollé, proprietor), Villa Montretout, Villa Peyronnet, and Villa Buffon.

Chaplain.—Rev. W. Radcliffe.

English Church, in the forest ; services every Sunday.

Cabs, during the day from 6 A.M. to 8 P.M. The course :

---

* i.p., including pourboire.
† The Chaplain, Mr. Radcliffe, has issued an excellent guide-book for the locality.

1½ frs. with one horse; 2 frs. with two horses; by the hour, 2½ and 3 frs. respectively.

Horses and **Donkeys**, 2 frs. and 1 fr. the hour, respectively.

Boats, from 2 frs. the hour, by arrangement.

Bankers and **Money Changers.**—Dubos and Mauriac, opposite Grand Hotel.

Post and **Telegraph Office, Chemists, Grocers,** &c.

Casino.

Principal Drives and **Excursion are :—**

To **Moulleau**, 2 miles through the forest.

To **La Teste**, 3 miles.

To the **Oyster Beds**, in the centre of the bay, on the Ile des Oiseaux.

To the **Lighthouse** at Cape Ferret, across the basin, whence the Biscay can be seen.

To the **Dune de la Grave** by boat, and across the forest to La Teste, visiting the giant trees (this must only be undertaken with an experienced guide).

ARGELÈS (1528 ft.), on the River Azun, in the Hautes-Pyrénées; with a genial climate that makes it a favourite resort very early in the year. Some few people use it as a winter abode also. Living costs "en pension" from 9 to 14 frs. per diem.

Hotels.—De France; D'Angleterre ‖ (cheaper than the France).

Carriages.—At Limoges', ‖ can be hired for the afternoon—with one horse, 5 frs.; 2 horses, 8 frs.; 4 horses, 10 frs.; or by the day, or for any special excursion.

Horses, also from M. Limoges. For the afternoon, 4 frs.; for the day, 8 to 10 frs. (N.B.—These are spring prices, and not those of the season.)

Chemist.—M. Bualé, near the Post Office.

Post and **Telegraph Office**, and a few shops.

The Chief Excursions are :—

To the Villages of Ges, Serres, Salles, and Ourous—a lovely ride, 2 hours; horses, 4 frs. each, pourboire, ½ fr.

Drive round the Valley, via Argelès station, the Chateau de Beaucens, Pierrefitte, and St. Savin, 2 hours 30 min.; carriage with 4 horses, 11 frs. 50 c., i.p.

Le Balandrau (1729 ft.). Lovely walk; one hour there and back.

Pic de Pibeste (4548 ft.) An easy climb : splendid view from the summit.

ARGELÈS-SUR-MER, 13¾ miles from Perpignan. In the midst of fertile fields. Ruins of the Castle de Pujols in the vicinity.

Hotels.—D'Angleterre, De France.

ARLES-SUR-TECH (909 ft.), in the Eastern Pyrenees. Chief town of the canton and the principal commercial centre in the Tech valley. 2½ miles from Amélie, which was formerly known as Arles-les-Bains. Trade with Algeria in apples; and in whip-handles with the whole of France. Old twelfth-century church in the town; and outside, behind a grating, lies the tomb of the Saints Abdon and Sennen.

Hotels.—Rousseau, Pujade.

ARREAU (2190 ft.), at the junction of the valley of Louron with the Aure valley, in the "Hautes-Pyrénées," 23¾ miles from Bagnères de Bigorre and 19¼ from Luchon, on the direct mountain road. (Route Thermale.)

Hotels.—De France, D'Angleterre.

Post and **Telegraph Office, Chemist, Grocer,** &c.

In the town are the Chapelle de St. Exupère, with a good view from the belfry; the Church of Notre Dame; and the ancient market-place. There are manganese mines in the vicinity.

Excursions to Cardiac, 2 miles. Sulphurous baths, with hotel accommodation.

To the forest of Riou-majou and the falls of Mail-Blanc and Ejet. Over the Col de Plan to the Spanish villages of St. Juan, Gestain, &c. Up the Vallée de Lastié to the Monné de Luchon (7044 ft.).

ARRENS (2950 ft.), in the valley of Azun, in the High Pyrenees, on the Route Thermale, between Eaux Bonnes (19 miles) and Argelès (7½ miles).

Hotels.—De France et de la Poste, De la Paix.

Guides.—Jean Lacoste, M. Gleyre.

Excursions (for which it is an excellent starting-point).—Mont Bälétous, 10,318 ft. (the most dangerous point for the ascent—from Eaux Bonnes it is much easier), 4 hours to the summit. Guide absolutely necessary.

Lac Miguelon and Pic d'Arrouy—11 hours there and back; a much-recommended trip.

Pic de Cambalés, 9 hours (9728 ft.); an easy ascension; recommended.

ARUDY, in the Basses-Pyrénées, on the direct road from Oloron to Eaux Bonnes or Chaudes; 17¼ miles from Oloron and 2 from Louvie-Juzon. Grotte d'Arudy in the vicinity.

ASPIN, a small village in the Aure valley, Hautes-Pyrénées, below the Col of the same name, on the road between Bigorre and Luchon.

ASTÉ, a village at the entrance to the Gorge de Lhéris, near Bagnères de Bigorre—to which refer. Ruins of an ancient castle in which Gabrielle d'Estrelle lived. Church of 16th century. Visited by Pitton de Tounefort, the naturalist.

BAGNÈRES DE BIGORRE (1808 ft.), standing at the mouth of the fine valley of Campan and the lesser one of

Salut. It is one of the most celebrated bathing resorts in the Pyrenees, and is very rich in springs. The **climate** is mild, and while the **season** only lasts from the 1st of June to the 15th of October, several English make it a residence all the year round. It is in a great measure protected from the winds, though they blow occasionally strongly and chillily; snow is a rare visitor in the town, and with Argelès it shares the honour of being among the earliest "changes of air" from the warmth of Pau. There are nearly 50 springs divided between 17 establishments, and there is hardly any known or unknown malady for which they cannot be recommended. They may be divided into four classes: 1st, saline; 2nd, ferruginous; 3rd, saline and ferruginous; 4th, sulphurous. They are all naturally heated. The temperature ranges from 64° to 123° Fahr.; and amongst the hottest is the "**Salies**," which contains a certain limited quantity of arsenic, and is only used for drinking purposes. It is said to be beneficial in laryngitis, ulcerous diseases, and affections of the mouth and throat.

The Principal Establishment is known as the Thermes de Marie-Therèse, and contains 7 different springs, and 38 baths of Pyrenean marble. In the winter the price for a bath (simple) varies from 1 fr. to 1 fr. 60 cents, including linen. For a douche-bath 1 fr.; a footbath 60 cents; and for other varieties from 1 fr. 25 cents to 3 frs. Every visit to the drinking-fountain costs 10 cents. In summer a simple bath costs from 1 fr. 25 cents to 2 frs., and douche-bath the same, while the others range from 1 fr. 25 cents to 5 frs.

The other most important establishments are those of Grand Pré, Santé, Salut, and Lassère, while the water of Labassère is brought daily to the town for drinking purposes.

This water of **Labassère** is sulphurous, and is considered highly beneficial in cases of chronic bronchial catarrh, congestion of the lungs, pulmonary consumption, spasmodic coughs, skin diseases, and chronic laryngitis. See Labassère in Appendix.

Grand Pré has three springs, in all of which iron is present; two are naturally heated, and are considered efficacious in scrofulous diseases, nervous rheumatism, and general debility. The other spring, which is cold and used only for drinking purposes, has a decided tonic action.

Santé possesses two sources, one of which is artificially heated; they are of a saline nature. These are *par excellence* the "Ladies' Springs," and have great efficacy in cases of overwork, shock to the nervous system, general nervousness, and neuralgia.

Salut possesses three sources of different temperatures, employed in baths and for drinking purposes, as well. Except in very hot weather the water is inodorous, but its sedative properties have placed it in the first rank. It has been used with great benefit in all nervous complaints, hypochondria, hysteria, intestinal complaints, indigestion, &c., its action being also diuretic.

Lasserre has one source only, slightly bitter and inodorous, containing sulphate of magnesia, which renders its action laxative. It is useful in cases of obesity, liver affections, and others of that type.

For the other establishments and springs, which have likewise their special uses, the reader is referred to the 'Guide to Bigorre,' and Joanne's Guide-book to the Pyrenees.

Hotels.—Beau Séjour ‖; Paris; De Londres et d'Angleterre; Du bon Pasteur; Frascati; &c. &c.

Banker and **Money Changer.**—D. Ortalis, 16 Place Lafayette.

Doctors.—(In summer only) Dr. Bagnall from Pau, Promenade St. Martin. Dr. Couzier, 27 Rue du Théâtre (all the year). Dr. Dejeau, 30 Allée de Coustous (ditto).

Chemists.—M. Nogues, Place Lafayette; and M. Jouaneton, 22 Place de Strasbourg.

Restaurant.—M. Vignes, Place Lafayette.

Nurses.—Les Sœurs de l'Esperance, 9 Avenue de Salut.

Draper.—Comet, Allée des Constons, No. 22.

Grocer (selling English goods of all kinds).—M. Peltier, 5 Boulevard du Collège.

Confectioners.—Mdme. Cheval, Rue du Centre, 19. M. Toujas, No. 10 same street.

Carriages.—Courtade, Place des Pyrenees, No. 14; Pourponnet, 3 Rue Labrun.

Horses.—Bourdettes, 25 Place Lafayette.

There is service all the year in the small English Church, and the present chaplain, the Rev. J. Grundy, M.A. Oxon., is always willing to assist visitors in any way, and glad to accept the offer of their services in the choir.

The cost of living in the winter averages 10 frs. in the best hotels, and between 7 and 9 in others; but the prices rise considerably in summer.

Post and Telegraph Office, Theatre, Casino, Museum and Reading-rooms in the town.

Guides.—Fages, senior and junior, 8 Rue de Lorry; Idrac, Rue Longue; Arnauné, Rue de Lorry.

Principal Excursions:—*

To Aste, Gerde, Lourdes, Campan, Baudean, Ste. Marie,

---

* For *full* particulars of these and all excursions, the reader is referred to P. Joanne's 'Pyrenees'; Mr. Packe's 'Guide to the Pyrenees for Mountaineers'; and Count Russell's 'Grandes Ascensions des Pyrénées' (French and English).

the Col d'Aspin, and up the Bédat and the Monné. Refer to Chapter II. for information.

Cæsar's Camp, 2 hrs. there and back, by the village of Pouzac.

Les Allées dramatiques, 2 hrs. there and back, riding—3 hrs. on foot; between the Bédat and the Monné, a pretty walk.

The Slate Quarries and Spring of Labassère, 6 hrs. there and back : 1¼ hrs. to Labassère ; 2 hrs. to the Quarries ; 3 hrs. to the Spring. Guide 6 frs. ; horses 10 frs. each.

The Mont-Aigu, 10 hrs. there and back, guide 15 frs. The view from the summit is immense; it extends over three valleys.

The Vallée de Lesponne and the "**Lac bleu,**" 9 hrs. there and back. Carriage-road to the end of valley ; mule-path the remainder of the way. Guide 8 frs., horse 10 frs.

Gripp (10 miles). Carriage-road all the way. Same road as far as Ste. Marie as that to Col d'Aspin.

Pic du Midi de Bigorre, 6 hrs. 45 min. to the summit ; Guide 6 frs., horse 10 frs. A magnificent excursion, but easier from Barèges.

Pêne de l'Heris, 2 hrs. 45 min. to summit. A pleasant excursion.

Houn Blanquo, 9 hrs. there and back. Guide 8 frs., horse 10 frs. A splendid mountain panorama in view, from the summit.

Puits de la Pindorle*—a natural ice-cave, spoken of by Mr. Packe as "unique in its kind in the Pyrenees"—8 hrs. there and back. Guide and ropes necessary.

BAGNERES DE LUCHON (2065 ft.).—A lovely town in the Western Pyrenees (Hautes), situated near the junction of the Pique with the One, at the mouth of the Larboust valley, and in the western angle of the valley of Luchon.

The most fashionable of all the Pyrenean watering-places.

Season.—1st of June to the end of October ; but most charming in May and early June.

The Bathing Establishment is a very ponderous building, containing accommodation second to none. The springs are nearly all naturally heated, varying from 103° to 150° Fahr. ; they may be divided into four classes : 1st, sodium sulphate ; 2nd, saline ; 3rd, bicarbonate of iron ; 4th, saline, but cold. The sulphur springs are considered the best and most complete series known ; and the iron are principally used for drinking purposes. The waters of Luchon are considered specially beneficial for chronic bronchitis, rheu-

* See footnote p. 226.

matism (articular and muscular), vesical catarrh, reopened wounds, fractures, scrofulous and cutaneous affections, and ulcers. In cases where there are complications, nervous excitement, or paralysis, a medical man should always be consulted before venturing to bathe.

There is an iron spring near the Castelvieil, 1½ miles from Luchon.

In the "Etablissement Thermal" the terms range from 60 cents to 4 frs. There are baths of all kinds, and it is advisable, if the bather wishes to bathe at any special time, that he should enter his name in the book kept for that purpose, as soon as he arrives. In the season there is always a great pressure of visitors, and otherwise the bather may have to wait an hour or two for his turn. There was once a **Museum** above the baths, this has now been removed to the splendid **Casino** which stands in beautiful grounds, not far from the **Post** and **Telegraph Office**—entrance 1 franc.

Hotels.—Canton,‖ Richelieu (very large but not recommended), Grand, Bonnemaison, Paris, d'Angleterre, d'Etigny, de France, des Bains, Monteil, du Parc, de la Paix.

Apartments.—Of all descriptions, in the Allée des Bains, Rue Neuve, Cours d'Etigny, Allée des Veuves, &c. &c.

Doctors.—Several, both attached to the baths and independent.

Carriage and **Horse Proprietors.**—Almost innumerable, but Jean Sanson is recommended, Rue d'Espagne.

Guides.—For the summits (French): Pierre Barrau, Rue de Pigué, Aurillon, Lafon fils, Capdeville senior and junior, Fermin Barrau. (Spanish) Francisco. For ordinary excursions and hunting: Jean and Luis Sanson; Jean Brunet, chamois-hunter (recommended for all ascensions from the Lac d'O).

Tariff for drinking the waters only.—During season, 8 days, 4 frs.; 20 days, 8 frs.; 30 days, 10 frs.

Carriage on Hire (from the stand).—The "course," 1 franc; the hour, 3 frs. for one horse; and 1 fr. 30 cents, and 3 frs. 75 cents respectively, for two horses—by day. By night, for one horse, 2 frs. 50 cents the "course," and 4 frs. the hour; for two horses, 3 frs. 25 cents and 5 frs. respectively.

For all excursions there is a recognised tariff, which may be seen at the Mairie; and an excellent local guide-book and map is published for 2 frs. by Lafont.

The Chief Excursions:—

For Superbagnères (horses and guide 5 frs. each respectively, hay on the summit 1 fr. out of the season, but 2 frs. more each person in the season), Vallée du Lys (20 to 25 frs. for a landau), Bosost (carriage *viâ* St. Béat, 45 frs., horses *viâ* the Portillon 5 frs. each, guide 6 frs.), Montauban (an easy walk), the Orphanage of Notre Dame du Rocher (a short and pleasant walk), St. Mamet (little more than ½ mile), the Rue d'Enfer (an easy climb from the Vallée du Lys), the Tour de Castelvieil (about two miles from Luchon), &c. &c. Refer to Chapter X.

The Val d'Esquierry (4839 ft.), 11 miles.—Carriage-road as far as Grange d'Astos (25 to 30 frs.) very rich in flora.

To the **Hospice de France** and the **Cascades—des Demoiselles, et du Parisien**, 9¼ miles. Carriage-road all the way. Landau, 25 frs.; but 4 frs. per seat in the Hospice diligence there and back.

To the **Port de Venasque** and the **Pic de Sauvegarde**, returning by the Port de la Picade; 10 miles to the Port de Venasque—1 hour further to the summit of the Pic de Sauvegarde; 11 miles from the Port de la Picade to Luchon. Time, 10 to 11 hours there and back; but this fine excursion is rendered more enjoyable by sleeping at the Hospice (*vide* above), and starting early next day for the summits.

The **Valley of Oueil** and the village of **Bourg** (9½ miles). Carriage there and back, 30 frs. From Bourg the **Pic de Montné** can be ascended. Splendid sunrise view from summit. Guide recommended if ascension is made by night; horses 7 frs., guides 10 frs.; or by day 7 frs.

Lac d'Oo (10 miles).—Carriage-road for 8 miles. Landau, 25 frs. This lake, also called Seculejo, is full of salmon-trout, and there is a very fine cascade (820 ft.) on the far side, to which visitors can be ferried. Fare for one person 1¼ frs.—for more, an arrangement can be made. There is a **small toll** levied on every person who visits this lake—no matter whether they patronise the little inn or not!

Saint Béat.—By carriage 25 frs., or by rail to Marignac and diligence afterwards (12½ miles). Refer to Chapter XI.

L'Antenac.—6½ hours to the summit and back. Horse and guide each 6 frs. An enjoyable excursion; and the whole distance can be ridden.

Pic Spijoles.—4½ hours from the Lac d'Oo—a difficult ascension.

Pic de Crabioules.—13 hours up and down. Guide necessary. Splendid view.

Pic Quairat.—5 hours from the Lac d'Oo. Guide necessary.

Le Céciré.—8 hours up and down. Guide and horses 6 frs. each.

Pic Sacroux.—8½ hours to the summit and back. Very fine view.

The **Peaks Bacanère** and the **Pales de Burat** (11¾ miles).—9 hours there and back. Horses and guides from

5 to 8 frs. each, according to season. One of the most charming of all the excursions from Luchon.

L'Entécade.—7 hours in all. Guides and horses 6 frs. each. A much-recommended climb. Splendid view from summit.

Pic de Poujastou.—$8\frac{1}{2}$ hours in all. Guides and horses 6 frs. each; an easy climb.

The **Mont Maudits** or **Maladetta Group**, the highest in the range, including the Pic de Nethou (11,169 ft.), Pic 'du Milieu (11,044 ft.), Pic de la Maladetta (10,867 ft.), Pic d'Albe (10,761 ft.), and the Pic Fourcanade (9456 ft.), are so difficult and perilous, and require such excellent guides, that the reader is referred for information to Mr. Packe's and Count Russell's books, previously mentioned.

Note.—Carriages from Bigorre to Luchon, $43\frac{1}{2}$ miles, *viâ* Arreau, 80 to 100 frs., 5 to 10 frs. pourboire, out of the season; 100 to 130 frs., and pourboire 10 frs., in the season.

BARÈGES (4084 ft.), situated in a barren rocky gorge above Luz, in the Hautes-Pyrénées. It may be called the "Old Soldier's Resort," as the waters are specially efficacious for gunshot wounds.

The fine **Bathing Establishment** contains 30 separate bath-rooms, besides 3 douche-rooms, a spray-room, foot-bath-room, &c. The springs vary in heat from 71° to 112° Fahr., and are of a similar nature, all containing large proportions of sulphur and baregine. Dr. Lee says, "The water when drunk has a diuretic, diaphoretic, and expectorant action; the bath, by its general and local stimulating properties, cleanses foul ulcers, . . . promotes the exfoliation of carious portions of bone and subsequent cicatrisation, and frequently causes foreign bodies which have been long imbedded . . . to make their way to the surface." It is also highly beneficial for old bullet-wounds, neuralgic affections, rheumatic pains, and stiff joints.

Hotels.—De l'Europe, De France, Des Pyrénées, Richelieu. Board and lodging from 10 to 15 frs. per day in the season (15th of June to September). No hotels open in winter, as the village is covered with snow.

The **Climate** even in summer is variable—great heat is frequently followed by great cold, necessitating the wearing of woollen under-clothing, which should always be taken.

Bathing Tariff, &c.—Baths and douches from 1 fr. to 2 frs. 50 cents. For each visit to the drinking-room 5 cents; subscription for one month, 10 frs.

Apartments.—One room, from 2 frs. 50 cents to 6 frs. per day, according to position and size.

Doctors at the Establishment, a few independent, and others from Luz.

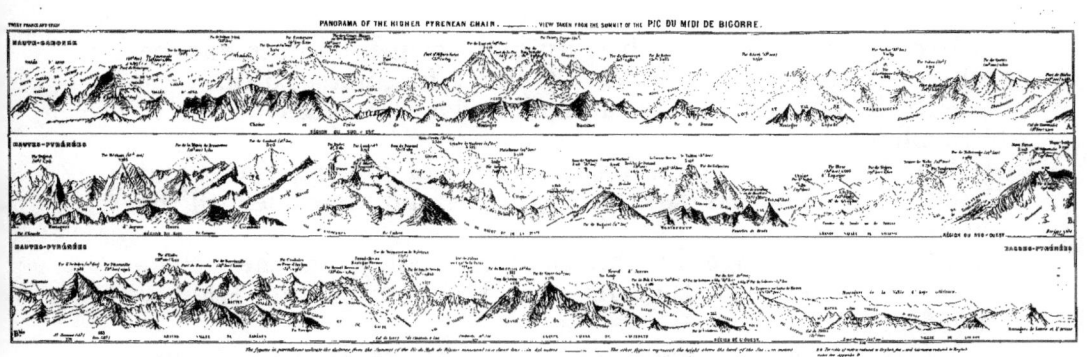

APPENDIX A. 231

Post and **Telegraph Office** in the season.

Carriages, Horses, and Asses in abundance; apply at the hotels.

Guides.—Of the 1st class: Bastien, Teinturier, Michael Pontis, Menvielle, &c. &c. for the lofty peaks; several of the 2nd class for minor excursions.

Chief Excursions:—

For the **Promenade Horizontale** and the Vallée de Lienz, refer to Chapter VI.

Pic de Néré.—6 hrs. there and back. Beware of vipers.

Pic du Midi de Bigorre.—8 hrs. up and down. Guide and horses, 5 frs. each. The favourite excursion in the vicinity, and one of the finest in the Pyrenees. The panorama which is annexed is on a fine day truly magnificent. Horses can be taken to the summit, where there is an excellent inn.

Lacs d'Escoubous.—2 hrs. to the Lac d'Escoubous; 2 hrs. 30 min. to the Lac Blanc; 2 hrs. return. Guide 4 to 6 frs., horses ditto.

Pic d'Ayré.—6 to 7 hrs. up and down. Horses can be taken within $\frac{1}{2}$ hr. of summit. Guide 6 frs., horses ditto.

Pic de Lienz.—5 hrs. up and down. A pleasant climb. See Chapter VI.

Le Néouville.—12 hrs. by the Col d'Aure, there and back. Guide necessary—10 frs. Splendid view over all the higher Pyrenees.

BAUDÉAN.—A village in the Campan valley on the Route Thermale, between Bigorre and Luchon, in the Hautes-Pyrénées.

BAYONNE.—City and first-class fortress in the Basses-Pyrénées, on the Adour and the Nive, standing some 2 miles from the shores of the terrible Biscay Bay. On the direct line from Bordeaux to Biarritz and Spain.

Hotels.—St. Etienne, Du Commerce, Ambassadeurs, St. Martin, De la Bilbaïna, De la Guipuzcoäna, and Du Panier fleuri. Rail to Négresse station for Biarritz; also narrow-gauge railway to Biarritz *viâ* Anglet.

Splendid twin-towered cathedral, ancient fortifications, &c. Excellent market and good shops, which are more reasonable than at Biarritz.

Post and **Telegraph Office**, English Vice-Consulate, &c.

Cabs.—The course 1 fr., the hour 2 frs.; 25 cents and 50 cents extra respectively for 2 horses.

Chocolate.—Fagalde.‖

Excursions to Cambo (10 miles), Croix de Mouguère, &c., see Chapter XIII.

BÉHOBIE.—A village in the Basses-Pyrénées, on the direct road to Spain, $14\frac{1}{4}$ miles from Biarritz.

BÉTHARRAM.—A pleasantly-situated village in the Basses-Pyrénées, once a favourite pilgrimage. There is a lovely bridge in the vicinity, and the Via Crucis just midway between the village and the bridge. It is situated on the direct road from Pau to Lourdes, and is 15 miles distant from the former, and $9\frac{1}{4}$ from the latter. The station on the railway, "Montaut-Bétharram," is about 2 miles from the village.

Inns.—De la Poste, De France. Celebrated grotto in the vicinity.

BIARRITZ, a favourite English winter resort on the shores of the Biscay, in the Basses-Pyrénées—2 miles from the Négresse station on the direct line to Spain, and 130 miles from Bordeaux. Living during the winter is considerably cheaper than at Pau, but the winds are much stronger and the air more bracing. Biarritz makes a valuable change from both Pau and Arcachon. It is free from epidemics, and beneficial in cases of paralysis, as well as chest and heart complaints.

Hotels.—De Paris et de Londres,‖ Grand Hotel, D'Angleterre (the favourite hotel with English people), Des Ambassadeurs, De France,‖ Des Princes, De l'Europe, De la Poste, &c.

Apartments.—All over the town, varying in price according to position. Maison Brocq,‖ Maison Larrodé,‖ Maison Broquedis.

English Pension.—Villa du Midi,‖ Rue des Champs.

Doctors.—Dr. Welby,‖ Rue Gambetta. Dr. Malpas; Dr. Girdlestone.

Carriages.—Maümus,‖ Place St. Eugenie. Larrondat, Place de la Marie.

Libraries.—One in connection with the English Church. Lending library at Victor Benquet's, Place de la Marie (stationer, &c.).

Confectioners.—Figué,‖ Rue Mazagran; Miremont.‖ Place de la Marie.

Photographer.—P. Frois, Rue du Port Vieux.

Banker.—E. H. Bellairs, Esq. (Vice Consul), International Bank.

"**Depôt Anglais,**" for wines, groceries, and English provisions, &c.

English Club, Post and **Telegraph Office.**

For principal excursions refer to Chapter XIII.

BIDART.—The first Basque village, 3 miles from Biarritz on the direct route to Spain—railway station, Bidart-Guétary.

BIELLE.—A village in the Basses-Pyrénées, on the road to Eaux Bonnes, in the Val d'Ossau, $18\frac{1}{4}$ miles from Pau. Inn, des Voyageurs.

BILHÈRES.—A village on the slopes of the Val d'Ossau, above Bielle, in the Basses-Pyrénées—celebrated for the copper mines in the vicinity. It lies in the direct track from the Val d'Ossau to the Vallée d'Aspe.

BILLÈRES.—A small village near Pau, in the Basses-Pyrénées on the road to the ancient town of Lescar: the locally well-known "Bois de Billères" take their name from it.

BIZANOS.—A village below Pau, on the Gave, in the Basses-Pyrénées, on the direct road to Lourdes.

BOO-SILHEN.—A village and railway station on the line from Lourdes to Pierrefitte, in the Hautes-Pyrénées. There is the site of an ancient camp in the vicinity.

BOSOST.—A village in Spain (18 miles from Luchon by the Portillon), under the shadow of the Eastern Pyrénées, in the valley of Aran. This is a most pleasing excursion from Luchon, either on horseback viâ the Portillon, or in a carriage viâ St. Béat. See Chapter X. **Inn,** Fonda d'España.

CAMBO.—A small picturesquely-situated bathing resort on the banks of the Nive, 10 miles from Bayonne, in the Basses-Pyrénées. A favourite excursion from Biarritz, with the extra attraction of good fishing.

Bathing Establishment, with a hot sulphur and cold ferruginous spring. The former has proved useful for its diuretic and laxative qualities, and efficacious in cases of languor following long illnesses: the latter is very rich in iron, and a useful tonic.

The **Climate** is exceedingly healthy in spring and autumn, but too warm in summer.

Hotel.—St. Martin.||

Chocolate Manufactory.—Monsieur Fagalde's.

Doctor.—M. Albert Dotézac.

Carriages, Horses, and **Asses,** at various rates.

CAMPAN (2192 ft.)—A village in the Hautes-Pyrénées (3¾ miles from Bigorre) situated in the valley of the same name—on the direct road from Bigorre to Luchon; possesses an ancient church and market-place.

CAPVERN.—A bathing resort in the Hautes-Pyrénées, built on a hill two miles distant from the bathing establishments, which are erected in a narrow ravine. One of the stations on the main line between Toulouse and Pau, being 78 miles distant from the former and 56 from the latter. The **climate** is mild, and the **season** lasts from the 15th of May to the 1st of November.

Two Bathing Establishments—De Hount-Caoudo and de Bouridé. The water principally contains sulphate of lime with a small proportion of carbonate of iron: its action is diuretic and laxative. It is an excellent and bracing tonic, stimulating to the digestion, and has also been beneficially employed in cases of catarrh and certain liver complaints. The Hount-Caoudo spring has an exciting tendency; that of Bouridé a sedative one.

Hotels.—Grand, Beau Séjour, De Fontaine, De la Paix, Des Bains, &c.

Post and **Telegraph Office** in the season.

CASTETS.—A small picturesquely-situated village in the Hautes-Pyrénées—off the high road between Pau and Eaux Bonnes—under a mile from Louvie Juzon. Lodging can be obtained at M. Fouga's.

CAUTERETS (3254 ft.)—A town situated in the gorge of the same name in the Hautes-Pyrénées, seven miles distant from Pierrefitte, the terminus of the line from Lourdes. It is said to be the most rich in mineral waters of any resort in the Pyrenees. From its position in a hollow, surrounded by lofty and beautiful mountains, it is frequently visited with a good deal of rain, and the climate is subject to severe changes in temperature, especially in spring, when the mornings and nights are cold. The season proper begins about the middle of June and lasts to the 15th of September. Living out of the season averages about 10 frs. per diem, but is much greater when once July has arrived, and consequently it is always best to write and make terms beforehand.

There are Nine Establishments for the Waters, among which twenty-four springs are divided. The springs may be classed under two heads—1stly, sodium sulphate; 2ndly, saline—both naturally heated.

The three most important establishments are—Les Œufs, La Raillère, and Les Thermes de Vieux César. The others are—Le Rocher-Rieumiset, Manhourat et Les Yeux, Pauze Vieux, Pauze Nouveaux, Petit St. Sauveur, and Le Pré; in addition to which there are two "buvettes," known as Buvette de César and Le Bois. The waters at the César Vieux are the most exciting of all, and prove beneficial in scrofulous and cutaneous affections, rheumatism, and tumours. Les Œufs are specially efficacious in lung complaints; La Raillère is used successfully in affections of the respiratory passages; Mauhourat is specially recommended to aid the digestion of La Raillère's water; while Les Yeux are beneficial for affections of the eyes—as the name suggests. Le Petit St. Sauveur is efficacious in cases of hysteria and similar complaints.

Hotels.—Du Parc,∥ Continental, De France, Richelieu, Des Promenades, Des Boulevards, De la Paix, De Londres, Des Bains, D'Angleterre, &c.

Apartments to be found in all parts. The price of a single-bedded room varies from 3 to 10 frs. in the season. Much less at other times.

Doctors, in connection with the "Thermes," and many independent ones.

Chemists.—J. Latapie and M. Broca—both in the Place St. Martin.

Confectioners.—Patisserie Suisse, Rue César; Patisserie Pyrénéenne, Rue de la Raillère.

Horses and **Carriages** in plenty—good steeds at Dominique's, Rue de la Raillère.

Guides.—Sarrettes, Clément Latour, Latapie, Barraga, Bordenare; and also Berret, Lac Dominique, and Pont Dominique.

Post and **Telegraph Office, Theatre, Casino**, &c. Tariff for bathing, &c., similar to other resorts.

Horses for **Excursions** cost about 12 frs. for the day, for an ordinary trip 6 frs.; and for a few hours' ride 4 to 5 frs., with 50 cents to the ostler.

Carriage from Argelès, 20 frs. with luggage; pourboire 3 frs.

The Chief Excursions are :—

To the Col de Riou.—Splendid view. Guide 6 frs., horses 6 frs. Can be prolonged down the opposite side to St. Sauveur.

To the Cascade de Cérizey, Pont d'Espagne, and **Lac de Gaube.**—Guides each 8 frs., horses 6 frs. The favourite trip.

Le Cabaliros.—6 hrs. up and down. Guide 10 frs., horses 10 frs.

Le Monné.—7 hrs. up and down. Horses and guide 10 frs. each, donkey 8 frs. Splendid view.

Pic d'Enfer.—8½ hrs. and 12 hrs. respectively by the two routes. Good guides necessary—a difficult climb.

For the Vallée de Lutour refer to Chapter V.

Pic d'Ardiden.—9 hrs. Guide essential—an interesting climb.

Pic de Vignemale.—18 to 20 hrs. not including rests. Guides, hatchets, and ropes necessary. Magnificent view from summit, but a very difficult trip.

CIER-de-Luchon.—A small village in the Haute Garonne, 4½ miles from Luchon on the railway from thence to Montrejeau.

CIERP.—A small village at the foot of a rock in the Pique valley—dep. Haute-Garonne—near Marignac, station for St. Béat on the line between Luchon and Montrejeau.

COARRAZE.—A village in the Basses-Pyrénées on the road between Pau and Lourdes. Railway station on line connecting the above places; 10½ miles from Pau. The ruins of a castle in the neighbourhood, in which Henry IV. spent his childhood. Refer to Chapter I.

DAX.—A town on the Adour, and junction for Bordeaux from the Bayonne and Pau lines. Celebrated for its baths, which are of three kinds, steam, mud, and water. There are several bathing establishments, but the Grand Etablissement is the best, where board and lodging can be also obtained, at an all-round figure, including baths, of from 10 to 15 frs. per diem. These baths are very useful for affections of the larynx, articular enlargements, and most kinds of rheumatism and neuralgia. When drunk the water has a tonic and diuretic effect.

Hotels.—De la Paix, Du Nord, De France, Figaro, De l'Europe.

There are enjoyable walks about the town and some old ruins; and in the vicinity a bed of fossil salt.

EAUX BONNES is a miniature Spa hemmed in by the sides of a wooded gorge in the Basses-Pyrénées—27½ miles from Pau and 6¼ from Eaux Chaudes; railway communication as far as Laruns ought now to be established: refer to Chapter XII. The waters, hot and cold, consist of five springs, sulphuret of sodium being largely present in all, and sulphate of lime in a less degree. There are **two establishments**—the Grand and the Ortech; but the former is far the most commodious, though the water is used for drinking purposes almost more than for bathing. The temperature varies in the different springs from 54° to 88° Fahr. The waters are specially recommended in cases of pulmonary consumption and affections of the air passages—also for chronic maladies of the abdominal viscera, intermittent fevers, hypochondria, and hysteria.

The Tariff is similar to that at the other Spas. **Season,** July and August.

The Climate is mild, but warm in summer.

Hotels.—De France,|| Princes, Empereurs, Richelieu, Poste, Europe, Sallenave, Des Touristes, D'Espagne et d'Orient, De l'Univers, &c.

Apartments all over the town. The following are a few of the houses that let rooms:—Bonnecaze, Pommé, Berdou, Tourné. Living in hotels during the season costs from 10 to 20 frs., according to *étage*, per diem.

Chemists.—Cazaux fils, and Tourné.

Confectioners.—Patisserie Suisse.

Post and **Telegraph Office.**—The Route Thermale runs from Eaux Bonnes to Argelès, 26½ miles: see Chapter XII.

Doctors in connection with the baths, and independent ones.

Horses and **Carriages** at the hotels, &c.

Guides.—Orteig, Lanusse, and Jean Pierre for lofty summits; also Maucor and Caillau, who, with Lanusse, are **Horse proprietors** as well. It is necessary to bargain about prices, as there is no fixed tariff, but 10 to 13 frs. per diem for ordinary trips ought to suffice, without providing food—with food, 3 or 4 frs. less.

The Chief Excursions are :—
For the Col de Gourzy and the Cascades du Valentin refer to Chapter XII.

Pic de Ger.—10 to 12 hours there and back. Guide 20 frs. and provisions necessary. Magnificent view.

Le Gabizos.—Whole day ; provisions, liquor, and guide necessary. A tiring climb, but one of the finest views in the Pyrenees.

Pic de Goupey.—7 hours up and down ; guide necessary.

Pic de St. Mont.—9 hours up and down, easy climb, guide not necessary.

Lacs d'Anglas et d'Uzious.—Guide and provisions necessary ; a whole day ; splendid excursion.

EAUX CHAUDES.—Another miniature Spa—less contracted in its position, but equally picturesquely situated in a wild gorge in the Basses-Pyrénées, 27½ miles from Pau. The climate is bracing, but on account of the situation of the town it is not so good a residence for invalids with chest complaints as Eaux Bonnes—as the wind sweeps up the valley unchecked. It is, however, a glorious place for healthy people to stay in, and a good centre for excursions.

The Bathing Establishment is a fine building with good accommodation. There are seven important springs and two of less consequence ; and they partake of the same nature as those of Eaux Bonnes, though the temperature extends about 10° Fahr. higher. They are largely charged with sulphur and lime, in combination with carbon and soda, and have an exciting action. They are especially useful in cases of catarrh, rheumatism, cutaneous diseases, and neuralgia. The "buvettes" of Baudot and Minvielle are largely patronised.

Hotels.—Baudot,|| De France; and more expensive accommodation at " L'Etablissement Thermal."

Prices are less than at Eaux Bonnes. In the season they range from 10 to 16 frs., but from 8 to 12 at other times, "**En Pension.**"—For one day or less than a week no fixed price can be quoted.

Doctors.—One in connection with the establishment.

Horses and **Carriages** to be obtained at the hotels or from the guides, who are mostly horse proprietors.

Guides.—Camy, Labarthe, Larrouy, Eugène Olivan, Jean Sallenave. Tariff not fixed, but 7 to 9 frs. per diem without providing food is sufficient, and 5 to 8 frs. for horses—though this is only for ordinary excursions and not perilous ones.

Bathing Tariff.—Similar to that of other Spas.

Chief Excursions are :—

Goust.—1 hour there and back ; mule track.

Grotte des Eaux Chaudes.—2 hours there and back—for lights and permit 1 fr. 50 c. each is charged, guide 2 frs.

Gabas and the Bious-Artigues.—See Chapter XII. Rather over 8 miles; carriage road to Gabas, fine and pleasant trip.

Baths of Panticosa.—13 to 15 hours by the mule track; a favourite way into Spain.

To Huesca by Sallent and Jaca, a very lengthy trip, requiring several days.

Pic Scarput.—10 hours up and down; a very fine climb.

Lac d'Artouste.—10 hours up and down; a viper region.

Pic d'Arriel.—10 hours up and down; an exceedingly fine view from summit, but not an easy climb.

Le Balaïtous —14 hours. For ascension only, it is necessary to have good guides (at least two), as well as provisions, and to pass the night on the mountain in the Cabanes near the Lac d'Artouste. A difficult excursion, not unattended with considerable danger.

FONTARABIE (Fuenterabia, Sp.). A quaint old Spanish town on the left bank of the Bidassoa, just across the frontier, well worthy of a visit. About equidistant from the stations of Hendaye (Fr.) and Irun (Sp.) on the direct line from Bordeaux to Madrid. A pleasant excursion from Biarritz.

GABAS.—A village in the Basses-Pyrénées, 5 miles from Eaux Chaudes, near the famous plateau of the Bious-Artigues. Inn accommodation can be had, and it is a good starting-point for several excursions.

GAN.—A village in the Val d'Ossau in the Basses-Pyrénées, 5 miles from Pau. The road from Pau forks here, one branch leading to Oloron (15½ miles), the other to Eaux Bonnes and Eaux Chaudes (22½ miles). There are some mosaics under a shed in the vicinity. Hôtel (such as it is), Des Voyageurs.

GAVARNIE (4380 ft.). An unpretentious village with good hotel accommodation, situated among some of the most magnificent scenery in the Hautes-Pyrénées, 13 miles from Luz. For full description of the Cirque of Gavarnie refer to Chapter VIII., also for the Falls of Marboré, 1380 ft.

Hotels.—Des Voyageurs ;‖ De la Cascade.

There are several Mountains to be ascended in the neighbourhood requiring experienced guides; among which are Le Piméné, the Brèche de Roland, Le Taillon, Le Gabiétou, Le Marboré, Pic d'Astazou, and the Mont Perdu; but for further information the traveller is referred to the previously recommended authorities.

No Guides have a better reputation than those of Gavarnie, and of these Henri Passet and Celestin Passet have made all the great ascents of the French and Spanish

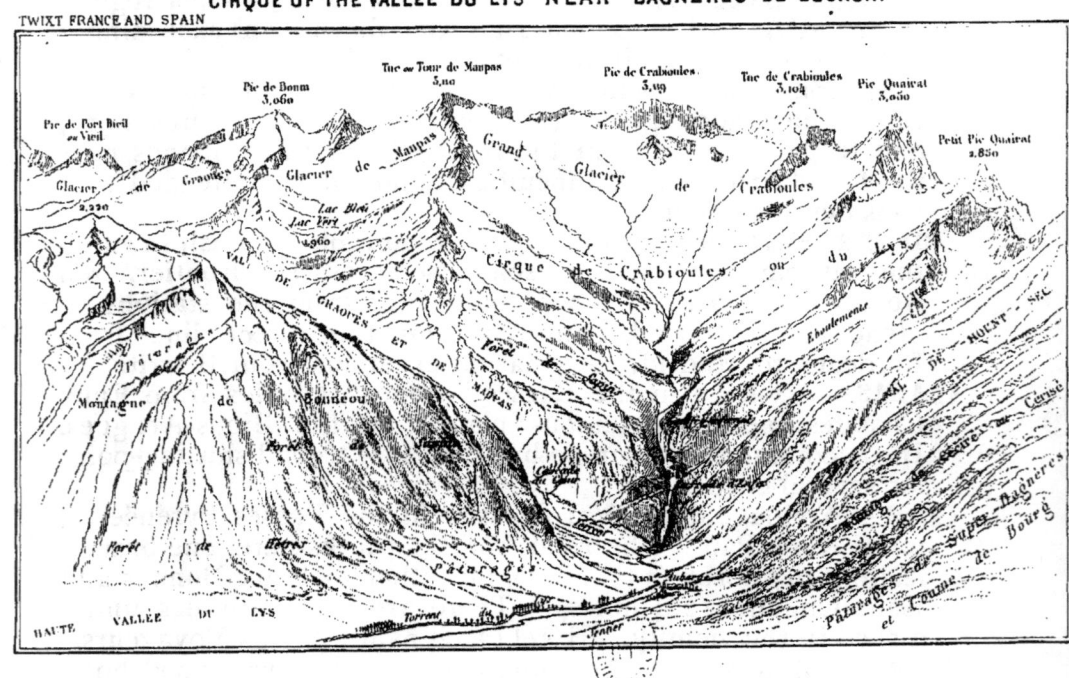

CIRQUE OF THE VALLÉE DU LYS NEAR BAGNÈRES-DE LUCHON.
TWIXT FRANCE AND SPAIN

Pyrenees; Pierre Pujo, Pierre Brioul, Poc, and Haurine are also men of experience in mountaineering.

Horses to the Cirque, 2 frs. each. **Guides,** 2 frs. each. Asses, 1½ fr. each.

GAZOST-les-Bains.—A village in the Vallée du Nez, 7½ miles from Lugagnan (the nearest station), on the line between Pierrefitte and Lourdes, in the Basses-Pyrénées. The baths, fed by four cold sulphurous springs, are less than ¾ of a mile from the village, where there is a large sawmill. Very few people visit the baths, and they are in a miserable state. There are copper, zinc, and argentiferous lead mines in the neighbourhood.

Rooms at the Châlet de la Scierie.

GÈDRE (3214 ft.).—A poor village in lovely scenery (see engraving, page 122), on the side of a rocky gorge in the Hautes-Pyrénées, 8 miles from Luz and 4 from Gavarnie, on the direct road between the two.

Hotels.—Des Voyageurs, Palasset.

For information on the so-called Grotte de Gèdre see Chapter VIII. The **two chief excursions** from Gèdre are those to the Vallée de Héas and the Cirque de Troumouse, though they may be considered as one trip here. From Gèdre to the chapel of Héas 2 to 2½ hours, from the chapel to the fork of the road ½ hour, and from thence to the Cirque 1 hour. This is a very fine excursion, occasionally undertaken from Luz and St. Sauveur.

GERDE.—A village in the Campan valley, in the Hautes-Pyrénées, near Bigorre. Known chiefly for the *palomières* or pigeon traps among the trees above it. See Chapter II.

GRIPP (3448 ft.).—A well-situated village in the Hautes-Pyrénées, on the Route Thermale, between Bigorre and Barèges, 2½ miles from Ste. Marie. Tourists often find the Hôtel des Voyageurs comfortable enough to keep them there for a few days. A little beyond the village on the old road are the **Baths of Bagnet,** supplied by a cold sulphurous spring; they do not, however, call for much mention. The Falls of Garet are in the immediate vicinity.

GRUST.—A small village in the Hautes-Pyrénées. Refer to Sazos in Appendix.

GUÉTARY.—A Basque village in the Basses-Pyrénées, 3 miles from Biarritz. The railway station, Bidart-Guétary, on the line between Bordeaux and Madrid, is not far from the village.

HÉAS.—A hamlet in the Hautes-Pyrénées, five miles from Gèdre and eight from Gavarnie, by the Piméné.

Inn.—De la Munia, kept by Victor Chappelle, hunter; besides whom, Jacques Canton and François Lavignolle, chamois-hunters, are excellent guides. Chief excursion to the Cirque de Troumouse. See Gèdre.

HENDAYE.—The French frontier town on the Bay of Biscay in the Basses-Pyrénées, known for the manufacture of a liqueur of the same name. French Custom-house; station on the line between Bordeaux and Madrid. Good beach and bathing. Boats can be hired to cross the Bidassoa to Fuenterabia, at about 2 frs. for 3 persons; for information concerning which see Chapter XIII.

Buffet at the station.
Money changed.
Hotels.—De France, Du Commerce, Americani.

IRUN.—The Spanish frontier town and railway station on the direct line between Bordeaux and Spain. Spanish Custom-house.

Buffet at the station, also a **money** changer.
Hotels.—Echenique, De Arupe.

IZESTE.—A village in the Basses-Pyrénées, near Louvie-Juzon and Arudy, on the road between Eaux Bonnes and Oloron.

JACA.—A fortified town of Spain on the banks of the Aragon, $52\frac{1}{2}$ miles from Oloron, on the direct route to **Huesca**, from which it is $57\frac{1}{2}$ miles distant.

LABASSÈRE.—A village in the Hautes-Pyrénées, celebrated for its waters and slate quarries (refer to Bagnères de Bigorre). It is $1\frac{1}{2}$ hrs. distant from Bigorre; but its quarries take $\frac{1}{2}$ hr. longer to reach, and the springs 1 hour after that. The celebrated water is bottled at the springs, but it is also sent in casks for use in Bagnères de Bigorre.

LAMOTHE.—A small village in the Landes, 25 miles from Bordeaux. Junction for Arcachon, 10 miles distant.

LARUNS.—An important though tumble-down village in the Val d'Ossau, in the Basses-Pyrénées, $3\frac{1}{4}$ miles from Eaux Bonnes and the same from Eaux Chaudes. The railway from Pau now extends to Laruns, 24 miles (see Chapter XII.), but the drive is more enjoyable, except on a dusty day. The picturesque costumes of the Ossau valley may still be seen occasionally at this village.

Hotels.—Des Touristes, Des Pyrénées. Living economical.

LESCAR.—An ancient and decaying town, $4\frac{1}{2}$ miles from Pau by rail. Several interesting ruins, &c., for which refer to Chapter I.

LOURDES.—A town in the Hautes-Pyrénées, and railway station on the direct line from Pau to Toulouse, and junction with the line to Pierrefitte. The great Roman Catholic Pilgrimage, having now quite eclipsed Bétharram, much visited formerly as a shrine. The grotto where the Virgin is supposed to have appeared is by the riverside. An admirable panorama represents the scene at one of these imaginary apparitions of the

Virgin—known as Notre Dame de Lourdes, and always represented in that connection with a blue sash. Five and twenty years and superstition have transformed Lourdes from a little village into a fair-sized town, overloaded with hotels, of which the traveller is advised to be wary, especially during the pilgrim season, when the beds are apt to have other occupants than the "weary traveller's form." The Hôtel des Pyrénées may be trusted.

Hotels.—Des Pyrénées ‖ (Mons. R. Lacrampe); Latapie; De la Grotte, De la Poste, De Paris, De l'Europe, De la Paix, D'Angleterre, &c.

Excellent Carriages on hire in the town and at the hotels.

Excursions to the Lac de Lourdes, &c.

LOURES (1445 ft.).—A village in the Hautes-Pyrénées, 17½ miles from Luchon and 3 from St. Bertrand de Comminges (see Chapter XI.), for which it is the station on the railway between Luchon and Montrejeau, and carriages await trains.

Hotels.—Pyrénées, Lassus.

LOUVIE-JUZON.—A village in the Val d'Ossau, Basses-Pyrénées, 16 miles from Pau, 11½ from Eaux Bonnes, and less than a mile from the ruins of the ancient castle of Géloz. There is a curious old church in the village, and the inn where the diligence daily halts is known as the Hôtel des Pyrénées.

LOUVIE SOUBIRON.—A small village at the foot of a mountain worked for its slates, 4 miles from the above.

LUZ (2410 ft.).—A well-situated village in a fertile valley in the Hautes-Pyrénées, 6¼ miles from Pierrefitte, the terminus of the line to Lourdes, 1¼ from St. Sauveur, and 3¾ from Barèges. From the last-named it receives water for its new **Bathing Establishment** (see Barèges in Appendix).

Hotels.—De l'Univers,‖ Des Pyrénées, De l'Europe, &c.

Apartments may also be obtained. Living is not on the whole expensive, but from July to September from 10 to 16 frs. may be charged—much less at other times (say from 7 to 10).

Carriages and **Horses**, **Asses** and **Guides** can be obtained for the various excursions (for which see St. Sauveur in Appendix).

Post and **Telegraph Office.**

For description of the old Church of the Templars and the Château St. Marie, &c., refer to Chapter VI.

MAULÉON-BAROUSSE.—In the valley of Barousse, Hautes-Pyrénées, 3¼ miles from Saléchan, on the line between Montrejeau and Luchon; 4½ miles from Ste. Marie (not to be confounded with the Ste. Marie near Bigorre).

Inn.—M. Grillon's.

MOLITG-les-Bains (1480 ft.).—Built on a terrace above the

Castellane Gorge in the Pyrénées Orientales, 5½ miles from Prades and 31 from Perpignan.

The **Bathing Establishments** (of which there are three) are situated a mile below the village, in the gorge, and they are supplied by 10 springs of a similar nature, largely charged with sulphate of soda, and of temperatures varying from 88° to 100° Fahr. The water has emollient and sedative properties, slightly diuretic, and is especially useful in diseases of the skin and nerves.

The **Climate** is very mild in winter, but hot in summer; and the **season** extends from May to October.

Hotels.—The best accommodation is to be had at the bathing establishments Barrère, Llupia, and Massia, all of which belong to M. Massia, who is a **doctor** by profession.

Chief Excursions are:—

To Olette by the Gourgs de Nohèdes (11 hours there and back).

To the **Baths** of **Carcanières** (about 11 hours there *only*) *viâ* Mosset.

MONTAUBAN.—A village in the Hautes-Pyrénées, 1½ miles from Luchon (see Chapter X.), known for its church and cascade.

MONTGAILLARD.—A village on the banks of the Adour, in the Hautes-Pyrénées, 5 miles from Bigorre: station on the line between Bigorre and Tarbes.

MONTREJEAU.—A town standing on an eminence above the river in the Haute-Garonne, junction for Luchon from the Pau-Toulouse line.

Hotels.—Leclair (fine situation); Pouget, well-known; &c.

Buffet at the station. Refer to Chapter XI. for further information.

MORCENZ.—A town in the "Landes" district, 68 miles from Bordeaux, and junction for the Tarbes-Bigorre line. There is a small bathing establishment in the town, supplied by a cold chalybeate spring; and a quarry of lithographic stone in the neighbourhood.

Buffet at station.

Inns.—Commerce, Ambassadeurs.

NAY.—An ancient village in the Basses-Pyrénées, on the left bank of the Gave de Pau. Station, **Coarraze-Nay**, on the line from Pau to Lourdes; 10½ miles from the former and 14 from the latter. Tanneries, &c., and ancient buildings. See Chapter I.

Inns.—Du Commerce, De France.

NÉGRESSE.—The station for Biarritz (2 miles from the town), on the direct line between Bordeaux and Madrid.

NESTALAS.—A village in the Hautes-Pyrénées, near Pierrefitte; the station being known as Pierrefitte-Nestalas, the terminus of the line from Lourdes. Hotel accommodation at Pierrefitte (which see in Appendix).

OLORON.—A town on a hill above the river of same name, in the Basses-Pyrénées, 20 miles from Pau, by Gan and Belair. Its suburb (across the river) Sainte Marie possesses a fine old church of the Transition style. The railway was to be opened this year (1883) in communication with Pau and Laruns. Oloron is celebrated for some exquisite pottery, that can be bought in all the chief Pyrenean resorts *except* the town itself.

 Hotels.—De la Poste, Des Voyageurs, De l'Aigle.

OO.—A small village with an ancient church, in the Haute-Garonne, $5\frac{1}{2}$ miles from Luchon, and $4\frac{1}{2}$ from the lake of the same name.

 Guide.—Jean Brunet.

ORTHEZ.—An ancient town situated on a hill above the Gave de Pau, in the Basses-Pyrénées. The Tour de Moncade, in the vicinity, has great historic interest, besides which there is an ancient bridge and other remains of olden days (see Chapter I.). Coach to Salies (10 miles), and Mauléon-Licharre (27 miles).

 Inns.—De la Belle-hôtesse, Des Pyrénées, &c.

PAILLOLE (or Payole).—A village in the Hautes-Pyrénées, $11\frac{1}{4}$ miles from Bigorre, on the Route Thermale, *viâ* the Col de Peyresourde to Luchon. See Chapters I. and IX.

 Inn.—De la Poste.

PANTICOSA.—A village in Spain, 24 miles from Cauterets, celebrated for its waters. The bathing establishments are fed by four springs of the sulphurous type. They are variously used for dyspepsia, rheumatism, skin diseases, scrofula, and chronic (non-tubercular) chest affections. They have a purgative and sedative action.

 Hotels.—Accommodation can be best obtained in the nine different bathing establishments belonging to the same proprietor; there are also the D'Espagne and Franco-Espagnol.

 Horses.—At about 5 to 7 francs per diem, at the Maison Borda.

 Doctors.—Attached to the establishments.

PASAGES.—A village on the shores of a tidal bay in Spain, 30 miles from Bayonne and $6\frac{3}{4}$ from Irun. It was once the safest port in the Biscay. Refer to Chapter XIII.

PAU (770 ft.).—A former capital, and most important town on the right bank of the Gave of same name, in the Basses-Pyrénées. A favourite winter resort with English and Americans, possessing hotels, markets, and shops of the best and most varied descriptions. An excellent starting-point for a tour in the Pyrenees. For history, &c., see Chapter I.

Hotels.—France,‖ Poste,‖ Gassion, De la Paix, Splendide Bellevue, Beau Séjour,‖ Grand Continental, De Londres, Henri IV., &c.

Pensions.—Colbert,‖ Hattersly, Etcherbest, Lecour, &c.

Apartments.—All over the town.

Season.—1st of October to end of May.

Villas. Can be hired furnished, for the season, at prices varying from £8 per month to £80.

Baths.—Rue Alexander Taylor, and 13 Rue d'Orleans, &c.

Carriage Proprietors.—Ranguedat,‖ Croharé,‖ &c. &c.

Horse Proprietors.—Estrade,‖ Peiho,‖ Lanusse.

T-Carts and Good Ponies.—Schürch, Rue de la Fontaine.

English Churches.—Trinity Church, Rue des Temples; Christ Church, Rue Serviez; St. Andrew's Church, Rue Calas; Presbyterian Church, Rue Montpensier.

Bankers.—Merillon,‖ will take English cheques, &c.; Mr. Church, English Vice-Consul; Mr. M. Clay, U. S. Vice-Consul; Tricou, &c.

Post and **Telegraph Office, Reading - Rooms, Theatre, Casino, &c.**

English Club.—Place Royale.

For the principal Excursions and sports and pastimes, refer to Chapter I.; for trips to Eaux Bonnes and Eaux Chaudes, refer to Chapter XIII.

PAYOLE.—See Paillole in Appendix.

PERPIGNAN.—A large town on the river Tet, in the Pyrénées Orientales, junction for Prades (station for Vernet), from the Toulouse line and starting-point of the coach for Amélie; 132 miles from Toulouse, 25½ from Prades, 29½ from Molitg, 32½ from Vernet, and 23½ from Amélie. It is fortified; celebrated for its garnet jewellery; and situated in a valley covered with groves of olive and pomegranate, and fruitful vineyards. Cathedral; château (splendid view from donjon tower) in the Citadol, entrance 1 fr.; theatre, Picture Gallery, &c.

Hotels.—Grand, De France, De l'Europe, Du Petit Paris, &c.

Post and **Telegraph Office.**

The **Chief Excursions** are :—

La Salanque, the whole day, by carriage *via* St. Laurent de la Salanque; Torreilles; Ste. Marie and Villelongue de la Salanque.

Castell Rossello et Canet.—6¼ miles; carriage-road part of the way.

PEYREHORADE.—Village in the Landes, and station on the line between Puyoo (13 miles) and Bayonne (19 miles).

Inns.—Lafond, Des Voyageurs.

PIERREFITTE.*—A village situated at the foot of the Pic de Soulom and the Gorge de Cauterets in the Hautes Pyrénées. Terminus of the railway line from Lourdes, and starting-point for the diligences to Cauterets, Luz, St. Sauveur, and Barèges.

 Hotels.—De la Poste,∥ Des Pyrénées, De France. Living more moderate than at any of the above-mentioned towns or Argelès. For further information see Chapter IV.

PRESTE-LES-BAINS.—A bathing-resort in the Eastern Pyrenees, 19 miles from Amélie (to which refer in Appendix), and 42½ from Perpignan, the nearest railway station.

 The **Bathing Establishment** is supplied by one sulphurous spring only, partaking of much the same properties as the more celebrated ones at the larger resorts, being specially beneficial, when drunk, for lithiasis and catarrh of the bladder.

 Hotel accommodation in the Bathing Establishment.
 Season.—June to October.

PUYOO.—A village in the Basses-Pyrénées, one mile distant from the station of same name ; junction for Bayonne from the line between Bordeaux and Pau ; from which it is 11½ miles and 32½ miles distant, respectively.

 Hotels.—Lafont, Voyageurs.

RÉBENAC.—A village in the Val de Néez, Basses-Pyrénées, 10 miles from Pau, and 17½ from Eaux Bonnes on the direct route, between the two.

 Inn.—Du Perigord.

SAINT AVENTIN (2805 ft.).—A village in the Haute-Garonne, 2¾ miles from Luchon, on the Route Thermale. Known for the chapel of same name, to which a legend is attached.

SAINT BÉAT.—A village in the Haute-Garonne, 3¼ miles from Marignac, a station on the line between Luchon and Montrejeau, from which it is 9½ and 13 miles distant respectively. A favourite drive from Luchon (see Chapter XI. and Luchon in Appendix), road to Viella *viâ* Bosost.

 Inn.—Commerce.

SAINT BERTRAND DE COMMINGES.—An ancient Roman town in the Haute-Garonne, 3 miles from Loures station on the Luchon-Montrejeau line. For information respecting the old cathedral, &c., refer to Chapter XI.

 Inn.—De Comminges.

 The Grotto de Gargas is in the vicinity. Guides must be hired at St. Bertrand.

SAINT CHRISTAU.—A village in the Basses-Pyrénées, 5 miles from Oloron, from which it is a lovely drive.

 Two **Bathing Establishments,** fed by four sources, one of which is calcareous, and the rest of a sulphurous

---

* The station is called Pierrefitte-Nestalas.

nature. They are useful for curing wounds, rheumatism, skin diseases, eczema, laryngitis, and affections of the eyes.

Hotels.—Poste, Grand Turc, Mogul; also **Châlets**, and rooms from 2 to 5 francs per diem.

There are many pleasant walks in the neighbourhood, and excellent fishing.

SAINTE MARIE (près Bigorre).—A village in the Campan valley, Hautes-Pyrénées, at the fork of the Route Thermale from Bigorre (see Chapter II.). It is distant $7\frac{1}{2}$ miles from Bigorre, $17\frac{1}{2}$ from Barèges by the Col de Tourmalet route, and 36 from Luchon by the Col d'Aspin.

SAINTE MARIE (près Oloron).—A suburb of Oloron, on the opposite bank of the river Aspe. See Oloron in Appendix.

SAINTE MARIE (près St. Laurent).—A small village on a hill in the Eastern Pyrenees, $2\frac{1}{2}$ miles from St. Laurent de la Salanque, and $7\frac{1}{2}$ from Perpignan.

SAINTE MARIE (près Saléchan).—A small bathing resort, situated in a lovely valley in the Hautes-Pyrénées about 1 mile from Saléchan station on the Luchon-Montrejeau line.

The **Bathing Establishment** is supplied by four cold springs, containing sulphate of lime principally, but also small quantities of magnesia and soda. The water is heated for bathing purposes, but drunk in its natural state. It is tonic in its action, but diuretic and purgative as well, and is used efficaciously in liver complaints, dyspepsia, neuralgia, and nervous irritability.

Hotel accommodation in the Bathing Establishment and **Apartments** in the houses near it.

SAINT JEAN DE LUZ.—A watering-place on the Bay of Biscay, in the Basses-Pyrénées, 8 miles from Biarritz, which it is very anxious to outrival. It is well protected from the winds, but is less free from dampness in its climate on the same account. It possesses an old church and several historical buildings, and is one of the favourite drives from Biarritz. Refer to Chapter XIII.

Hotels.—De la Poste, De France, D'Angleterre et de la Plage, De l'Ocean, De Madrid.

Apartments and **Houses** furnished in the town.

Sea-Bathing Establishment, Casino, &c.

SAINT LAURENT DE LA SALANQUE.—A town in the Eastern Pyrenees, with a good agricultural and commercial industry, $8\frac{3}{4}$ miles from Perpignan.

Hotels.—Got, Garriques.

SAINT MAMET.—A village in the Haute-Garonne, $\frac{3}{4}$ mile from Luchon (see Chapter X.). The church is interesting.

SAINT PÉ.—A village built on an eminence in the Hautes-Pyrénées, and station on the railway between Pau and Lourdes, 18 miles from the one and $6\frac{1}{4}$ from the other.

SAINT PÉE-sur-Nivelles.—A village in the Basses-Pyrénées, on the route between St. Jean de Luz and Cambo—8¾ miles from the former, and 10 miles from the latter.

SAINT SAUVEUR (2525 ft.).—A bathing and mountain resort in the Hautes-Pyrénées, 7 miles from Pierrefitte—the nearest station—1¼ from Luz, and 5 from Barèges. A most charming place for a spring or summer residence, being beautifully situated and possessing numerous pleasant walks in the vicinity. See Chapter VII.

Two Bathing Establishments, each supplied by one spring, in which sulphuret of sodium predominates. The water is largely diuretic in its action, having at the same time a tonic and anti-spasmodic effect. Its sedative properties are beneficial to the nervous system generally, and it proves useful in removing the after-effects of long illnesses, hæmorrhages, &c., besides being pleasant to the skin.

Hotels.—De France,‖ Des Bains,‖ Du Parc, Des Princes, De Paris.

Guides (living at Luz).—Martin, Noguez, Fortanet, and Bernard senior. For lofty summits, such as the Pic d'Ardiden, and for other excursions, Lons, Pratdessus, and Cramp Brothers.

Horses may generally be obtained from them, and **Carriages** (at Luz) as well.

Post and **Telegraph** during the season only, but letters and telegrams are forwarded from Luz at other times, there being one delivery and one collection of the former daily.

Chief Excursions :—

To Barèges.—10 to 15 frs. landau ; 2 frs. pourboire. See Chapter VI.

To Sazos and Grust.—See Chapter VII.

To Gavarnie.—Landau and four horses, 15 to 25 frs. ; pourboire, 3 frs. Horses and guide to the Cirque, each 2 frs. from Gavarnie. See Chapter VIII.

The **Pic de Bergons.**—4 frs. each horse, guide 5 frs. out of season, 6 frs. each in season. Refer to Chapter VII.

The **Pic de Viscos.**—7 hours up and down. Guide 10 frs., horse 8 frs. Viâ Grust ; a pleasant excursion.

Pic de Néré.—8 hours there and back. Horse 10 frs., guide 12 frs. Horse-track three-quarters of the way ; an easy and pleasant climb.

Pic d'Ardiden.—8½ hours up and down. Guide necessary. A fine but difficult climb.

SAINT SAVIN.—A very ancient village in the Argelès valley, in the Hautes-Pyrénées ; fully described in Chapter IV.

SAINT SÉBASTIEN.—A town in the north of Spain, on the shores of the Biscay, 163½ miles from Bordeaux, 35 from Biarritz, and 19 from Hendaye (the French frontier town).

Possessing a fine citadel, bull-ring, beach, and bathing establishment, and two fine churches. See Chapter XIII.

Hotels.—De Londres,‖ De Escurra, Anglais, De Arrese, De Berdejo, &c.

SALÉCHAN.—A village in the Garonne valley, in the Hautes-Pyrénées, and station on the Montrejeau-Luchon line for Ste. Marie (baths) and Siradan (baths).

SALIES.—A town on the river of same name, in the Basses-Pyrénées, 10 miles from Orthez, the nearest station.

It is celebrated for its salt springs; and Bayonne hams are said to owe their fine (?) flavour to the use of the salt produced from them.

Hotels.—Du Cheval Blanc, De France, De Paris.

SAZOS.—A small village near St. Sauveur, in the Hautes-Pyrénées, below the hamlet of Grust. For description of church, &c., refer to Chapter VII.

SIRADAN.—A small bathing resort in the valley of same name, in the Hautes-Pyrénées, with a bathing establishment and hotel in one building, 2 miles from Saléchan station on the Luchon-Montrejeau line. The springs contain sulphuret of lime and bicarbonate of iron. They have a similar effect to those of Ste. Marie (1 mile distant), but tend to excite more strongly. The water stands bottling well.

SOULOM.—A small village at the foot of the peak of same name, in the Hautes-Pyrénées, near Pierrefitte, possessing a curious old church. See Chapter IV.

TARBES.—A large town on the Adour, in the Hautes-Pyrénées. Station on the railway between Pau and Toulouse, and junction for the Bigorre and Morcenz lines.

Cavalry barracks, cathedral, &c. Buffet at the station. See Chapter III.

Hotels.—De la Paix, France, Commerce.

URRUGNE.—A village in the Basses-Pyrénées, 2½ miles from St. Jean de Luz.

USTARITZ.—The name of two villages, formerly separate, in the Basses-Pyrénées, 8¾ miles from Bayonne, on the carriage-road thence *via* Elizondo to Pampeluna (63 miles).

VALCABRÈRE.—A small village in the Haute-Garonne, 2 miles from Loures station on the Luchon-Montrejeau line, celebrated for the Church of St. Just, a venerable pile in the vicinity.

VENASQUE.—A small and prosperous town in Spain, 9 hours from Luchon (21 miles) by the *Port* of the same name. There are some baths similar in their uses to those of Luchon, fed by sulphurous springs at some distance from the town, and 2½ hours nearer Luchon.

Excellent accommodation can be obtained at the Casa san Mimi (Antonio Saora) for travellers.

VERNET-LES-BAINS (2050 ft.), a bathing resort situated in a hollow in the Eastern Pyrenees, 7 miles from the nearest railway station.

There are several springs which supply the **large Bathing Establishment** and the smaller **Thermes Mercader.** The water is largely charged with sulphate of lime, and possesses properties similar to other waters of that type. It is especially useful in affections of the air-passages and skin complaints, and is more or less exciting according to the springs. The climate is mild, and therefore Vernet has some reputation as a winter resort, being very little colder than Amélie (to which refer in Appendix).

Hotels.—Des Commandants (in the bathing establishment), Du Parc, Ibrahim Pacha et des Bains, Du Canigou, &c.

Villas furnished to be let.

Carriages and **Horses.**

Post and **Telegraph Office, Theatre, Clubs,** &c.

Guide.—Michael Nou.

Chief Excursions:—

The Canigou (9144 ft.).—11 hours up and down. Guide recommended, also provisions. Horses 10 frs., guide 10 frs. Horses can go within a mile of the top, from which the view is splendid. The ascent is long but not difficult.

The Fountain des Esquereyres.—*Viâ* Castell, ½ hour; a pleasant walk.

Tour de Goa.—4 hours up and down. An interesting battlemented tower, with a fine view.

Vallée de Sahorre.—3 hours there and back; an enjoyable trip.

Cascade de Cadi.—6 hours there and back; guide recommended.

The Abbey of Canigou.—2½ hours there and back; guide unnecessary. An interesting ruin.

Vieuzac.—A suburb of Argelès, in the Hautes-Pyrénées, possessing a donjon tower. The station on the line from Lourdes is called Argelès-Vieuzac.

Villelongue.—A small village in the Argelès valley, in the Hautes-Pyrénées, near Pierrefitte. See Chapter IV.

APPENDIX B.

RAILWAY INFORMATION AND SKELETON ROUTES TO THE CHIEF RESORTS IN THE PYRENEES.

For the ordinary traveller a "Continental Bradshaw" is as useful a railway guide as any, especially if his knowledge of French is limited, but the time tables published by Chaix and Cie. are also most excellent in every way. Of these the best and most expensive is the "Livret-Chaix Continental," price 2 frs., containing all continental railways and a complete index. A cheaper time table is the "Indicateur des Chemins de Fer," published by the same firm, price ½ fr., which gives the French railways only, with map and index. Besides these, all the principal lines have time tables of their own, price 30 cents.

It is advisable, when people are travelling as a party, that they should have their luggage all weighed together, presenting the whole of the tickets at the same time; this not only frequently saves expense, but, as the number of persons is marked by the luggage clerk on their baggage receipt, it is a guarantee that each has bought a ticket, which saves trouble if one should happen to be lost.

When people are stopping the night *en route* at a place, and do not wish to take their registered luggage to the hotel, only to have to bring it back for re-registration next day, they have simply to leave it in the station, and when starting again on the morrow to tell the porter—when they give him the baggage ticket—that it was left overnight (for which the charge is 1d. per package), whereupon he will register it without further trouble.

If a ticket is taken for the wrong station (by mistake) and the luggage is accordingly registered wrongly too, the passenger must represent the same to the station-master and ask him to allow a change to be made; if there is not time to do this the luggage clerk may take the responsibility—if the urgency of the case is made *argentiferously* clear—but the plan is not recommended. *It is important to know* that if a traveller misses his train he *must present* his *ticket* at the ticket office to be *restamped* in order to make it again available—otherwise it is liable to be forfeited.

Travellers will also save themselves much trouble by settling which hotel they intend to go to, before arriving at their destination; and it must be fully understood that for the carrying of small parcels taken into the carriage, the aid of porters can *never* be counted on. See Chapter XI.

Luggage not exceeding 30 kilogrammes (*i.e.* 66 lbs. Eng.) is carried free; 1d. being charged for the registration thereof.

Routes from London to Paris.

Route 1.—*Viâ* Dover, Calais, Montreuil, Abbeville, Amiens, Claremont, and Creil: the quickest route.

Route 2.—*Viâ* Folkestone, Boulogne, Montreuil, &c. as above.

Route 3.—*Viâ* Newhaven, Dieppe, Rouen, Gaillon, Mantes, and Poissy: the least expensive route.

From Liverpool to Bordeaux.

Route 4.—Per Pacific Steam Navigation Co.'s steamers, fortnightly, sailing on Wednesdays; average passage $2\frac{1}{2}$ days.

From London to Bordeaux.

Route 5.—Per General Steam Navigation Co.'s steamers, average passage 3 to 4 days.

Route 6.—*Viâ* Weymouth, Cherbourg, Caen, Alençon, Le Mans, Tours and Angoulême.

From Paris to Bordeaux.

Route 7.—*Viâ* Orleans, Blois, St. Pierre les Corps (for Tours), Poitiers, Angoulême, and Libourne.

From Paris to Bagnères de Bigorre.

Route 8.—*Viâ* Orléans, Nexon, Perigueux, Les Eyzies, Libos, Agen, Lectoure, Auch, Mirande, and Tarbes: the most direct route from Paris to the Pyrénées.

From Paris to Toulouse.

Route 9.—*Viâ* Issoudun, Argenton, Limoges, Nexon, Brives, Rocamadour, Assier, Figeac, Villefranche, and Tessonières: the quickest and best route for the Pyrénées Orientales, and resorts of Vernet, Amélie, &c.

From Bordeaux to Arcachon.

Route 10.—*Viâ* Gazinet, Facture, Lamothe, and La Teste.

From Bordeaux to Bagnères de Bigorre.

Route 11.—*Viâ* Morcenx, Arjuzaux, Arengosse, Mont de Marsan, Aire, Vic-Bigorre, Tarbes, Salles, Adour, and Montgaillard: a longer route from Paris, by a few miles only, than Route 8.

From Bordeaux to Biarritz.

Route 12.—*Viâ* Ychoux, Morcenx, Dax, Saint Geours, and Bayonne.

From Bordeaux to Pau.

Route 13.—*Viâ* Ychoux, Morcenx, Dax, Puyoo, Orthez, Lacq, and Lescar.

From Pau to Eaux Bonnes and Eux Chaudes.

Route 14.—By carriage *viâ* Gan, Louvie-Juzon, and Laruns.
Route 15.—By rail *viâ* Gan and Laruns,* and carriage from Laruns.

From Pau to Lourdes.

Route 16.—*Viâ* Coarraze-Nay, Montaut-Bétharram, and St. Pé.

From Pau to Oloron.

Route 17.—*Viâ* Gan and Belair.

From Lourdes to Argelès.

Route 18.—*Viâ* Soum, Lugagnan, and Boo-Silhen.

From Lourdes to Pierrefitte.

Route 19.—*Viâ* Soum, Lugagnan, Boo-Silhen and Argelès.

* This railway was to be opened this year (1883).

From Lourdes to Cauterets, Luz, St. Sauveur, Barèges, and Gavarnie.

Route 20.—By Route 19 to Pierrefitte, thence by diligence or private carriage to Cauterets.

Route 21.—By Route 19 to Pierrefitte, thence by diligence or private carriage to Luz.

Route 22.—By Route 19 to Pierrefitte, thence by similar conveyances to St. Sauveur.

Route 23.—By Route 21 to Luz and continuation to Barèges.

Route 24.—By Route 22 to St. Sauveur and continuation to Gavarnie.

From Bagnères de Bigorre to Barèges.

Route 25.—By carriage *viâ* Ste. Marie, Gripp, Tramesaïgues, and the Col de Tourmalet. This route is only open in midsummer.

From Bagnères de Bigorre to Bagnères de Luchon.

Route 26.—By carriage *viâ* Campan, Ste. Marie, Payole, Col d'Aspin, Arreau, Bordères, Col de Peyresourde, and Garin. Considered the finest drive in the Pyrenees.

Route 27.—By rail *viâ* Montgaillard, Tarbes, Montrejeau, Saléchan, Marignac, and Luchon. An exceedingly long round.

From Bagnères de Luchon to St. Bertrand de Comminges.

Route 27.—By carriage *viâ* Cier, Marignac, Saléchan, Loures, and Labroquère.

Route 28.—By train *viâ* Marignac and Saléchan to Loures, and carriage thence to St. Bertrand. The rail continues from Loures to Montrejeau.

From St. Bertrand to Montrejeau.

Route 29.—By carriage to Loures station, thence by train to Montrejeau.

Route 30.—By carriage direct to Montrejeau.

From Toulouse to Perpignan.

Route 31.—Via Castelnaudary, Carcassone, Narbonne, La Nouvelle, Salses, and Rivesaltes.

From Perpignan to Amélie-les-Bains.

Route 32.—By diligence or carriage *viâ* Pollestres, Le Boulou, and Le Pont de Ceret.

From Perpignan to Molitg.

Route 33.—By rail *viâ* Millas, Ille, Bouleternère, and Vinca, to Prades, thence by diligence or carriage *viâ* Catlar to Molitg.

From Perpignan to Vernet.

Route 34.—By Route 33 to Prades and coach to Vernet.
Route 35.—By rail *viâ* Prades to Villefranche, and carriage thence to Vernet.

APPENDIX C.

SOME LOCAL PYRENEAN TERMS AND THEIR ENGLISH EQUIVALENTS.

Artigue, pasturage, prairie.
Barranque, a deep hollow or ravine.
Borde, Bourdette, farm-house, barn, cot.
Caire, Quaire, Quaïrat, a cone-shaped peak, rocky and bare.
Canaou, narrow ravine worn by the snow.
Cap, mountain tip.
Clot, a valley without exit.
Colline, a small valley, a dale.
Cortal, Courtaou, sheep-fold, sheep-pen.
Couila, Couillade, shepherd's cabin, hut, fertile vale.
Estibe, pasturage, feeding-ground.
Estibère, a well-pastured mountain.
Fitte, pointed summit.
Montagne, feeding-ground (on a mountainside).
Neste, mountain torrent.
Orrhy, Orri, shepherd's hut.
Oule, a bowl-shaped valley.
Pech, Pouey, Puy, a mountain of no great height, in the Western Pyrenees; but also applied to loftier summits, in the Eastern range.
Pène, Peña, Penne, pointed rock.
Peyre, a large crag.
Piche, Pisse, a cascade waterfall.
Pinède, Pinade, pine forest, site of pine forest.
Pique, synonymous with *Fitte*, pointed summit, peak.
Pla, Plan, a valley with level meadows.
Prade, Pradère, similar to *Estibe*, feeding-ground, meadow.
Raillère, steep decline, avalanche channel.
Roque, a mountain, steep and covered with crags.
Sarrat, Serre, Serrère, a sharp-toothed crest, backbone of mountain.
Sarre, a small hill.

Séoube, Scube, wood, forest.
Tausse, Truc, Truque, Tuc, a steep and lofty peak with large buttresses.

The *Defiles* and *Passes* of the mountains for which the word *Col* is generally applied, bear many other names, of which the following, with their special significations, are the chief :—

Core, a pass on a side range or small lateral chain.
Fourque, Fourquette, Hourque, Hourquette, generally applied to passes on the small side ranges.
Pas, a pass difficult of approach.
Port, a pass in the principal chain.
Porteil, Portillon, Pourtet, passes in the principal or side chains.

APPENDIX D.

GENERAL INFORMATION, AND TABLES OF METRES, GRAMMES, DEGREES, &c. &c.

IT would be difficult to speak with *too* much weight on the subject of *bread*, especially where invalids are concerned, and that article in the Pyrenees is essentially *bad*—we might almost say *unfit for food*. With the exception of Bagnères de Bigorre —and then only when specially ordered—and *in the season*, Bagnères de Luchon, the bread throughout the mountain resorts is abominably sour. Travellers *do* eat it, because they have no other, but to invalids it is positively nauseous. In our opinion it is the only real drawback to enjoying a Pyrenean trip! But it would be foolish to bring it into such prominence when we have all along recommended a stay amid these lovely scenes, unless we could suggest a remedy, and the remedy is as simple as, with us, it proved complete. There are several bakers in Pau selling bread as good as one could wish for, and doubtless any of these would be glad to meet the wishes of travellers; in our case we addressed ourselves to Mr. Otto Kern, Vienna Bakery, Rue de la Préfecture, Pau, requesting him to supply us with a certain quantity of bread daily, at whatever place we might be. We had previously decided on our route on broad lines, so that a postcard as a rule was sufficient to give notice of a change in our address; while if a sudden alteration occurred in our plans, a half-franc telegram told him the news, and *our bread* never failed to be at the *right* place on the *right day*. The bread sufficient for four people, carriage thereof, and a trifle for commission (i.e. paper and trouble) cost on an average 2 frs. 50 cents per diem, which was a little over 80 centimes each. Perhaps in time hotel-keepers will resort to this method; in fact, we were assured that it would be so; but in the meantime every traveller is recommended to do so on his own account; though in all other respects he will find most of the hotels throughout the mountains very well found. When once in the Pyrenees, after Pau had been left behind, we found an average price of 10 frs. per day—perhaps a shade less

—was what our hotel expenses amounted to ; including—coffee and milk, bread and butter, eggs *or* kidneys *or* chops for the first breakfast ; table d'hôte luncheon and table d'hôte dinner, with a good bedroom not higher than 2nd floor. These prices must be understood as only those of a spring or autumn tour—*out of the season*—and rather easier than a traveller would pay at many of the hotels if he arrived without having previously written and made terms. *We* invariably wrote, and at all the hotels marked thus ‖ received every attention, good rooms, good food, and *dry beds*.

It is difficult to give a hard-and-fast amount per diem as to expenditure, as it depends so much on the drives, excursions, &c. ; as above stated 10 frs. per day paid all hotel expenses (including *vin ordinaire*), and we consider that in the spring, with several excursions, and "a landau and four" for the principal drives—such as Bigorre to Luchon, Lourdes to St. Sauveur, St. Sauveur to Gavarnie, &c. &c.—25 frs. or £1 per day ought to cover the whole daily expense of each person. In the summer of course 35 frs., or even 40 frs., would be required for the same period. Horses and carriages are cheap in the spring, but even then a little judicious bargaining is required, as it is in nearly every transaction, in the Pyrenees.

Jam, marmalade, bloater-paste, and small luxuries of that kind, not excluding *whiskey*, are difficult to obtain, and it is well to take them all from Pau or Biarritz, wherever the start is made. Bagnères de Bigorre, chez M. Peltier, is fairly well supplied, but other resorts know not the sound of their names! It is also worth knowing that a system of "Parcels Post" is in operation, whereby any moderate-sized parcel can be dispatched from any station for 85 cents, and delivered at any place within reach of the railway or diligence ; but it must be understood at the same time that *bread* will in like manner be delivered *only* where the railway or diligence runs ; if travellers therefore go to places where there is no *official* communication, they must depute some agent to receive letters or parcels where the diligence last stops, and then forward them by special messenger. This can be done of course, but it will prove costly.

The rate of postage is 2½d. the 15 grammes (a shade over ½ oz.), and 2½d. for every additional 15 grammes.

Money orders are issued at all the principal towns to which (see Appendix A) a post-office belongs.

Telegrams, ½d = 5 cents, per word, the address being charged for the same as the rest ; but no telegram can cost less than 50 centimes.

The rate to England is variable ; usually 2½d. per word.

Money is reckoned at 25 frs. to the £1 English, and banknotes or gold will be accepted in nearly all hotels, and circular notes as well, at the larger resorts.

Table of Litres and Pints.

$\frac{1}{2}$ litre = $\frac{7}{8}$ pint.
1   „   = $1\frac{3}{4}$ pints.
2 litres = $3\frac{1}{2}$ pints.
4   „   = 7 pints.
8   „   = 7 quarts.

Tables of Grammes and Ounces.

29 grammes = 1 oz.
57   „   = 2 oz.
86   „   = 3 oz.
114   „   = 4 oz. = $\frac{1}{4}$ lb.
227   „   = 8 oz. = $\frac{1}{2}$ lb.
454   „   = 16 oz. = 1 lb.
908   „   = 32 oz. = 2 lbs.
1000 „   = $35\frac{1}{5}$ oz. = 2 lbs. $3\frac{1}{5}$ oz.
1 kilogramme = 1000 grammes = 2 lbs. $3\frac{1}{5}$ oz.

Table of Centimetres and Inches.

100 centimetres = 1 metre = $39\frac{1}{3}$ inches ; 1 centimetre = $\frac{2}{5}$ inch as near as possible.

5 centimetres = 2 inches.
10   „   = 4   „
15   „   = 6   „
20   „   = 8   „
25   „   = 10 „
30   „   = 12 „   = 1 foot.
45   „   = 18 „   = $1\frac{1}{2}$ feet.
50   „   = 20 „   = 1 ft. 8 in.
60   „   = 24 „   = 2 feet.
90   „   = 36   = 3 feet.
100   „   = $39\frac{1}{3}$ „ = 3 ft. $3\frac{1}{3}$ in.

Table of Metres and Feet, for Determining the Height of Mountains, &c.

1 metre = 3 ft. 3⅓ in. as near as possible, without using decimals; but at this computation 2 inches are lost in every 25 metres, which however have been duly supplied in the following table, but the fractions omitted:—

Metres.	Ft.	in.	Metres.	Ft.	in.	Metres.	Ft.	in.
1 =	3	3	26 =	85	4	140 =	459	4
2 =	6	7	27 =	88	7	150 =	492	2
3 =	9	10	28 =	91	10	160 =	524	11
4 =	13	1	29 =	95	2	170 =	557	9
5 =	16	5	30 =	98	8	175 =	574	3
6 =	19	8	35 =	114	10	180 =	590	7
7 =	22	11	40 =	131	2	190 =	623	4
8 =	26	3	45 =	147	7	200 =	656	3
9 =	29	6	50 =	164	1	300 =	984	4
10 =	32	9	55 =	180	5	400 =	1,312	6
11 =	36	1	60 =	196	10	500 =	1,640	7
12 =	39	4	65 =	213	3	600 =	1,968	8
13 =	42	7	70 =	229	7	700 =	2,296	9
14 =	45	11	75 =	246	1	800 =	2,624	11
15 =	49	2	80 =	262	6	900 =	2,953	0
16 =	52	5	85 =	278	10	1,000 =	3,281	1
17 =	55	9	90 =	295	3	2,000 =	6,562	2
18 =	59	0	95 =	311	8	3,000 =	9,843	3
19 =	62	3	100 =	328	2	3,100 =	10,171	5
20 =	65	7	105 =	344	6	3,200 =	10,499	6
21 =	68	10	110 =	360	11	3,300 =	10,827	7
22 =	72	1	115 =	377	4	3,400 =	11,155	8
23 =	75	5	120 =	393	8	3,500 =	11,483	9
24 =	78	8	125 =	410	2	4,000 =	13,124	4
25 =	82	0	130 =	426	6			

Table of Kilometres and Miles.

1 kilometre = 1,000 metres = 1,093 yards = $\frac{5}{8}$ mile, as nearly as possible, without employing decimals; but at this computation the kilometre gains 11 yards, 40 kilometres gain $\frac{1}{4}$ mile, and 160 kilometres gain 1 mile. This gain has been deducted in the following table, and all fractions less than $\frac{1}{4}$ omitted :—

Kilos.	Miles.	Kilos.	Miles.
1 =	$\frac{5}{8}$	19 =	$11\frac{3}{4}$
2 =	$1\frac{1}{4}$	20 =	$12\frac{1}{4}$
3 =	2	30 =	$18\frac{1}{2}$
4 =	$2\frac{1}{2}$	40 =	$24\frac{3}{4}$
5 =	3	50 =	31
6 =	$3\frac{3}{4}$	60 =	37
7 =	$4\frac{1}{4}$	70 =	$43\frac{1}{4}$
8 =	5	80 =	$55\frac{3}{4}$
9 =	$5\frac{1}{2}$	100 =	62
10 =	$6\frac{1}{4}$	120 =	$74\frac{1}{4}$
11 =	7	160 =	99
12 =	$7\frac{1}{2}$	200 =	$123\frac{3}{4}$
13 =	8	300 =	$185\frac{1}{2}$
14 =	$8\frac{3}{4}$	320 =	198
15 =	$9\frac{1}{4}$	400 =	$247\frac{1}{2}$
16 =	10	500 =	$309\frac{1}{4}$
17 =	$10\frac{1}{2}$	1,000 =	$618\frac{3}{4}$
18 =	$11\frac{1}{4}$		

Comparison Table of the Centigrade and Fahrenheit Thermometers.

1° Centigrade = 1⅘° Fahr.; 5° Cent. = 9° Fahr. It must be understood that, as the freezing-point of Centigrade is Zero and of Fahrenheit 32°, these 32° must be taken into account in all calculations above freezing-point : thus +5° Cent. are equivalent to a temperature of 41° Fahr.

	Cent.		Fahr.		Cent.		Fahr.	
Below Zero.	−15	=	+ 3		17	=	63	
	−10	=	+12		18	=	64	
	− 5	=	+21		19	=	65	
	0	=	32	Freezing-point.	20	=	67	
	1	=	34		25	=	76	
	2	=	36		30	=	85	
	3	=	37		35	=	94	
	4	=	39		35½	=	95	Blood heat.
	5	=	41		40	=	103	
	6	=	43		45	=	112	
	7	=	45		50	=	121	
	8	=	47		55	=	130	
	9	=	48		60	=	139	
	10	=	50		65	=	148	
	11	=	52		70	=	156	
	12	=	54		75	=	165	
	13	=	55		80	=	174	
	13½	=	56	Temperate.	85	=	183	
	14	=	57		90	=	192	
	15	=	59		95	=	201	
	16	=	61		100	=	210	Boiling-point.

INDEX.

A.

Abbé's song, the, 40
A dirty avalanche, 125
A "double stroke" (St. Sauveur), 117
Adour, basin of, 134
Allée d'Etigny (Luchon), 142, 159
　,,　de Barcugna, 159
　,,　des Bains, 142, 144
　,,　Verte (Barèges), 105
Allées de Cambasque, 89
Amélie-les-Bains, 214 ; A 221
　,,　excursions from, A 222
　,,　general information, A 222
　,,　hotels at, &c., A 221
Amoy, Valley of Ten Thousand Rocks, 123
Ancient church of the Templars (Luz), 98
Anemone vernalis, 107
　,,　scarlet, 207
　,,　wood, 106, 118
A new "diet of worms," 101
An excited dog-fancier, 93
An extraordinary detachment, 90
Anglêt, 212
Appendix A, 221
　,,　B, 250
　,,　C, 255
　,,　D, 257
Aran, valley of, 156
Arboust, valley of, 139
Arcachon, 3 ; A 222

Arcachon, excursions from, A 223
　,,　general information, A 222
　,,　hotels at, A 222
Argelès, 60 ; A 223
　,,　drive round valley of, 71
　,,　excursions from, A 223
　,,　hotels at, 61 ; A 223
　,,　valley of, 36, 83, 132
Argelès-sur-Mer, A 223
Arles-sur-Tech, A 223
Arlos, 160
Arreau, 137 ; A 224
　,,　hotels at and excursions from, A 224
Arrens, A 224
　,,　excursions from, A 224
　,,　hotels at, A 224
Arrieuzé (river), 176
Arroudet, cascade of, 123
Artigues-Tellin, 156
Arudy, 173, 176 ; A 224
Ascent of the Col de Riou, 82
Ascent of the Pic de Bergons, 113
Aspe, valley of, 175
Aspin, 137, A 224
　,,　col of, 42, 137
Asphodel, 158
Assat, 25
Asté, 36, 47, A 224
Atalaya, cape, 197
Auberge du Lys (Luchon), 146
Auch, road of, 161
Aure, valley of, 44, 137
Avajan, 139
Avalanche, a dirty, 125
Avenue de Salut, 35
Ax, road of, 161

B.

Bagnères de Bigorre to Bagnères de Luchon, B 253
Bagnères de Luchon to Barèges, B 253
Bagnères de Bigorre, 32, 134; A 224
Bagnères de Bigorre, bathing establishment of, A 225
Bagnères de Bigorre, excursions from, A 226
Bagnères de Bigorre, hotels of, A 226
Bagnères de Bigorre, springs of, A 225
Bagnères de Luchon to Montrejeau, B 253
Bagnères de Luchon to St. Bertrand de Comminges, B 253
Bagnères de Luchon, 140; A 227
Bagnères de Luchon, baths of, A 227
Bagnères de Luchon, casino of, 144; A 228
Bagnères de Luchon, excursions from, A 228
Bagnères de Luchon, general information, A 228
Bagnères de Luchon, hotels at, A 228
Ballooning, 19
Barbe de Bouch, 115
Barèges, 103; A 230
  ,, bathing establishment of, A 230
  ,, excursions from, A 231
  ,, hotels of, A 230
Barousse, valley of, 160
Basin of Adour, 134
  ,, Echez, 134
Baths of Amélie, 214; A 221
  ,, Barèges, 105; B 230
  ,, Capvern, 214
  ,, César, 79
Baths of Grand Pré, 35; A 225
  ,, Hontalade, 116
  ,, Le Pré, 86
  ,, Luchon, 141
  ,, Luz, 101
  ,, Marie Therèse, 35; A 225
  ,, Mauhourat, 86
  ,, Molitg, 214
  ,, Œufs, 79
  ,, Panticosa, 214
  ,, Pauze Nouveaux, 83
  ,,   ,, Vieux, 83
  ,, Petit St. Sauveur, 86
  ,, Preste, 214
  ,, Raillère, 86
  ,, Ste. Marie (near Luchon), 160
  ,, St. Sauveur, 116
  ,, Salut, 35; A 225
  ,, Santé, 35; A 225
  ,, Siradan, 161
  ,, Vernet, 214
Baudéan, 36, 41; A 231
Bayonne, 194; A 231
  ,, general information, A 231
  ,, hotels at, A 231
Beaucens, castle of, 71, 132
Bédat, 36
Bee orchids, 111, 116, 118
Béhobie, 209; A 231
Bélesten, 175
Bernadette Soubirons, 58
Bétharram, 24; A 232
  ,, bridge near, 24
Betpouey (Barèges), 103
Biarritz, 195; A 232
  ,, amusements of, 195
  ,, Cape Atalaya at, 197
  ,, general information, A 232
  ,, hotels at, A 232
  ,, Port Vieux at, 196
Bidart, 206; A 232
Bidassoa, 209
Bielle, 174; A 232
Bilhères, 175; A 233
Billères (Pau), A 233

INDEX.

Billères plains of, 16
„ woods of, 17
Bious-Artigues, 187
Bishop's arrival, the, 90
Bizanos, 28 ; A 233
Black Forest (Bosost), 156
Black Prince, 101
Boo-Silhen, A 233
Bordeaux to Arcachon, B 252
Bordeaux to Bagnères de Bigorre, B 252
Bordeaux to Biarritz, B 252
„ **to Pau,** B 252
Bordeaux, 2
„ hotels at, 2
„ steamers to, 2
„ trains to, B 251
Bordères, 139
Bosost, 157 ; A 233
„ chapel of St. Antoine at, 157
„ church of, 157
„ Fonda (inn) d'España at, 157
Box plants, 116
Brada (mountain), 120
Bread, 76 ; D 257
„ arrival of, 76
Brêche d'Allanz, 126
„ Fausse, 126
„ de Roland, 121, 126
Broussette, valley of, 187
Bué, 121
Bugaret (mountain), 114, 115
„ torrent of, 121
Burbe, valley of, 154
Burnished toes, 133
Butte du Trésor, 180
Buvette de Minvieille, 189

C.

CABALIROS, the, 71, 83, 89
Cabanes du Lys, 146
Cagots, 73, 99
Cambo, 206 ; A 233
„ hotels at, 206 ; A 233

Campan, 36, 41 ; A 233
Canine absurdity, 85
„ feat, a, 197
Canton, odours of, 58
Capercailzie, 44
Capvern, 214 ; A 233
„ baths of, A 233
„ hotels at, A 234
Carmelites, church of the (Bigorre), 50
Carnival time (Pau), 28
Cascade d'Arroudet, 123
„ de Cérizey, 87
„ du Cœur, 147
„ de Discoo, 181
„ des Eaux Bonnes, 182
„ d'Enfer, 146
„ du Groshêtre, 182
„ de Laressec, 182
„ de Lassariou, 120
„ du Lutour, 86
„ du Marboré, 126
„ de Montauban, 143
„ de Pisse-Arros, 87
„ de Rioumaou, 120
„ du Serpent, 182
„ de Sidonie, 154
„ du Valentin, 179
Casino (Luchon), 142, 144
„ (Pau), 19
„ du Portillon (Luchon), 156
„ de Roulette (Luchon), 156
Castel-Géloos, 174
Castel-Mouly, 36
Castel-Vieilh (or Castelvieil) 146, 154
Castets, 174 ; A 234
Catarabe, 89
Cat-fight, 39
Cauterets, 79 ; A 234
„ baths of, 79, 86 ; A 234
„ excursions from, A 235
„ Fruitière of, 87
„ Gorge of, 78
„ hotels of, A 234
Cazaril, 161
Cazaux, 139

Céciré (Bosost), 150, 151, 156
" (Superbagnères), 150
Cemetery, Luz, 112
" Pau, 19
Cercle des Etrangers (Barèges), 103
Cérizey, cascade of, 86
Chambre d'Amour (inn), 204
Chamois, 75
Chandelles du Marboré, 126
Chaos, the, 123
Chapelle de Piétad, 72
" de St. Antoine, 157
" de St. Exupère, 137
" de St. Roch, 99
" de Solferino, 111
Château de Beaucens, 71, 132
" de Despourrins, 72
" de Géloz, 174
" de Miramont, 74
" de Ste. Marie, 100
Chester, resemblance to, 72
Cheval, Madame, 50
Chinaougue, 199
Church of Montauban, 143
" Notre Dame, Arreau, 137
" Notre Dame, Lourdes, 57, 133
" Piétat, 28
" St. Jacques, Pau, 20
" St. Martin, Pau, 11, 20
" St. Savin, Argelès, 72
" St. Vincent, Bigorre, 33
" Sazos, 117
" Soulom, 71
Chute de Lapaca, 126
" la Pique, 142
Cier de Luchon, 160; A 235
Cierp, 160; A 235
Cirque de Gavarnie, 127
" Troumouse, 121, 123
Clerical sensation, 90
Coarraze, 24; A 235
Coffre d'Ossau, 174
Col d'Arbéousse, 115
" d'Aspin, 42, 137
" d'Aubiste, 111, 120

Col de Bué, 121
" d'Estom Soubiran, 89
" de Gourzy, 189
" de Marie Blanque, 175
" de Peyresourde, 42, 139
" de Portillon, 156, 158
" de Riou, 82, 86, 111, 115
" de Tortes, 71
" de Tourmalet, 42
Columbine (*aquilegia*), 158
Confirmation at Cauterets, 90
Coteaux, the (Pau), 26, 192
Cottin, Madame, 36
Coumélie (mountain), 123
Couradilles, the, 156
Coustous, the, 33
" music on the, 135
Cowslips, 139
Crabé (bridge), 183
Crabioules, glacier of, 150
Crête d'Ordincède, 36, 42
"Crocodile of St. Bertrand," the, 164
Croix de Manse, 37
" de Mouguère, 205
"Cry of the Lourdes Shopkeepers," the, 55
Cucurlon rock (Biarritz), 198
Cylindre (du Marboré), 126

D.

DAX, 3; A 235
" baths of, A 236
" hotels at, A 236
Daffodils, 36, 118, 123
Dangerous footing, 115, 202
Dear travelling, 135
Dog-fancier, an excited, 93
Dragon's-mouth Rock, 199

E.

EAUX BONNES, 178; A 236
" bathing establishment of, A 236
" cascade of, 181
" excursions from, A 237

Eaux Bonnes, hotels at, A 236
Eaux Chaudes, 185 ; A 237
   ,,   baths at, A 237
   ,,   excursions from, A 237
   ,,   grotto of, 189
   ,,   hotels at, A 237
Echez, basin of, 134
Echo, wonderful, 120
English Church (Bigorre), 40
Entécade, peak, 156
Espelette, 206
Esplanade des Œufs, 79, 89
Esquiez, 98
Esterre, 103
"Exhortation to the First Snow," 85

F.

FASHION on a donkey, 155
Fausse Brêche (Gavarnie), 126
Feather moss, 28
Females, importunate, 125
Fête de Payole, 136
Flight of lizards, 155
Fontaine de Marnières (Pau), 19, 22
Fos, 160
French sportsmen (Pau), 17
Fuenterabia (*Fr.* Fontarabie), 209 ; A 238

G.

GABAS, 187 ; A 238
Gabrielle d'Estrelle, 48
Gan, 27, 171, 192 ; A 238
Garin, 139
Garonne, river, 156, 160
   ,,   valley of, 44, 160
Gavarnie, 125 ; A 238
   ,,   Cirque of, 126
   ,,   hotels of, A 238
   ,,   Port de, 126
Gave d'Azun, 62
Gave de Barèges, 95

Gave de Bastan, 98, 103
   ,,   Cauterets, 71, 86
   ,,   Gavarnie, 121
   ,,   Héas, 121
   ,,   Lutour, 86
   ,,   Marcadau, 86
   ,,   d'Ossau, 173, 177
   ,,   de Pau, 9, 71
Gazost-les-Bains, A 239
Gèdre, 121 ; A 239
   ,,   excursions from, &c., A 239
   ,,   grotto of, 121
Géloos, Castel, 174
Gélos, 25
General information, Appendix D, 257
Gentians, 116, 118, 123, 130, 158
Gerde, 36, 47 ; A 239
Géruzet's marble works, 34
Ges, 63
Glacier de Crabioules, 150
Gorge de Bacheviron, 120
   ,,   ,,   Cauterets, 78
   ,,   du Hourat, 182
Gouffre d'Enfer, 146
Granges de Gouron, 148
Grange de la Reine Hortense, 83, 86
Gripp, 42 ; A 239
Grocer's opinion, the (Cauterets), 92
Grotto of Eaux Chaudes, 189
   ,,   Gèdre, 121
   ,,   Lourdes, 56, 133
   ,,   the Néez, 172
Grust (St. Sauveur), 117 ; A 239
Guétary, 206 ; A 239
"Guide's Auction," the, 129

H.

HÉAS, A 239
   ,,   inn, &c., A 239
   ,,   valley of, 121
Hendaye, 209 ; A 240
Hepaticas, 106
Hermitage of St. Peter (St. Sauveur), 112

INDEX.

Herrère, stream, 19, 22
Hospice Civil (Bigorre), 50
   ,,   de France (Luchon), 146
   ,,   de Ste. Eugénie (Barèges), 105
Hôtel d'Angleterre, Argelès, 61
   ,,   Baudot, Eaux Chaudes, 185
   ,,   Beau Séjour (Bigorre), 32
   ,,   Canton, Luchon, 144
   ,,   de Comminges, 162
   ,,   d'España, Bosost, 157
   ,,   de France, Argelès, 61
   ,,   ,,   Arreau, 138
   ,,   ,,   Eaux Bonnes, 178
   ,,   ,,   St. Sauveur, 108
   ,,   du Parc, Cauterets, 79
   ,,   de Paris, Biarritz, 195
   ,,   de la Poste, Payole, 42
   ,,   ,,   Pierrefitte, 72
   ,,   des Pyrénées, Lourdes, 54
   ,,   ,,   Louvie-Juzon, 173
   ,,   de l'Univers, Luz, 100
   ,,   des Voyageurs, Gavarnie, 125
Houn Blanquo, 47
Hourat, Gorge de, 182
Hungry guardian, a, 112
Hyacinths, 118

I.

"IDYLLIC COLBERT" (Pau), 29
Importunate females, 125
Irun, 211; A 240
Itsatsou, 207
Izeste, 173; A 240

J.

JACA, A 240
"Jackdaw's Causerie," 100
Jardin à l'Anglaise (St. Sauveur), 113
   ,,   Darralde, 178
   ,,   des Quinconces, 141, 152
"Jay of Barèges," the, 105

"Jeannette's Lamb," 70
Jonquils, 118
Jurançon, 25, 26, 171

L.

LABASSÈRE, A 240
   ,,   waters of (see Bagnères de Bigorre)
La Brune (Cauterets), 83
La Casque du Marboré, 115, 121, 126
Lac Bleu, 41
   ,,   d'Estibaoute, 87
   ,,   d'Estom, 87
   ,,   d'Estom Soubiran, 87
   ,,   de Gaube, 87
   ,,   Vert, 147
"Lady's Farewell to her Asinine Steed," the, 37
Lagas, fountain of, 189
Lamothe 3; A 240
Lapaca, Chute de, 126
Laressec, cascade of,
Laruns, 176; A 240
   ,,   church of, 176
   ,,   inns at, A 240
Lassariou, cascade of, 120
La Tour du Marboré, 115, 121, 126
Lès, 160
Lescar, 5, 18; A 240
"Lesson of the Mountains," the, 217
Lime-works (Eaux Bonnes), 172
Linaria, 118
Liverpool to Bordeaux, B 251
Lizards, flight of, 155
Llanberis Pass, resemblance to, 78
London to Bordeaux, B 251
London to Paris, B 251
Louderville, 139
Lourdes to Argelès, B 252
   ,,   **Barèges,** B 253
   ,,   **Cauterets,** B 253
   ,,   **Gavarnie,** B 253
   ,,   **Luz,** B 253

INDEX.

Lourdes to Pierrefitte, B 252
    „   **St. Sauveur,**
           B 253
Lourdes, 36, 52, 133 ; A 240
   „   castle of, 58
   „   chapel of, 133
   „   church of, 37, 133
   „   grotto of, 56, 133
   „   hotels at, A 241
   „   panorama of, 57
Loures, 161 ; A 241
   „   inns of, A 241
Louron, valley of, 139
Louvie-la-Haute, 176
Louvie-Juzon, 173 ; A 241
Louvie-Soubiron, A 241
Luchon (see Bagnères de Luchon)
Lunch on the Bergons, 114
Lutour, cascade of, 86
   „   valley of, 83
Luz, 98 ; A 241
   „   hotels at, A 241
   „   baths of, A 241
Lys, valley of, 145

M.

MARBLE Works, Géruzet's, 34
Marboré, the, 126
   „   Cascade du, 126
   „   Chandelles du, 126
   „   Epaule du, 126
   „   La Casque du, 115, 121, 126
   „   La Tour du, 115, 121, 126
"March of the Men of Garlic," the, 23
Marignac, 160
Marion, Lake, 204
Marnières, Fontaine de, 19, 22
Maucapéra, 114, 115
Mauléon-Barousse, 161 ; A 241
   „   Licharre, 5
Médiabat, bridge of, 78
Menu (Cauterets), 81
   „   (Payole), 45

Mill conduits, 103
Milord, a, 133
Minvieille, Buvette de, 189
Molitg, 214 ; A 241
   „   baths of, &c., A 242
   „   excursions from, A 242
   „   hotels at, A 242
Monné, Bigorre, 35
   „   Cauterets, 83
   „   Rouge, 42
Montagne de Brada, 120
Mont Arrouye, 115
Montaigu, Pic de (see Pic)
Montauban, 143 ; A 242
   „   church of, 143
   „   cascade of, 143
Mont Bédat, 36
   „   Ferrat, 121
Montgaillard, 134 ; A 242
Montrejeau, 168 ; A 242
   „   buffet of, 168 ; A 242
Mont Ségu, Bosost, 151, 156
Morcenx, 3 ; A 242
Mouguère (cross of), 205
Mountain rhododendrons, 107
   „   violets, 116
Mouriscot, Lake, 204
Museum (Luchon), A 228
   „   (Luz), 99

N.

NAPOLEON'S pillar (St. Sauveur), 111
Narcissus, 139
Nature's voice, 97
Nay, 24 ; A 242
Néez, grotto of the, 172
   „   stream, 172
   „   valley of, 172
Négresse (station), 204 ; A 242
Nestalas, A 242
Neste (river), 138
Nethou, Pic de, 145, 150
New "diet of worms," a, 101
Nivelle (river), 206
Noah's ark landscape, a, 195

O.

"OLD world and the new," the (Pau), 20
Oloron, A 243
„ general information, A 243
„ hotels at, A 243
„ roads to, 171, 173
Oo, A 243
Open-air concert, 135
Ordincède, Crête d', 36, 42
Orphanage of Notre Dame du Rocher (Luchon), 146, 153
Orphanage, church of, 153
Orphéon, the, 135
Orthez, 3 ; A 243
Osmunda regalis (fern), 204
Ossau, Gave d', 173
„ Val d', 173
Ourous, 65
"Oxen's Appeal," the, 152
Oxslips, 118, 139, 158

P.

PAILLOLE (see Payole)
Pagoda Villa, the (Cauterets), 89
Palais de Justice, Pau, 20
Palomières de Gerde, 36, 49
Panorama of Lourdes, 57
Panticosa, 187, 188, 214 ; A 243
„ hotels at, A 243
Parc Beaumont, Pau, 19
„ du Château, Pau, 11, 16
Paris to Bagnères de Bigorre, B 251
Paris to Bordeaux, B 251
„ **Toulouse**, B 251
Pasages, 211 ; A 243
Pas de l'Echelle, 120
„ l'Escalette, 151
„ Roland, 206
Pau to Eaux Bonnes and Chaudes, B 252
Pau to Lourdes, B 252

Pau to Oloron, B 252
Pau, 1, 193 ; A 243
„ amusements at, 8, 17
„ castle of, 11
„ drives, &c., at, 21, 28
„ general information, A 244
„ history of, 12
„ hotels of, 6 ; A 244
Payole, 42, 136 ; A 243
„ en fête, 136
Peasants and their ways, 22, 47
Peculiar teams, 190
Peguère, the, 83, 89
Peña Blanca, 151
Pêne de l'Heris, 36, 42
„ Montarqué, 150
Perpignaa, 26
Perpignan to Amélie, B 253
„ **Molitg**, B 254
„ **Vernet**, B 254
Perpignan, A 244
„ chief excursions from, A 244
„ hotels at, A 244
Peyrehorade, A 244
Peyresourde, Col de, 42, 139
Pic d'Antenac, 160
„ d'Arbizon, 137
„ d'Ardiden, 115
„ d'Arrens, 71
„ d'Aspé, 126
„ d'Astazou, 126
„ d'Aubiste, 115
„ d'Ayré, 103, 106, 111
„ de Bergons, 111
„ de Boum, 150
„ de Bugaret, 114, 115
„ de Campbieil, 123
„ de Clarabide, 44
„ de Crabioules, 150
„ de Gabiétou, 126
„ de Gabizos, 71, 182
„ de Gar, 160
„ de Gaube, 87
„ de Ger, 179, 190
„ de Gourzy, 189
„ de Labassa, 71, 83
„ du Lac Grand, 111, 115

Pic de Laruns, 185, 190
„ de Lienz, 106
„ de Litouèse, 115
„ de Maladetta, 145, 150
„ de Maucapéra, 114, 115
„ du Midi d'Arrens (see Pic d'Arrens)
„ du Midi de Bigorre, 36, 42, 134
„ du Midi d'Ossau, 172, 188
„ du Milieu, 145, 150
„ de la Mine, 150
„ de Montaigu (near Bigorre), 36, 42
„ de Montaigu (near Saint Sauveur), 103, 111
„ de Néouville, 107
„ de Néré, 111, 115
„ de Néthou, 145, 150
„ Rouge de Pailla, 126
„ de Pez, 44
„ de la Pique, 151
„ de Posets, 137, 151
„ Poujastou, 156
„ Sacroux, 150
„ de Sarradets, 126
„ de Sauvegarde, 150
„ de Soulom, 71
„ de Villelongue, 71
„ de Viscos, 71, 83, 111, 115
Picnicking (Pau), 27
Pie de Mars, 59
Pierrefitte, 72 ; A 245
„ hotels at, A 245
„ road to, 76
Piétat, 26
Pilgrims, 91
Piméné, the, 121, 126
Pique, valley of, 160
Pitton de Tournefort, 48
Place Royale, Pau, 9, 11, 19
„ Ste. Eugénie, Biarritz, 198
"Plaint of the Weather-beaten Pine," 44
Plateau of the Bious-Artigues, 187
Poc (guide), 125
Polygala amara, 116, 118, 158

Polygala rosea, 116, 118
Pont d'Arrougé, 146
„ de Benquès, 87
„ de Crabé, 183
„ de Desdouroucat, 120
„ d'Enfer (near Eaux Chaudes), 187
„ d'Enfer (near Luz), 97
„ d'Espagne, 87
„ de la Hiladère, 97
„ de Lestelle, 24
„ de Nadie, 147
„ Napoléon, 109, 111, 113
„ de Pescadère, 108
„ de Ravi, 145, 148
„ de Sia, 120
„ de Villelongue, 95
"Poor Pillicoddy," 29
Port de Gavarnie, 126
„ de Peyresourde (see Col de)
„ de la Picade, 151
„ de Venasque, 146, 148, 151
Posets, the Peak, 137, 151
Post-office (Luz), 112
Potentilla, 118
Pragnères, 121
Preste-les-Bains, 214 ; A 245
„ baths and hotels of, A 245
Primula farinosa, 118, 123
Promenade Horizontale (Barèges), 105
„ de l'Imperatrice, 180
Puyoo, 3 ; A 245
Pyramide de Peyrelance, 71, 83
Pyrenean dogs, 92
„ „ prices of, 92
„ „ treatment of, 92
„ local terms translated, some, C 255
„ songs, 135

Q.

QUAIRAT, Pic, 150
Quatre Moulins de Sia, 120

R.

RAILWAY information and skeleton routes to the Pyrenees, B 250
Ramondia pyrenaïca, 118
Ravin d'Araillé, 87
Rébénac, 172, 192; A 245
Red tape, 53
"Riou," 215
Rioumaou, cascade of, 120
"Roads up again," 90
Rocks at Biarritz, 200
Rue d'Enfer (Luchon), 145
" de la Fontaine (Pau), 20

S.

SAINT ANTOINE, chapel of, 157
" Aventin, 139, 148; A 245
" Béat, 160; A 245
" Bernard, statue of, 57
" **Bertrand de Comminges to Montrejeau,** B 253
" Bertrand de Comminges, 161; A 245
" " cathedral of, 163
" " cloisters of, 167
" " history of, 161
St. Christau, A 245
" hotels at, A 246
" Etienne, 205
" Jacques Church (Pau), 20
" Jean de Luz, 206; A 246
" " dogs of, 197
" " general information, A 246
" Laurent de la Salanque, A 246
" Mamet, 154; A 246
" " church of, 154
" Martin's Church (Pau), 20
" Pé, A 246
" Pée, 206; A 247
" Peter's statue (Lourdes), 133
" Pierre, 205

St. Sauveur, 108; A 247
" " baths of, A 247
" " excursions from, A 247
" " hotels at, A 247
" Savin, 71; A 247
" Vincent's Church (Bigorre), 33
Ste. Marie (near Bigorre), 36, 42; A 246
" (near Oloron), A 246
" (near St. Laurent), A 246
" (near Saléchan), 160; A 246
" baths of, A 246
Sakurazawa, memories of, 186
Salies, 5; A 248
Saléchan, 160
Salluz (Argelès), 64
Salut, avenue of, 35
San Sebastian, 211; A 247
" chief features of, 212; A 247
" hotels at, A 248
Sarsaparilla, 204
Sassis (St. Sauveur), 108
Sazos (St. Sauveur), 108, 117; A 248
Scabii, 182
Sère (Luz), 98
Serres, 64
Sévignac, 173, 192
Sia, 120
" bridge of, 120
" Quatre Moulins de, 120
Sidonie, cascade of, 154
Silver beeches, 139
Siradan, A 248
" valley of, 160
Skeleton routes and railway information, B 250
Sketching advice, 67
" with a donkey-cart, 26
Snow, 84, 114
Some Pyrenean local terms translated, C 255
Songs, Pyrenean, 135
Soulom, 71; A 248

INDEX. 273

Soulom, Pic de, 71
Soum de Secugnac, 125
Sour grapes (Pau), 23
Sourde, valley of, 179
Spanish mules and peasants, 154
Sport, French, 136, 185
"Spring's Bitters and Sweets," 67
Sugar-loaf Mountain (Gavarnie), 125
Superbagnères, 148
     „   view from, 150
Swine-feeding, 167

T.

Tables of centigrade and Fahrenheit thermometers, D 262
  „ of centimetres and inches, D 259
  „ of grammes and ounces, D 259
  „ of kilometres and miles, D 261
  „ of litres and pints, D 259
  „ of metres and feet, D 260
Taillon, the, 123, 126
Tapère (stream), 36
Tarbes, 52 ; A 248
  „ road, 134
Templars' church at Luz, 98
"The Abbé's Song," 40
"The Argelès Shepherd's Reply," 62
The Bishop's arrival, 90
The Chaos, 123
"The Crocodile of St. Bertrand," 164
The Couradilles, 156
"The Guide's Auction," 129
"The Jackdaw's Causerie," 100
"The Jay of Barèges," 105
"The Lady's Farewell to her Asinine Steed," 37
"The Lesson of the Mountains," 217
"The March of the Men of Garlic," 23

"The Organ's Tale," 73
"The Oxen's Appeal," 152
"The Plaint of the Weather-beaten Pine," 44
"The Three Cormorants," 199
The "witch of the hills," 68
"Three Cormorants," the, 199
Torrent of Bugaret, 121
Toulouse to Perpignan, B 253
    „   road to, 161
Tour des Lacs (Biarritz), 204
Tour de la Monnaie (Pau), 15
Tourmalet, Col de, 42
Trained vines, 23
Tramesaïgues, 42
Travellers' troubles, 125, 168
Troumouse, Cirque of, 121, 123
Trous d'Enfer, 150
Tuc de Maupas, 150

U.

URRUGNE, 209 ; A 248
Ustaritz, A 248

V.

VALCABRÈRE, A 248
Val d'Ossau, 171
Valentin (river), 181
Vallée d'Aran, 156
  „ d'Arboust, 139
  „ d'Argelès, 38, 83, 132
  „ d'Aspe, 175
  „ d'Aure, 44, 137
  „ de Barèges, 111
  „ de Barousse, 160
  „ de Broussette, 187
  „ de Campan, 36
  „ de Garonne, 44
  „ de Héas, 121
  „ de l'Hospice, 151
  „ de Lesponne, 36, 41
  „ de Lienz, 106
  „ de Louron, 139
  „ de Luchon, 159
  „   „   history of, 160

T

Vallée du Lutour, 83
" de Luz, 111
" du Lys, 146
" de Marcadau, 86
" du Néez, 172
" de la Pique, 160
" de Séoube, 44
" de Serris, 36, 41
" de Siradan, 160
" de Sourde (or Soude), 179
Valley of the Ten Thousand Rocks (Amoy), 123
Venasque, A 248
" Port de, 146, 148, 151
Vernet-les-Bains, 214 ; A 249
" " baths of, A 249
" " excursions from, A 249
" " hotels at, A 249
Via Crucis (Bétharram), 25
Viella (near Barèges), 103
" (near St. Béat), 156, 160

Vieuzac, A 249
Vignemale, Pic de, 87, 125
Villelongue, 71 ; A 249
" Pic de, 71
Villenave, 113
Vines trained by the roadside, 23
Violets, 118

W.

WASHERWOMEN and their gamps, 22, 173
Wonderful echo, 120
Wood anemones, 106

Y.

YANKEE tale, a, 130

Z.

ZINC mines, 78

A Catalogue of American and Foreign Books Published or Imported by MESSRS. SAMPSON LOW & CO. *can be had on application.*

Crown Buildings, 188, Fleet Street, London,
September, 1883.

A Selection from the List of Books
PUBLISHED BY
SAMPSON LOW, MARSTON, SEARLE, & RIVINGTON.

ALPHABETICAL LIST.

ABOUT Some Fellows. By an ETON BOY, Author of "A Day of my Life." Cloth limp, square 16mo, 2s. 6d.

Adams (C. K.) Manual of Historical Literature. Crown 8vo, 12s. 6d.

Alcott (Louisa M.). Jack and Jill. 16mo, 5s.
—— *Proverb Stories.* 16mo, 3s. 6d.
—— *Old-Fashioned Thanksgiving Day.* 3s. 6d.
—— *Shawl Straps.* 2s. 6d.
—— See also "Low's Standard Novels" and "Rose Library."

Aldrich (T. B.) Friar Jerome's Beautiful Book, &c. Very choicely printed on hand-made paper, parchment cover, 3s. 6d.
—— *Poetical Works. Édition de Luxe.* Very handsomely bound and illustrated, 21s.

Allen (E. A.) Rock me to Sleep, Mother. With 18 full-page Illustrations, elegantly bound, fcap. 4to, 5s.

American Men of Letters. Lives of Thoreau, Irving, Webster. Small post 8vo, cloth, 2s. 6d. each.

Andersen (Hans Christian) Fairy Tales. With 10 full-page Illustrations in Colours by E. V. B. Cheap Edition, 5s.

Angler's Strange Experiences (An). By COTSWOLD ISYS. With numerous Illustrations, 4to, 5s.

Angling. See "British Fisheries Directory," "Cutcliffe," "Lambert," "Martin," and "Theakston."

Archer (William) English Dramatists of To-day. Crown 8vo, 8s. 6d.

Arnold (G. M.) Robert Pocock, the Gravesend Historian. Crown 8vo, cloth, 5s.

Art Education. See "Biographies of Great Artists," "Illustrated Text Books," "Mollett's Dictionary."

Audsley (G. A.) Ornamental Arts of Japan. 90 Plates, 74 in Colours and Gold, with General and Descriptive Text. 2 vols., folio, £16 16s.

A

Audsley (G. A.) *The Art of Chromo-Lithography.* Coloured Plates and Text. Folio, 63s.

Audsley (W. and G. A.) *Outlines of Ornament.* Small folio, very numerous Illustrations, 31s. 6d.

Auerbach (B.) *Spinoza.* Translated. 2 vols., 18mo, 4s.

BALDWIN (J.) *Story of Siegfried.* Emblematical binding, 6s.

Bankruptcy: Inutility of the Laws. Lord Sherbrooke's Remedy. Crown 8vo, 1s.

Bathgate (Alexander) *Waitaruna: A Story of New Zealand Life.* Crown 8vo, cloth, 5s.

Batley (A. W.) *Etched Studies for Interior Decoration.* Imperial folio, 52s. 6d.

THE BAYARD SERIES.

Edited by the late J. HAIN FRISWELL.

Comprising Pleasure Books of Literature produced in the Choicest Style as Companionable Volumes at Home and Abroad.

"We can hardly imagine better books for boys to read or for men to ponder over."—*Times.*

Price 2s. 6d. each Volume, complete in itself, flexible cloth extra, gilt edges, with silk Headbands and Registers.

The Story of the Chevalier Bayard. By M. De Berville.
De Joinville's St. Louis, King of France.
The Essays of Abraham Cowley, including all his Prose Works.
Abdallah; or, The Four Leaves. By Edouard Laboullaye.
Table-Talk and Opinions of Napoleon Buonaparte.
Vathek: An Oriental Romance. By William Beckford.
Words of Wellington: Maxims and Opinions of the Great Duke.
Dr. Johnson's Rasselas, Prince of Abyssinia. With Notes.
Hazlitt's Round Table. With Biographical Introduction.
The Religio Medici, Hydriotaphia, and the Letter to a Friend. By Sir Thomas Browne, Knt.
Ballad Poetry of the Affections. By Robert Buchanan.
Coleridge's Christabel, and other Imaginative Poems. With Preface by Algernon C. Swinburne.
Lord Chesterfield's Letters, Sentences, and Maxims. With Introduction by the Editor, and Essay on Chesterfield by M. de Ste.-Beuve, of the French Academy.
The King and the Commons. A Selection of Cavalier and Puritan Songs. Edited by Professor Morley.
Essays in Mosaic. By Thos. Ballantyne.
My Uncle Toby; his Story and his Friends. Edited by P. Fitzgerald.
Reflections; or, Moral Sentences and Maxims of the Duke de la Rochefoucauld.
Socrates: Memoirs for English Readers from Xenophon's Memorabilia. By Edw. Levien.
Prince Albert's Golden Precepts.

A Case containing 12 Volumes, price 31s. 6d.; or the Case separately, price 3s. 6d.

Bell (Major) : *Rambla—Spain. From Irun to Cerbere.* Crown 8vo, 8s. 6d.

Beumers' German Copybooks. In six gradations at 4d. each.

Biart (Lucien) Adventures of a Young Naturalist. Edited and adapted by PARKER GILLMORE. With 117 Illustrations on Wood. Post 8vo, cloth extra, gilt edges, New Edition, 7s. 6d.

Bickersteth's Hymnal Companion to Book of Common Prayer may be had in various styles and bindings from 1d. to 21s. Price List and Prospectus will be forwarded on application.

Bickersteth (Rev. E. H., M.A.) The Clergyman in his Home. Small post 8vo, 1s.

———— *Evangelical Churchmanship and Evangelical Eclecticism.* 8vo, 1s.

———— *From Year to Year: a Collection of Original Poetical* Pieces. Small post 8vo.

———— *The Master's Home-Call; or, Brief Memorials of Alice* Frances Bickersteth. 20th Thousand. 32mo, cloth gilt, 1s.

———— *The Master's Will.* A Funeral Sermon preached on the Death of Mrs. S. Gurney Buxton. Sewn, 6d.; cloth gilt, 1s.

———— *The Shadow of the Rock.* A Selection of Religious Poetry. 18mo, cloth extra, 2s. 6d.

———— *The Shadowed Home and the Light Beyond.* 7th Edition, crown 8vo, cloth extra, 5s.

Bilbrough (E. J.) "*Twixt France and Spain.*" [*In the press.*

Biographies of the Great Artists (Illustrated). Crown 8vo, emblematical binding, 3s. 6d. per volume, except where the price is given.

Claude Lorrain.*
Correggio, by M. E. Heaton, 2s. 6d.
Della Robbia and Cellini, 2s. 6d.
Albrecht Dürer, by R. F. Heath.
Figure Painters of Holland.
Fra Angelico, Masaccio, and Botticelli.
Fra Bartolommeo, Albertinelli, and Andrea del Sarto.
Gainsborough and Constable.
Ghiberti and Donatello, 2s. 6d.
Giotto, by Harry Quilter.
Hans Holbein, by Joseph Cundall.
Hogarth, by Austin Dobson.
Landseer, by F. G. Stevens.
Lawrence and Romney, by Lord Ronald Gower, 2s. 6d.
Leonardo da Vinci.
Little Masters of Germany, by W. B. Scott.
Mantegna and Francia.
Meissonier, by J. W. Mollett, 2s. 6d.
Michelangelo Buonarotti, by Clément.
Murillo, by Ellen E. Minor, 2s. 6d.
Overbeck, by J. B. Atkinson.
Raphael, by N. D'Anvers.
Rembrandt, by J. W. Mollett.
Reynolds, by F. S. Pulling.
Rubens, by C. W. Kett.
Tintoretto, by W. R. Osler.
Titian, by R. F. Heath.
Turner, by Cosmo Monkhouse.
Vandyck and Hals, by P. R. Head.
Velasquez, by E. Stowe.
Vernet and Delaroche, by J. R. Rees.
Watteau, by J. W. Mollett, 2s. 6d.
Wilkie, by J. W. Mollett.

* *Not yet published.*

Bird (F. J.) American Practical Dyer's Companion. 8vo, 42s.

Bird (H. E.) Chess Practice. 8vo, 2s. 6d.

Black (Wm.) Novels. See "Low's Standard Library."

Blackburn (Henry) Breton Folk : An Artistic Tour in Brittany. With 171 Illustrations by RANDOLPH CALDECOTT. Imperial 8vo, cloth extra, gilt edges, 21s.; plainer binding, 10s. 6d.

—— *Pyrenees (The).* With 100 Illustrations by GUSTAVE DORÉ, corrected to 1881. Crown 8vo, 7s. 6d.

Blackmore (R. D.) Lorna Doone. Édition de luxe. Crown 4to, very numerous Illustrations, cloth, gilt edges, 31s. 6d.; parchment, uncut, top gilt, 35s. Cheap Edition, small post 8vo, 6s.

—— *Novels.* See "Low's Standard Library."

Blaikie (William) How to get Strong and how to Stay so. A Manual of Rational, Physical, Gymnastic, and other Exercises. With Illustrations, small post 8vo, 5s.

Boats of the World, Depicted and Described by one of the Craft. With Coloured Plates, showing every kind of rig, 4to, 3s. 6d.

Bock (Carl). The Head Hunters of Borneo: Up the Mahakkam, and Down the Barita; also Journeyings in Sumatra. 1 vol., super-royal 8vo, 32 Coloured Plates, cloth extra, 36s.

—— *Temples and Elephants.* A Narrative of a Journey through Upper Siam and Lao. With numerous Coloured and other Illustrations, 8vo.

Bonwick (James) First Twenty Years of Australia. Crown 8vo, 5s.

—— *Port Philip Settlement.* 8vo, numerous Illustrations, 21s.

Borneo. See BOCK.

Bosanquet (Rev. C.) Blossoms from the King's Garden : Sermons for Children. 2nd Edition, small post 8vo, cloth extra, 6s.

Boussenard (L.) Crusoes of Guiana; or, the White Tiger. Illustrated by J. FERAT. 7s. 6d.

Boy's Froissart. King Arthur. Mabinogion. Percy. See LANIER.

Bradshaw (J.) New Zealand as it is. 8vo, 12s. 6d.

Brassey (Lady) Tahiti. With 31 Autotype Illustrations after Photos. by Colonel STUART-WORTLEY. Fcap. 4to, very tastefully bound, 21s.

Braune (Wilhelm) Gothic Grammar. Translated by G. H. BULG. 3s. 6d.

Brisse (Baron) Menus (366, one for each day of the year). Each Ménu is given in French and English, with the recipe for making every dish mentioned. Translated from the French of BARON BRISSE, by Mrs. MATTHEW CLARKE. 2nd Edition. Crown 8vo, 5s.

British Fisheries Directory, 1883-84. Small 8vo, 2s. 6d.

Brittany. See BLACKBURN.

Broglie (Duc de) Frederick II. and Maria Theresa. 2 vols., 8vo, 30s.

Browne (G. Lathom) Narratives of Nineteenth Century State Trials. First Period: From the Union with Ireland to the Death of George IV., 1801—1830. 2nd Edition, 2 vols., crown 8vo, cloth, 26s.

Browne (Lennox) and Behnke (Emil) Voice, Song, and Speech. Medium 8vo, cloth.

Bryant (W. C.) and Gay (S. H.) History of the United States. 4 vols., royal 8vo, profusely Illustrated, 60s.

Bryce (Rev. Professor) Manitoba: its History, Growth, and Present Position. Crown 8vo, with Illustrations and Maps, 7s. 6d.

Bunyan's Pilgrim's Progress. With 138 original Woodcuts. Small post 8vo, cloth gilt, 3s. 6d.

Burnaby (Capt.) On Horseback through Asia Minor. 2 vols., 8vo, 38s. Cheaper Edition, crown 8vo, 10s. 6d.

Burnaby (Mrs. F.) High Alps in Winter; or, Mountaineering in Search of Health. By Mrs. FRED BURNABY. With Portrait of the Authoress, Map, and other Illustrations. Handsomely bound in cloth, 14s.

Butler (W. F.) The Great Lone Land; an Account of the Red River Expedition, 1869-70. With Illustrations and Map. Fifth and Cheaper Edition, crown 8vo, cloth extra, 7s. 6d.

—— *Invasion of England, told twenty years after, by an Old* Soldier. Crown 8vo, 2s. 6d.

—— *Red Cloud; or, the Solitary Sioux.* Imperial 16mo, numerous illustrations, gilt edges, 7s. 6d.

—— *The Wild North Land; the Story of a Winter Journey* with Dogs across Northern North America. Demy 8vo, cloth, with numerous Woodcuts and a Map, 4th Edition, 18s. Cr. 8vo, 7s. 6d.

Buxton (H. J. W.) Painting, English and American. With numerous Illustrations. Crown 8vo, 5s.

Cadogan (Lady A.) Illustrated Games of Patience. Twenty-four Diagrams in Colours, with Descriptive Text. Foolscap 4to, cloth extra, gilt edges, 3rd Edition, 12s. 6d.

California. See "Nordhoff."

Cambridge Staircase (A). By the Author of "A Day of my Life at Eton." Small crown 8vo, cloth, 2s. 6d.

Cambridge Trifles; or, Splutterings from an Undergraduate Pen. By the Author of "A Day of my Life at Eton," &c. 16mo, cloth extra, 2s. 6d.

Capello (H.) and Ivens (R.) From Benguella to the Territory of Yacca. Translated by ALFRED ELWES. With Maps and over 130 full-page and text Engravings. 2 vols., 8vo, 42s.

Carleton (W.). See "Rose Library."

Carlyle (T.) Reminiscences of my Irish Journey in 1849. Crown 8vo, 7s. 6d.

Carnegie (A.) American Four-in-Hand in Britain. Small 4to, Illustrated, 10s. 6d.

Chairman's Handbook (The). By R. F. D. PALGRAVE, Clerk of the Table of the House of Commons. 5th Edition, enlarged and re-written, 2s.

Challamel (M. A.) History of Fashion in France. With 21 Plates, coloured by hand, satin-wood binding, imperial 8vo, 28s.

Changed Cross (The), and other Religious Poems. 16mo, 2s. 6d.

Charities of London. See Low's.

Chattock (R. S.) Practical Notes on Etching. Second Edition, 8vo, 7s. 6d.

Chess. See BIRD (H. E.).

China. See COLQUHOUN.

Choice Editions of Choice Books. 2s. 6d. each. Illustrated by C. W. COPE, R.A., T. CRESWICK, R.A., E. DUNCAN, BIRKET FOSTER, J. C. HORSLEY, A.R.A., G. HICKS, R. REDGRAVE, R.A., C. STONEHOUSE, F. TAYLER, G. THOMAS, H. J. TOWNSHEND, E. H. WEHNERT, HARRISON WEIR, &c.

Bloomfield's Farmer's Boy.	Milton's L'Allegro.
Campbell's Pleasures of Hope.	Poetry of Nature. Harrison Weir.
Coleridge's Ancient Mariner.	Rogers' (Sam.) Pleasures of Memory.
Goldsmith's Deserted Village.	Shakespeare's Songs and Sonnets.
Goldsmith's Vicar of Wakefield.	Tennyson's May Queen.
Gray's Elegy in a Churchyard.	Elizabethan Poets.
Keat's Eve of St. Agnes.	Wordsworth's Pastoral Poems.

"Such works are a glorious beatification for a poet."—*Athenæum.*

Christ in Song. By Dr. PHILIP SCHAFF. A New Edition, revised, cloth, gilt edges, 6*s.*

Chromo-Lithography. See "Audsley."

Cid (Ballads of the). By the Rev. GERRARD LEWIS. Fcap. 8vo, parchment, 2*s.* 6*d.*

Clay (Charles M.) Modern Hagar. 2 vols., crown 8vo, 21*s.* See also "Rose Library."

Colquhoun (A. R.) Across Chrysê; From Canton to Mandalay. With Maps and very numerous Illustrations, 2 vols., 8vo, 42*s.*

Composers. See "Great Musicians."

Confessions of a Frivolous Girl (The): A Novel of Fashionable Life. Edited by ROBERT GRANT. Crown 8vo, 6*s.* Paper boards, 1*s.*

Cook (Dutton) Book of the Play. New and Revised Edition. 1 vol., cloth extra, 3*s.* 6*d.*

—— *On the Stage: Studies of Theatrical History and the* Actor's Art. 2 vols., 8vo, cloth, 24*s.*

Coote (W.) Wanderings South by East. Illustrated, 8vo, 21*s.* New and Cheaper Edition, 10*s.* 6*d.*

—— *Western Pacific.* Illustrated, crown 8vo, 2*s.* 6*d.*

Costume. See SMITH (J. MOYR).

Cruise of the Walnut Shell (The). An instructive and amusing Story, told in Rhyme, for Children. With 32 Coloured Plates. Square fancy boards, 5*s.*

Curtis (C. B.) Velazquez and Murillo. With Etchings &c., Royal 8vo, 31*s.* 6*d.*; large paper, 63*s.*

Cutcliffe (H. C.) Trout Fishing in Rapid Streams. Cr. 8vo, 3*s.* 6*d.*

D'ANVERS (N.) An Elementary History of Art. Crown 8vo, 10*s.* 6*d.*

—— *Elementary History of Music.* Crown 8vo, 2*s.* 6*d.*

—— *Handbooks of Elementary Art—Architecture; Sculp-* ture; Old Masters; Modern Painting. Crown 8vo, 3*s.* 6*d.* each.

Day of My Life (A); or, Every-Day Experiences at Eton. By an ETON BOY, Author of "About Some Fellows." 16mo, cloth extra, 2*s.* 6*d.* 6th Thousand.

Day's Collacon: an Encyclopædia of Prose Quotations. Imperial 8vo, cloth, 31*s.* 6*d.*

Decoration. Vol. II., folio, 6*s.* Vols. III., IV., V., and VI., New Series, folio, 7*s.* 6*d.* each.

—— See also BATLEY.

De Leon (E.) Egypt under its Khedives. With Map and Illustrations. Crown 8vo, 4s.

Don Quixote, Wit and Wisdom of. By EMMA THOMPSON. Square fcap. 8vo, 3s. 6d.

Donnelly (Ignatius) Atlantis; or, the Antediluvian World. Crown 8vo, 12s. 6d.

—— *Ragnarok: The Age of Fire and Gravel.* Illustrated, Crown 8vo, 12s. 6d.

Dos Passos (J. R.) Law of Stockbrokers and Stock Exchanges. 8vo, 35s.

Dougall (James Dalziel, F.S.A., F.Z.A.) Shooting: its Appliances, Practice, and Purpose. New Edition, revised with additions. Crown 8vo, cloth extra, 7s. 6d.

"The book is admirable in every way..... We wish it every success."—*Globe.*
"A very complete treatise..... Likely to take high rank as an authority on shooting."—*Daily News.*

Drama. See ARCHER, COOK (DUTTON), WILLIAMS (M.).

Durnford (Col. A. W.) A Soldier's Life and Work in South Africa, 1872-9. 8vo, 14s.

Dyeing. See BIRD (F. J.).

EDUCATIONAL Works published in Great Britain. Classified Catalogue. Second Edition, revised and corrected, 8vo, cloth extra, 5s.

Egypt. See "De Leon," "Foreign Countries," "Senior."

Eidlitz (Leopold) Nature and Functions of Art (The); and especially of Architecture. Medium 8vo, cloth, 21s.

Electricity. See GORDON.

Emerson Birthday Book. Extracts from the Writings of R. W. Emerson. Square 16mo, cloth extra, numerous Illustrations, very choice binding, 3s. 6d.

Emerson (R. W.) Life. By G. W. COOKE. Crown 8vo, 8s. 6d.

English Catalogue of Books. Vol. III., 1872—1880. Royal 8vo, half-morocco, 42s.

English Philosophers. Edited by E. B. IVAN MÜLLER, M.A.

A series intended to give a concise view of the works and lives of English thinkers. Crown 8vo volumes of 180 or 200 pp., price 3s. 6d. each.

Francis Bacon, by Thomas Fowler.
Hamilton, by W. H. S. Monck.
Hartley and James Mill, by G. S. Bower.
*John Stuart Mill, by Miss Helen Taylor.
Shaftesbury and Hutcheson, by Professor Fowler.
Adam Smith, by J. A. Farrer.

* *Not yet published.*

Episodes in the Life of an Indian Chaplain. Crown 8vo, cloth extra, 12s. 6d.

Episodes of French History. Edited, with Notes, Maps, and Illustrations, by GUSTAVE MASSON, B.A. Small 8vo, 2s. 6d. each.
    1. Charlemagne and the Carlovingians.
    2. Louis XI. and the Crusades.
    3. Part I. Francis I. and Charles V.
       ,, II. Francis I. and the Renaissance.
    4. Henry IV. and the End of the Wars of Religion.

Esmarch (Dr. Friedrich) Handbook on the Treatment of Wounded in War. Numerous Coloured Plates and Illustrations, 8vo, strongly bound, 1l. 8s.

Etcher (The). Containing 36 Examples of the Original Etched-work of Celebrated Artists, amongst others: BIRKET FOSTER, J. E. HODGSON, R.A., COLIN HUNTER, J. P. HESELTINE, ROBERT W. MACBETH, R. S. CHATTOCK, &c. Vols. for 1881 and 1882, imperial 4to, cloth extra, gilt edges, 2l. 12s. 6d. each.

Etching. See BATLEY, CHATTOCK.

Etchings (Modern) of Celebrated Paintings. 4to, 31s. 6d.

FARM Ballads, Festivals, and Legends. See "Rose Library."

Fashion (History of). See "Challamel."

Fawcett (Edgar) A Gentleman of Leisure. 1s.

Fechner (G. T.) On Life after Death. 12mo, vellum, 2s. 6d.

Felkin (R. W.) and Wilson (Rev. C. T.) Uganda and the Egyptian Soudan. With Map, numerous Illustrations, and Notes. By R. W. FELKIN, F.R.G.S., &c., &c.; and the Rev. C. T. WILSON, M.A. Oxon., F.R.G.S. 2 vols., crown 8vo, cloth, 28s.

Fenn (G. Manville) Off to the Wilds: A Story for Boys. Profusely Illustrated. Crown 8vo, 7s. 6d.

Ferguson (John) Ceylon in 1883. With numerous Illustrations. Crown 8vo.

Ferns. See HEATH.

Fields (J. T.) Yesterdays with Authors. New Ed., 8vo., 16s.

Florence. See "Yriarte."

Flowers of Shakespeare. 32 beautifully Coloured Plates, with the passages which refer to the flowers. Small 4to, 5s.

Foreign Countries and British Colonies. A series of Descriptive Handbooks. Each volume will be the work of a writer who has special acquaintance with the subject. Crown 8vo, 3s. 6d. each.

Australia, by J. F. Vesey Fitzgerald.
Austria, by D. Kay, F.R.G.S.
*Canada, by W. Fraser Rae.
Denmark and Iceland, by E. C. Otté.
Egypt, by S. Lane Poole, B.A.
France, by Miss M. Roberts.
Germany, by S. Baring-Gould.
Greece, by L. Sergeant, B.A.
*Holland, by R. L. Poole.
Japan, by S. Mossman.
*New Zealand.
*Persia, by Major-Gen. Sir F. Goldsmid.
Peru, by Clements R. Markham, C.B.
Russia, by W. R. Morfill, M.A.
Spain, by Rev. Wentworth Webster.
Sweden and Norway, by F. H. Woods.
*Switzerland, by W. A. P. Coolidge, M.A.
*Turkey-in-Asia, by J. C. McCoan, M.P.
West Indies, by C. H. Eden, F.R.G.S.

* *Not ready yet.*

Fortunes made in Business. 2 vols., demy 8vo, cloth, 32s.

Franc (Maud Jeanne). The following form one Series, small post 8vo, in uniform cloth bindings, with gilt edges:—

Emily's Choice. 5s.
Hall's Vineyard. 4s.
John's Wife: A Story of Life in South Australia. 4s.
Marian; or, The Light of Some One's Home. 5s.
Silken Cords and Iron Fetters. 4s.
Vermont Vale. 5s.
Minnie's Mission. 4s.
Little Mercy. 4s.
Beatrice Melton's Discipline. 4s.
No Longer a Child. 4s.
Golden Gifts. 4s.
Two Sides to Every Question. 4s.

Francis (F.) War, Waves, and Wanderings, including a Cruise in the "Lancashire Witch." 2 vols., crown 8vo, cloth extra, 24s.

Frederick the Great. See "Broglie."

French. See "Julien."

Froissart. See "Lanier."

GENTLE Life (Queen Edition). 2 vols. in 1, small 4to, 6s.

THE GENTLE LIFE SERIES.

Price 6s. each; or in calf extra, price 10s. 6d.; Smaller Edition, cloth extra, 2s. 6d., except where price is named.

The Gentle Life. Essays in aid of the Formation of Character of Gentlemen and Gentlewomen.

About in the World. Essays by Author of "The Gentle Life."

Like unto Christ. A New Translation of Thomas à Kempis' "De Imitatione Christi."

Familiar Words. An Index Verborum, or Quotation Handbook. 6s.

Essays by Montaigne. Edited and Annotated by the Author of "The Gentle Life."

The Gentle Life. 2nd Series.

The Silent Hour: Essays, Original and Selected. By the Author of "The Gentle Life."

Half-Length Portraits. Short Studies of Notable Persons. By J. HAIN FRISWELL.

Essays on English Writers, for the Self-improvement of Students in English Literature.

Other People's Windows. By J. HAIN FRISWELL. 6s.

A Man's Thoughts. By J. HAIN FRISWELL.

The Countess of Pembroke's Arcadia. By Sir PHILIP SIDNEY. New Edition, 6s.

George Eliot: a Critical Study of her Life. By G. W. COOKE. Crown 8vo, 10s. 6d.

German. See BEUMER.

Germany. By S. BARING-GOULD. Crown 8vo, 3s. 6d.

Gibbs (J. R.) British Honduras, Historical and Descriptive. Crown 8vo, 7s. 6d.

Gilder (W. H.) Ice-Pack and Tundra. An Account of the Search for the "Jeannette." 8vo, 18s.

────── *Schwatka's Search.* Sledging in quest of the Franklin Records. Illustrated, 8vo, 12s. 6d.

Gilpin's Forest Scenery. Edited by F. G. HEATH. Large post 8vo, with numerous Illustrations. Uniform with "The Fern World," re-issued, 7s. 6d.

Glas (John) The Lord's Supper. Crown 8vo, 5s.

Gordon (J. E. H., B.A. Cantab.) Four Lectures on Electric Induction. Delivered at the Royal Institution, 1878-9. With numerous Illustrations. Cloth limp, square 16mo, 3s.

────── *Electric Lighting.* [*In preparation.*

────── *Physical Treatise on Electricity and Magnetism.* New Edition, revised and enlarged, with coloured, full-page, and other Illustrations. 2 vols., 8vo, 42s.

Gouffé. The Royal Cookery Book. By JULES GOUFFÉ; translated and adapted for English use by ALPHONSE GOUFFÉ, Head Pastrycook to Her Majesty the Queen. Illustrated with large plates printed in colours. 161 Woodcuts, 8vo, cloth extra, gilt edges, 42s.

────── Domestic Edition, half-bound, 10s. 6d.

Great Artists. See "Biographies."

Great Historic Galleries of England (The). Edited by LORD RONALD GOWER, F.S.A., Trustee of the National Portrait Gallery. Illustrated by 24 large and carefully executed *permanent* Photographs of some of the most celebrated Pictures by the Great Masters. Vol. I., imperial 4to, cloth extra, gilt edges, 36s. Vol. II., with 36 large permanent photographs, 2l. 12s. 6d.

Great Musicians. Edited by F. HUEFFER. A Series of Biographies, crown 8vo, 3s. each :—

Bach.	Handel.	Purcell.
*Beethoven.	*Haydn.	Rossini.
*Berlioz.	*Marcello.	Schubert.
English Church Composers. By BARETT.	Mendelssohn.	*Schumann.
	Mozart.	Richard Wagner.
*Gluck.	*Palestrina.	Weber.

* *In preparation.*

Grohmann (W. A. B.) Camps in the Rockies. 8vo, 12s. 6d.

Guizot's History of France. Translated by ROBERT BLACK. Super-royal 8vo, very numerous Full-page and other Illustrations. In 8 vols., cloth extra, gilt, each 24s. This work is re-issued in cheaper binding, 8 vols., at 10s. 6d. each.

"It supplies a want which has long been felt, and ought to be in the hands of all students of history."—*Times.*

—————————————— *Masson's School Edition.* The History of France from the Earliest Times to the Outbreak of the Revolution; abridged from the Translation by Robert Black, M.A., with Chronological Index, Historical and Genealogical Tables, &c. By Professor GUSTAVE MASSON, B.A., Assistant Master at Harrow School. With 24 full-page Portraits, and many other Illustrations. 1 vol., demy 8vo, 600 pp., cloth extra, 10s. 6d.

Guizot's History of England. In 3 vols. of about 500 pp. each, containing 60 to 70 Full-page and other Illustrations, cloth extra, gilt, 24s. each; re-issue in cheaper binding, 10s. 6d. each.

"For luxury of typography, plainness of print, and beauty of illustration, these volumes, of which but one has as yet appeared in English, will hold their own against any production of an age so luxurious as our own in everything, typography not excepted."—*Times.*

Guyon (Mde.) Life. By UPHAM. 6th Edition, crown 8vo, 6s.

HALL (W. W.) *How to Live Long; or,* 1408 *Health Maxims,* Physical, Mental, and Moral. By W. W. HALL, A.M., M.D. Small post 8vo, cloth, 2s. 2nd Edition.

Harper's Christmas No., 1882. Elephant folio, 2s. 6d.

Harper's Monthly Magazine. Published Monthly. 160 pages, fully Illustrated. 1s.
  Vol. I. December, 1880, to May, 1881.
  ,, II. June to November, 1881.
  ,, III. December, 1881, to May, 1882.
  ,, IV. June to November, 1882.
  ,, V. December, 1882, to May, 1883.
Super-royal 8vo, 8s. 6d. each.

"'Harper's Magazine' is so thickly sown with excellent illustrations that to count them would be a work of time; not that it is a picture magazine, for the engravings illustrate the text after the manner seen in some of our choicest *éditions de luxe*."—*St. James's Gazette*.

"It is so pretty, so big, and so cheap. . . . An extraordinary shillingsworth—160 large octavo pages, with over a score of articles, and more than three times as many illustrations."—*Edinburgh Daily Review*.

"An amazing shillingsworth . . . combining choice literature of both nations."—*Nonconformist*.

Hatton (Joseph) Journalistic London: with Engravings and Portraits of Distinguished Writers of the Day. Fcap. 4to, 12s. 6d.

———— *Three Recruits, and the Girls they left behind them.* Small post 8vo, 6s.

"It hurries us along in unflagging excitement."—*Times*.

———— See also "Low's Standard Novels."

Heath (Francis George). Autumnal Leaves. New Edition, with Coloured Plates in Facsimile from Nature. Crown 8vo, 14s.

———— *Burnham Beeches.* Illustrated, small 8vo, 1s.

———— *Fern Paradise.* New Edition, with Plates and Photos., crown 8vo, 12s. 6d.

———— *Fern World.* With Nature-printed Coloured Plates. New Edition, crown 8vo, 12s. 6d.

———— *Gilpin's Forest Scenery.* Illustrated, 8vo, 12s. 6d.; New Edition, 7s. 6d.

———— *Our Woodland Trees.* With Coloured Plates and Engravings. Small 8vo, 12s. 6d.

———— *Peasant Life in the West of England.* Crown 8vo, 10s. 6d.

———— *Sylvan Spring.* With Coloured, &c., Illustrations. 12s. 6d.

———— *Trees and Ferns.* Illustrated, crown 8vo, 3s. 6d.

———— *Where to Find Ferns.* Crown 8vo, 2s.

Heber (Bishop) Hymns. Illustrated Edition. With upwards of 100 beautiful Engravings. Small 4to, handsomely bound, 7s. 6d. Morocco, 18s. 6d. and 21s. New and Cheaper Edition, cloth, 3s. 6d.

Heldmann (Bernard) Mutiny on Board the Ship "Leander." Small post 8vo, gilt edges, numerous Illustrations, 7s. 6d.

Henty (G. A.) Winning his Spurs. Numerous Illustrations Crown 8vo, 5s.

—— *Cornet of Horse : A Story for Boys.* Illustrated, crown 8vo, 5s.

—— *Jack Archer: Tale of the Crimea.* Illust., crown 8vo, 5s.

Herrick (Robert) Poetry. Preface by AUSTIN DOBSON. With numerous Illustrations by E. A. ABBEY. 4to, gilt edges, 42s.

History and Principles of Weaving by Hand and by Power. With several hundred Illustrations. By ALFRED BARLOW. Royal 8vo, cloth extra, 1l. 5s. Second Edition.

Hitchman (Francis) Public Life of the Right Hon. Benjamin Disraeli, Earl of Beaconsfield. New Edition, with Portrait. Crown 8vo, 3s. 6d.

Hole (Rev. Canon) Nice and Her Neighbours. Small 4to, with numerous choice Illustrations, 16s.

Holmes (O. W.) The Poetical Works of Oliver Wendell Holmes. In 2 vols., 18mo, exquisitely printed, and chastely bound in limp cloth, gilt tops, 10s. 6d.

Hoppus (J. D.) Riverside Papers. 2 vols., 12s.

Hovgaard (A.) See "Nordenskiöld's Voyage." 8vo, 21s.

Hugo (Victor) "Ninety-Three." Illustrated. Crown 8vo, 6s.

—— *Toilers of the Sea.* Crown 8vo, fancy boards, 2s.

—— *and his Times.* Translated from the French of A. BARBOU by ELLEN E. FREWER. 120 Illustrations, many of them from designs by Victor Hugo himself. Super-royal 8vo, cloth extra, 24s.

—— *History of a Crime (The) ; Deposition of an Eye-witness.* The Story of the Coup d'État. Crown 8vo, 6s.

Hundred Greatest Men (The). 8 portfolios, 21s. each, or 4 vols., half-morocco, gilt edges, 10 guineas.

Hutchinson (Thos.) Diary and Letters. Demy 8vo, cloth, 16s.

Hutchisson (W. H.) Pen and Pencil Sketches: Eighteen Years in Bengal. 8vo, 18s.

Hygiene and Public Health (A Treatise on). Edited by A. H. BUCK, M.D. Illustrated by numerous Wood Engravings. In 2 royal 8vo vols., cloth, 42s.

Hymnal Companion of Common Prayer. See BICKERSTETH.

ILLUSTRATED Text-Books of Art-Education. Edited by EDWARD J. POYNTER, R.A. Each Volume contains numerous Illustrations, and is strongly bound for the use of Students, price 5s. The Volumes now ready are:—

PAINTING.

Classic and Italian. By PERCY R. HEAD. | French and Spanish.
German, Flemish, and Dutch. | English and American.

ARCHITECTURE.

Classic and Early Christian.
Gothic and Renaissance. By T. ROGER SMITH.

SCULPTURE.

Antique: Egyptian and Greek. | Renaissance and Modern.
Italian Sculptors of the 14th and 15th Centuries.

ORNAMENT.

Decoration in Colour. | Architectural Ornament.

Irving (Washington). Complete Library Edition of his Works in 27 Vols., Copyright, Unabridged, and with the Author's Latest Revisions, called the "Geoffrey Crayon" Edition, handsomely printed in large square 8vo, on superfine laid paper. Each volume, of about 500 pages, fully Illustrated. 12s. 6d. per vol. *See also* "Little Britain."

—————————— ("American Men of Letters.") 2s. 6d.

JAMES (C.) Curiosities of Law and Lawyers. 8vo, 7s. 6d.

Japan. See AUDSLEY.

Jarves (J. J.) Italian Rambles. Square 16mo, 5s.

Johnson (O.) W. Lloyd Garrison and his Times. Crown 8vo, 12s. 6d.

Jones (Major) The Emigrants' Friend. A Complete Guide to the United States. New Edition. 2s. 6d.

Jones (Mrs. Herbert) Sandringham: Past and Present. Illustrated, crown 8vo, 8s. 6d.

Julien (F.) English Student's French Examiner. 16mo. 2s.

—————— *First Lessons in Conversational French Grammar.* Crown 8vo, 1s.

—————— *Conversational French Reader.* 16mo, cloth, 2s. 6d.

—————— *Petites Leçons de Conversation et de Grammaire.* New Edition, 3s. 6d.; without Phrases, 2s. 6d.

—————— *Phrases of Daily Use.* Limp cloth, 6d.

Jung (Sir Salar) Life of. [*In the press*

KEMPIS (*Thomas à*) *Daily Text-Book.* Square 16mo, 2s. 6d.; interleaved as a Birthday Book, 3s. 6d.

Kingston (*W. H. G.*) *Dick Cheveley.* Illustrated, 16mo, gilt edges, 7s. 6d.; plainer binding, plain edges, 5s.

—— *Fresh and Salt Water Tutors: A Story.* 3s. 6d.

—— *Heir of Kilfinnan.* Uniform, 7s. 6d.; also 5s.

—— *Snow-Shoes and Canoes.* Uniform, 7s. 6d.; also 5s.

—— *Two Supercargoes.* Uniform, 7s. 6d.; also 5s.

—— *With Axe and Rifle.* Uniform, 7s. 6d.; also 5s.

Knight (*E. F.*) *Albania and Montenegro.* Illust. 8vo. 12s. 6d.

Knight (*E. J.*) *The Cruise of the "Falcon."* A Voyage round the World in a 30-Ton Yacht. Numerous Illust. 2 vols., crown 8vo.

LAMBERT (*O.*) *Angling Literature in England; and* Descriptions of Fishing by the Ancients. With a Notice of some Books on other Piscatorial Subjects. Fcap. 8vo, vellum, top gilt, 3s. 6d.

Lanier (*Sidney*) *The Boy's Froissart, selected from the Chronicles* of England, France, and Spain. Illustrated, extra binding, gilt edges, crown 8vo, 7s. 6d.

—— *Boy's King Arthur.* Uniform, 7s. 6d.

—— *Boy's Mabinogion; Original Welsh Legends of King* Arthur. Uniform, 7s. 6d.

—— *Boy's Percy: Ballads of Love and Adventure, selected* from the "Reliques." Uniform, 7s. 6d.

Lansdell (*H.*) *Through Siberia.* 2 vols., demy 8vo, 30s.; New Edition, very numerous illustrations, 8vo, 10s. 6d.

Larden (*W.*) *School Course on Heat.* Second Edition, Illustrated, crown 8vo, 5s.

Lathrop (*G. P.*) *In the Distance.* 2 vols., crown 8vo, 21s.

Legal Profession: Romantic Stories. 7s. 6d.

Lennard (*T. B.*) *To Married Women and Women about to be* Married, &c. 6d.

Lenormant (*F.*) *Beginnings of History.* Crown 8vo, 12s. 6d.

Leonardo da Vinci's Literary Works. Edited by Dr. JEAN PAUL RICHTER. Containing his Writings on Painting, Sculpture, and Architecture, his Philosophical Maxims, Humorous Writings, and Miscellaneous Notes on Personal Events, on his Contemporaries, on Literature, &c.; for the first time published from Autograph Manuscripts. By J. P. RICHTER, Ph.Dr., Hon. Member of the Royal and Imperial Academy of Rome, &c. 2 vols., imperial 8vo, containing about 200 Drawings in Autotype Reproductions, and numerous other Illustrations. Twelve Guineas.

Leyland (R. W.) Holiday in South Africa. Crown 8vo, 12s. 6d.

Library of Religious Poetry. A Collection of the Best Poems of all Ages and Tongues. Edited by PHILIP SCHAFF, D.D., LL.D., and ARTHUR GILMAN, M.A. Royal 8vo, 1036 pp., cloth extra, gilt edges, 21s.; re-issue in cheaper binding, 10s. 6d.

Lindsay (W. S.) History of Merchant Shipping and Ancient Commerce. Over 150 Illustrations, Maps, and Charts. In 4 vols., demy 8vo, cloth extra. Vols. 1 and 2, 11s. each; vols. 3 and 4, 14s. each. 4 vols. complete, 50s.

Lillie (Lucy E.) Prudence: a Story of Æsthetic London. Small 8vo, 5s.

Little Britain; together with *The Spectre Bridegroom,* and *A* Legend of Sleepy Hollow. By WASHINGTON IRVING. An entirely New *Edition de luxe,* specially suitable for Presentation. Illustrated by 120 very fine Engravings on Wood, by Mr. J. D. COOPER. Designed by Mr. CHARLES O. MURRAY. Re-issue, square crown 8vo, cloth, 6s.

Logan (Sir William E.) Life. By BERNARD J. HARRINGTON. 8vo, 12s. 6d.

Long (Mrs. W. H. C.) Peace and War in the Transvaal. 12mo, 3s. 6d.

Low's Standard Library of Travel and Adventure. Crown 8vo, bound uniformly in cloth extra, price 7s. 6d., except where price is given.

1. **The Great Lone Land.** By Major W. F. BUTLER, C.B.
2. **The Wild North Land.** By Major W. F. BUTLER, C.B.
3. **How I found Livingstone.** By H. M. STANLEY.
4. **Through the Dark Continent.** By H. M. STANLEY. 12s. 6d.
5. **The Threshold of the Unknown Region.** By C. R. MARKHAM. (4th Edition, with Additional Chapters, 10s. 6d.)
6. **Cruise of the Challenger.** By W. J. J. SPRY, R.N.
7. **Burnaby's On Horseback through Asia Minor.** 10s. 6d.
8. **Schweinfurth's Heart of Africa.** 2 vols., 15s.
9. **Marshall's Through America.**
10. **Lansdell's Through Siberia.** Illustrated and unabridged, 10s. 6d.

Low's Standard Novels. Small post 8vo, cloth extra, 6s. each, unless otherwise stated.

Work. A Story of Experience. By LOUISA M. ALCOTT.

A Daughter of Heth. By W. BLACK.

In Silk Attire. By W. BLACK.

Kilmeny. A Novel. By W. BLACK.

Low's Standard Novels—continued.

Lady Silverdale's Sweetheart. By W. BLACK.
Sunrise. By W. BLACK.
Three Feathers. By WILLIAM BLACK.
Alice Lorraine. By R. D. BLACKMORE.
Christowell, a Dartmoor Tale. By R. D. BLACKMORE.
Clara Vaughan. By R. D. BLACKMORE.
Cradock Nowell. By R. D. BLACKMORE.
Cripps the Carrier. By R. D. BLACKMORE.
Erema; or, My Father's Sin. By R. D. BLACKMORE.
Lorna Doone. By R. D. BLACKMORE.
Mary Anerley. By R. D. BLACKMORE.
An English Squire. By Miss COLERIDGE.
Mistress Judith. A Cambridgeshire Story. By C. C. FRASER-TYTLER.
A Story of the Dragonnades; or, Asylum Christi. By the Rev. E. GILLIAT, M.A.
A Laodicean. By THOMAS HARDY.
Far from the Madding Crowd. By THOMAS HARDY.
The Hand of Ethelberta. By THOMAS HARDY.
The Trumpet Major. By THOMAS HARDY.
Two on a Tower. By THOMAS HARDY.
Three Recruits. By JOSEPH HATTON.
A Golden Sorrow. By Mrs. CASHEL HOEY. New Edition.
Out of Court. By Mrs. CASHEL HOEY.
History of a Crime: The Story of the Coup d'État. VICTOR HUGO.
Ninety-Three. By VICTOR HUGO. Illustrated.
Adela Cathcart. By GEORGE MAC DONALD.
Guild Court. By GEORGE MAC DONALD.
Mary Marston. By GEORGE MAC DONALD.
Stephen Archer. New Edition of "Gifts." By GEORGE MAC DONALD.
The Vicar's Daughter. By GEORGE MAC DONALD.
Weighed and Wanting. By GEORGE MAC DONALD.
Diane. By Mrs. MACQUOID.
Elinor Dryden. By Mrs. MACQUOID.
My Lady Greensleeves. By HELEN MATHERS.
John Holdsworth. By W. CLARK RUSSELL.
A Sailor's Sweetheart. By W. CLARK RUSSELL.

Wreck of the Grosvenor. By W. CLARK RUSSELL.
The Lady Maud. By W. CLARK RUSSELL.
Little Loo. By W. CLARK RUSSELL.
My Wife and I. By Mrs. BEECHER STOWE.
Poganuc People, Their Loves and Lives. By Mrs. B. STOWE.
Ben Hur: a Tale of the Christ. By LEW. WALLACE.
Anne. By CONSTANCE FENIMORE WOOLSON.
For the Major. By CONSTANCE FENIMORE WOOLSON. 5s.

Low's Handbook to the Charities of London (Annual). Edited and revised to date by C. MACKESON, F.S.S., Editor of "A Guide to the Churches of London and its Suburbs," &c. Paper, 1s.; cloth, 1s. 6d.

McCORMICK (R., R.N.). Voyages of Discovery in the Arctic and Antarctic Seas in the "Erebus" and "Terror," in Search of Sir John Franklin, &c., with Autobiographical Notice by R. McCORMICK, R.N., who was Medical Officer to each Expedition. With Maps and very numerous Lithographic and other Illustrations. 2 vols., royal 8vo, 52s. 6d.

Macdonald (A.) "Our Sceptred Isle" and its World-wide Empire. Small post 8vo, cloth, 4s.

MacDonald (G.) Orts. Small post 8vo, 6s.

—— See also "Low's Standard Novels."

Macgregor (John) "Rob Roy" on the Baltic. 3rd Edition, small post 8vo, 2s. 6d.; cloth, gilt edges, 3s. 6d.

—— *A Thousand Miles in the "Rob Roy" Canoe.* 11th Edition, small post 8vo, 2s. 6d.; cloth, gilt edges, 3s. 6d.

—— *Description of the "Rob Roy" Canoe.* Plans, &c., 1s.

—— *Voyage Alone in the Yawl "Rob Roy."* New Edition, thoroughly revised, with additions, small post 8vo, 5s.; boards, 2s. 6d.

Macquoid (Mrs.). See LOW'S STANDARD NOVELS.

Magazine. See DECORATION, ETCHER, HARPER, UNION JACK.

*Magyarland. A Narrative of Travels through the Snowy Car-*pathians, and Great Alföld of the Magyar. By a Fellow of the Carpathian Society (Diploma of 1881), and Author of "The Indian Alps." 2 vols., 8vo, cloth extra, with about 120 Woodcuts from the Author's own sketches and drawings, 38s.

Manitoba. See RAE.

Maria Theresa. See BROGLIE.

Marked "In Haste." A Story of To-day. Crown 8vo, 8s. 6d.

Markham (Admiral) A Naval Career during the Old War. 8vo, cloth, 14*s*.

Markham (C. R.) The Threshold of the Unknown Region. Crown 8vo, with Four Maps, 4th Edition. Cloth extra, 10*s*. 6*d*.

———— *War between Peru and Chili*, 1879-1881. Crown 8vo, with four Maps, &c. Third Edition. 10*s*. 6*d*. See also "Foreign Countries."

Marshall (W. G.) Through America. New Edition, crown 8vo, with about 100 Illustrations, 7*s*. 6*d*.

Martin (J. W.) Float Fishing and Spinning in the Nottingham Style. Crown 8vo, 2*s*. 6*d*.

Marvin (Charles) Russian Advance towards India. 8vo, 16*s*.

Maury (Commander) Physical Geography of the Sea, and its Meteorology. Being a Reconstruction and Enlargement of his former Work, with Charts and Diagrams. New Edition, crown 8vo, 6*s*.

Men of Mark: a Gallery of Contemporary Portraits of the most Eminent Men of the Day taken from Life, especially for this publication Complete in Seven Vols., handsomely bound, cloth, gilt edges, 25*s*. each.

Mendelssohn Family (The), 1729—1847. From Letters and Journals. Translated from the German of SEBASTIAN HENSEL. 3rd Edition, 2 vols., 8vo, 30*s*.

Mendelssohn. See also "Great Musicians."

Mitford (Mary Russell) Our Village. Illustrated with Frontispiece Steel Engraving, and 12 full-page and 157 smaller Cuts. Crown 4to, cloth, gilt edges, 21*s*.; cheaper binding, 10*s*. 6*d*.

Mollett (J. W.) Illustrated Dictionary of Words used in Art and Archæology. Explaining Terms frequently used in Works on Architecture, Arms, Bronzes, Christian Art, Colour, Costume, Decoration, Devices, Emblems, Heraldry, Lace, Personal Ornaments, Pottery, Painting, Sculpture, &c., with their Derivations. Illustrated with 600 Wood Engravings. Small 4to, strongly bound in cloth, 15*s*.

Morley (H.) English Literature in the Reign of Victoria. The 2000th volume of the Tauchnitz Collection of Authors. 18mo, 2*s*. 6*d*.

Muller (E.) Noble Words and Noble Deeds. Containing many Full-page Illustrations by PHILIPPOTEAUX. Square imperial 16mo, cloth extra, 7*s*. 6*d*.; plainer binding, plain edges, 5*s*.

Music. See "Great Musicians."

NEWBIGGIN'S Sketches and Tales. 18mo, 4s.

New Child's Play (A). Sixteen Drawings by E. V. B. Beautifully printed in colours, 4to, cloth extra, 12s. 6d.

New Zealand. See BRADSHAW.

Newfoundland. See RAE.

Norbury (Henry F.) Naval Brigade in South Africa. Crown 8vo, cloth extra, 10s. 6d.

Nordenskiöld's Voyage around Asia and Europe. A Popular Account of the North-East Passage of the "Vega." By Lieut. A. HOVGAARD, of the Royal Danish Navy, and member of the "Vega" Expedition. 8vo, with about 50 Illustrations and 3 Maps, 21s.

Nordhoff (C.) California, for Health, Pleasure, and Residence. New Edition, 8vo, with Maps and Illustrations, 12s. 6d.

Northern Fairy Tales. Translated by H. L. BRAEKSTAD. 5s.

Nothing to Wear; and Two Millions. By W. A. BUTLER. New Edition. Small post 8vo, in stiff coloured wrapper, 1s.

Nursery Playmates (Prince of). 217 Coloured Pictures for Children by eminent Artists. Folio, in coloured boards, 6s.

O'BRIEN (P. B.) Fifty Years of Concessions to Ireland. 8vo.

—— *Irish Land Question, and English Question.* New Edition, fcap. 8vo, 2s.

Our Little Ones in Heaven. Edited by the Rev. H. ROBBINS. With Frontispiece after Sir JOSHUA REYNOLDS. Fcap., cloth extra, New Edition—the 3rd, with Illustrations, 5s.

Outlines of Ornament in all Styles. A Work of Reference for the Architect, Art Manufacturer, Decorative Artist, and Practical Painter. By W. and G. A. AUDSLEY, Fellows of the Royal Institute of British Architects. Only a limited number have been printed and the stones destroyed. Small folio, 60 plates, with introductory text, cloth gilt, 31s. 6d.

Owen (Douglas) Marine Insurance Notes and Clauses. 10s. 6d.

Palgrave (*R. F. D.*). See "Chairman's Handbook."

Palliser (*Mrs.*) *A History of Lace, from the Earliest Period.* A New and Revised Edition, with additional cuts and text, upwards of 100 Illustrations and coloured Designs. 1 vol., 8vo, 1*l*. 1*s*.

—— *Historic Devices, Badges, and War Cries.* 8vo, 1*l*. 1*s*.

—— *The China Collector's Pocket Companion.* With upwards of 1000 Illustrations of Marks and Monograms. 2nd Edition, with Additions. Small post 8vo, limp cloth, 5*s*.

Perseus, the Gorgon Slayer. Numerous coloured Plates, square 8vo, 5*s*.

Pharmacopœia of the United States of America. 8vo, 21*s*.

Photography (*History and Handbook of*). See TISSANDIER.

Pinto (*Major Serpa*) *How I Crossed Africa : from the Atlantic* to the Indian Ocean, Through Unknown Countries ; Discovery of the Great Zambesi Affluents, &c.—Vol. I., The King's Rifle. Vol. II., The Coillard Family. With 24 full-page and 118 half-page and smaller Illustrations, 13 small Maps, and 1 large one. 2 vols., demy 8vo, cloth extra, 42*s*.

Pocock. See ARNOLD (G. M.).

Poe (*E. A.*) *The Raven.* Illustrated by GUSTAVE DORÉ. Imperial folio, cloth, 63*s*.

Poems of the Inner Life. Chiefly from Modern Authors. Small 8vo, 5*s*.

Polar Expeditions. See KOLDEWEY, MARKHAM, MACGAHAN, NARES, NORDENSKIÖLD, GILDER, MCCORMICK.

Politics and Life in Mars. 12mo, 2*s*. 6*d*.

Powell (*W.*) *Wanderings in a Wild Country ; or, Three Years* among the Cannibals of New Britain. Demy 8vo, Map and numerous Illustrations, 18*s*.

Prisons, Her Majesty's, their Effects and Defects. New and cheaper Edition, 6*s*.

Poynter (*Edward J., R.A.*). See "Illustrated Text-books."

Publishers' Circular (*The*), *and General Record of British and* Foreign Literature. Published on the 1st and 15th of every Month, 3*d*.

RAE (*W. Fraser*) *From Newfoundland to Manitoba;* a Guide through Canada's Maritime, Mining, and Prairie Provinces. With Maps. Crown 8vo, 6s.

Rambaud (*A.*) *History of Russia.* 2 vols., 8vo, 36s.

Reber (*F.*) *History of Ancient Art.* 8vo, 18s.

Redford (*G.*) *Ancient Sculpture.* Crown 8vo, 5s.

Reid (*T. W.*) *Land of the Bey.* Post 8vo, 10s. 6d.

Rémusat (*Madame de*), *Memoirs of*, 1802—1808. By her Grandson, M. PAUL DE RÉMUSAT, Senator. Translated by Mrs. CASHEL HOEY and Mr. JOHN LILLIE. 4th Edition, cloth extra. 2 vols., 8vo, 32s.

—————— *Selection from the Letters of Madame de Rémusat to her* Husband and Son, from 1804 to 1813. From the French, by Mrs. CASHEL HOEY and Mr. JOHN LILLIE. In 1 vol., demy 8vo (uniform with the "Memoirs of Madame de Rémusat," 2 vols.), cloth extra, 16s.

Richter (*Dr. Jean Paul*) *Italian Art in the National Gallery.* 4to. Illustrated. Cloth gilt, 2l. 2s.; half-morocco, uncut, 2l. 12s. 6d.

—————— See also LEONARDO DA VINCI.

Robin Hood; Merry Adventures of. Written and illustrated by HOWARD PYLE. Imperial 8vo, cloth. [*In the press.*

Robinson (*Phil*) *In my Indian Garden.* With a Preface by EDWIN ARNOLD, M.A., C.S.I., &c. Crown 8vo, limp cloth, 4th Edition, 3s. 6d.

—————— *Noah's Ark. A Contribution to the Study of Unnatural* History. Small post 8vo, 12s. 6d.

—————— *Sinners and Saints: a Tour across the United States of* America, and Round them. Crown 8vo, 10s. 6d.

—————— *Under the Punkah.* Crown 8vo, limp cloth, 5s.

Robinson (*Sergeant*) *Wealth and its Sources. Stray Thoughts.* 5s.

Roland; the Story of. Crown 8vo, illustrated, 6s.

Romantic Stories of the Legal Profession. Crown 8vo, cloth, 7s. 6d.

Rose (*J.*) *Complete Practical Machinist.* New Edition, 12mo, 12s. 6d.

Rose Library (*The*). Popular Literature of all Countries. Each volume, 1s.; cloth, 2s. 6d. Many of the Volumes are Illustrated—

Little Women. By LOUISA M. ALCOTT. Dble. vol., 2s.

Little Women Wedded. Forming a Sequel to "Little Women."

Little Women and Little Women Wedded. 1 vol., cloth gilt, 3s. 6d.

Little Men. By L. M. ALCOTT. 2s.; cloth gilt, 3s. 6d.

An Old-Fashioned Girl. By LOUISA M. ALCOTT. 2s.; cloth, 3s. 6d.

Work. A Story of Experience. By L. M. ALCOTT. 2 vols., 1s. each.

Stowe (Mrs. H. B.) The Pearl of Orr's Island.

────── **The Minister's Wooing.**

────── **We and our Neighbours.** 2s.; cloth, 3s. 6d.

────── **My Wife and I.** 2s.; cloth gilt, 3s. 6d.

Hans Brinker; or, the Silver Skates. By Mrs. DODGE.

My Study Windows. By J. R. LOWELL.

The Guardian Angel. By OLIVER WENDELL HOLMES.

My Summer in a Garden. By C. D. WARNER.

Dred. Mrs. BEECHER STOWE. 2s.; cloth gilt, 3s. 6d.

Farm Ballads. By WILL CARLETON.

Farm Festivals. By WILL CARLETON.

Farm Legends. By WILL CARLETON.

The Clients of Dr. Bernagius. 2 parts, 1s. each.

The Undiscovered Country. By W. D. HOWELLS.

Baby Rue. By C. M. CLAY.

The Rose in Bloom. By L. M. ALCOTT. 2s.; cloth gilt, 3s. 6d.

Eight Cousins. By L. M. ALCOTT. 2s.; cloth gilt, 3s. 6d.

Under the Lilacs. By L. M. ALCOTT. 2s.; also 3s. 6d.

Silver Pitchers. By LOUISA M. ALCOTT.

Jimmy's Cruise in the "Pinafore," and other Tales. By LOUISA M. ALCOTT. 2s.; cloth gilt, 3s. 6d.

Jack and Jill. By LOUISA M. ALCOTT. 2s.

Hitherto. By the Author of the "Gayworthys." 2 vols., 1s. each; 1 vol., cloth gilt, 3s. 6d.

Friends: a Duet. By E. STUART PHELPS.

A Gentleman of Leisure. A Novel. By EDGAR FAWCETT.

The Story of Helen Troy.

Round the Yule Log: Norwegian Folk and Fairy Tales. Translated from the Norwegian of P. CHR. ASBJÖRNSEN. With 100 Illustrations after drawings by Norwegian Artists, and an Introduction by E. W. Gosse. Imperial 16mo, cloth extra, gilt edges, 7s. 6d.

Rousselet (Louis) Son of the Constable of France. Small post 8vo, numerous Illustrations, 5s.

—————— *The Drummer Boy: a Story of the Days of Washington.* Small post 8vo, numerous Illustrations, 5s.

Russell (W. Clark) The Lady Maud. 3 vols., crown 8vo, 31s. 6d. New Edition, small post 8vo, 6s.

—————— *Little Loo.* 6s.

—————— *My Watch Below; or, Yarns Spun when off Duty.* 2nd Edition, crown 8vo, 2s. 6d.

—————— *Sailor's Language.* Illustrated. Crown 8vo, 3s. 6d.

—————— *Sea Queen.* 3 vols., crown 8vo, 31s. 6d.

—————— *Wreck of the Grosvenor.* 4to, sewed, 6d.

—————— See also LOW'S STANDARD NOVELS.

Russell (W. H., LL.D.) Hesperothen: Notes from the Western World. A Record of a Ramble through part of the United States, Canada, and the Far West, in the Spring and Summer of 1881. By W. H. RUSSELL, LL.D. 2 vols., crown 8vo, cloth, 24s.

—————— *The Tour of the Prince of Wales in India.* By W. H. RUSSELL, LL.D. Fully Illustrated by SYDNEY P. HALL, M.A. Super-royal 8vo, cloth extra, gilt edges, 52s. 6d.; Large Paper Edition, 84s.

S*AINTS and their Symbols: A Companion in the Churches and Picture Galleries of Europe.* With Illustrations. Royal 16mo, cloth extra, 3s. 6d.

Scherr (Prof. J.) History of English Literature. Translated from the German. Crown 8vo, 8s. 6d.

Schuyler (Eugène). The Life of Peter the Great. By EUGÈNE SCHUYLER, Author of "Turkestan." 2 vols., 8vo.

Schweinfurth (Georg) Heart of Africa. Three Years' Travels and Adventures in the Unexplored Regions of Central Africa, from 1868 to 1871. With Illustrations and large Map. 2 vols., crown 8vo, 15s.

Scott (Leader) Renaissance of Art in Italy. 4to, 31s. 6d.

Sedgwick (Major W.) Light the Dominant Force of the Universe. 7s. 6d.

Senior (Nassau W.) Conversations and Journals in Egypt and Malta. 2 vols., 8vo, 24s.

Shadbolt (S. H.) South African Campaign, 1879. Compiled by J. P. MACKINNON (formerly 72nd Highlanders) and S. H. SHADBOLT; and dedicated, by permission, to Field-Marshal H.R.H. the Duke of Cambridge. Containing a portrait and biography of every officer killed in the campaign. 4to, handsomely bound in cloth extra, 2l. 10s.

—— *The Afghan Campaigns of* 1878—1880. By SYDNEY SHADBOLT, Joint Author of "The South African Campaign of 1879." 2 vols., royal quarto, cloth extra, 3l.

Shakespeare. Edited by R. GRANT WHITE. 3 vols., crown 8vo, gilt top, 36s.; *édition de luxe*, 6 vols., 8vo, cloth extra, 63s.

—— See also "Flowers of Shakespeare."

Sidney (Sir P.) Arcadia. New Edition, 6s.

Siegfried: The Story of. Crown 8vo, illustrated, cloth, 6s.

Sikes (Wirt). Rambles and Studies in Old South Wales. With numerous Illustrations. Demy 8vo, 18s.

—— *British Goblins, Welsh Folk Lore.* New Edition, 8vo, 18s.

—— *Studies of Assassination.* 16mo, 3s. 6d.

Sir Roger de Coverley. Re-imprinted from the "Spectator." With 125 Woodcuts, and steel Frontispiece specially designed and engraved for the Work. Small fcap. 4to, 6s.

Smith (G.) Assyrian Explorations and Discoveries. By the late GEORGE SMITH. Illustrated by Photographs and Woodcuts. Demy 8vo, 6th Edition, 18s.

—— *The Chaldean Account of Genesis.* By the late G. SMITH, of the Department of Oriental Antiquities, British Museum. With many Illustrations. Demy 8vo, cloth extra, 6th Edition, 16s. An entirely New Edition, completely revised and re-written by the Rev. PROFESSOR SAYCE, Queen's College, Oxford. Demy 8vo, 18s.

Smith (J. Moyr) Ancient Greek Female Costume. 112 full-page Plates and other Illustrations. Crown 8vo, 7s. 6d.

—— *Hades of Ardenne: a Visit to the Caves of Han.* Crown 8vo, Illustrated, 5s.

Smith (T. Roger) Architecture, Gothic and Renaissance. Illustrated, crown 8vo, 5s.

―――――― *Classic and Early Christian.* Illustrated. Crown 8vo, 5s.

South Kensington Museum. Vol. II., 21s.

Spanish and French Artists. By GERARD SMITH. (Poynter's Art Text-books.) 5s. [*In the press.*

Spry (W. J. J., R.N.) The Cruise of H.M.S. "Challenger." With Route Map and many Illustrations. 6th Edition, demy 8vo, cloth, 18s. Cheap Edition, crown 8vo, with some of the Illustrations, 7s. 6d.

Stack (E.) Six Months in Persia. 2 vols., crown 8vo, 24s.

Stanley (H. M.) How I Found Livingstone. Crown 8vo, cloth extra, 7s. 6d. ; large Paper Edition, 10s. 6d.

―――― *"My Kalulu," Prince, King, and Slave.* A Story from Central Africa. Crown 8vo, about 430 pp., with numerous graphic Illustrations after Original Designs by the Author. Cloth, 7s. 6d.

―――― *Coomassie and Magdala.* A Story of Two British Campaigns in Africa. Demy 8vo, with Maps and Illustrations, 16s.

―――― *Through the Dark Continent.* Cheaper Edition, crown 8vo, 12s. 6d.

Stenhouse (Mrs.) An Englishwoman in Utah. Crown 8vo, 2s. 6d.

Stoker (Bram) Under the Sunset. Crown 8vo, 6s.

Story without an End. From the German of Carové, by the late Mrs. SARAH T. AUSTIN. Crown 4to, with 15 Exquisite Drawings by E. V. B., printed in Colours in Fac-simile of the original Water Colours; and numerous other Illustrations. New Edition, 7s. 6d.

―――― square 4to, with Illustrations by HARVEY. 2s. 6d.

Stowe (Mrs. Beecher) Dred. Cheap Edition, boards, 2s. Cloth, gilt edges, 3s. 6d.

―――― *Footsteps of the Master.* With Illustrations and red borders. Small post 8vo, cloth extra, 6s.

―――― *Geography.* With 60 Illustrations. Square cloth, 4s. 6d.

―――― *Little Foxes.* Cheap Edition, 1s.; Library Edition, 4s. 6d.

―――― *Betty's Bright Idea.* 1s.

Stowe (Mrs. Beecher) My Wife and I; or, Harry Henderson's History. Small post 8vo, cloth extra, 6s.*

―――― *Minister's Wooing.* 5s.; Copyright Series, 1s. 6d.; cl., 2s.*

―――― *Old Town Folk.* 6s.; Cheap Edition, 2s. 6d.

―――― *Old Town Fireside Stories.* Cloth extra, 3s. 6d.

―――― *Our Folks at Poganuc.* 6s.

―――― *We and our Neighbours.* 1 vol., small post 8vo, 6s. Sequel to "My Wife and I."*

―――― *Pink and White Tyranny.* Small post 8vo, 3s. 6d. Cheap Edition, 1s. 6d. and 2s.

―――― *Poganuc People: their Loves and Lives.* Crown 8vo, cloth, 6s.

―――― *Queer Little People.* 1s.; cloth, 2s.

―――― *Chimney Corner.* 1s.; cloth, 1s. 6d.

―――― *The Pearl of Orr's Island.* Crown 8vo, 5s.*

―――― *Woman in Sacred History.* Illustrated with 15 Chromo-lithographs and about 200 pages of Letterpress. Demy 4to, cloth extra, gilt edges, 25s.

Sullivan (A. M., late M.P.) Nutshell History of Ireland. From the Earliest Ages to the Present Time. Paper boards, 6d.

TACCHI (A.) Madagascar and the Malagasy Embassy. Demy 8vo, cloth.

Taine (H. A.) "Les Origines de la France Contemporaine." Translated by JOHN DURAND.
   Vol. 1. **The Ancient Regime.** Demy 8vo, cloth, 16s.
   Vol. 2. **The French Revolution.** Vol. 1. do.
   Vol. 3. **Do.** do. Vol. 2. do.

Talbot (Hon. E.) A Letter on Emigration. 1s.

Tauchnitz's English Editions of German Authors. Each volume, cloth flexible, 2s.; or sewed, 1s. 6d. (Catalogues post free on application.)

Tauchnitz (B.) German and English Dictionary. Paper, 1s. 6d.; cloth, 2s.; roan, 2s. 6d.

* *See also* Rose Library.

Tauchnitz (B.) French and English Dictionary. Paper, 1*s.* 6*d.*; cloth, 2*s.*; roan, 2*s.* 6*d.*

────── *Italian and English Dictionary.* Paper, 1*s.* 6*d.*; cloth, 2*s.*; roan, 2*s.* 6*d.*

────── *Spanish and English.* Paper, 1*s.* 6*d.*; cloth, 2*s.*; roan, 2*s.* 6*d.*

Taylor (W. M.) Paul the Missionary. Crown 8vo, 7*s.* 6*d.*

Thausing (Prof.) Preparation of Malt and the Fabrication of Beer. 8vo, 45*s.*

Theakston (Michael) British Angling Flies. Illustrated. Cr. 8vo, 5*s.*

Thoreau. By SANBORN. (American Men of Letters.) Crown 8vo, 2*s.* 6*d.*

Thousand Years Hence (A). By NUNSOWE GREENE. Crown 8vo, 6*s.*

Tolhausen (Alexandre) Grand Supplément du Dictionnaire Technologique. 3*s.* 6*d.*

Tolmer (Alexander) Reminiscences of an Adventurous and Chequered Career. 2 vols., 21*s.*

Trials. See BROWNE.

Tristram (Rev. Canon) Pathways of Palestine: A Descriptive Tour through the Holy Land. First Series. Illustrated by 44 Permanent Photographs. 2 vols., folio, cloth extra, gilt edges, 31*s.* 6*d.* each.

Tuckerman (Bayard) History of English Prose and Fiction. 8*s.* 6*d.*

Tunis. See REID.

Turner (Edward) Studies in Russian Literature. Crown 8vo, 8*s.* 6*d.*

*U*NION *Jack (The). Every Boy's Paper.* Edited by G. A. HENTY. Profusely Illustrated with Coloured and other Plates. Vol. I., 6*s.* Vols. II., III., IV., 7*s.* 6*d.* each.

Up Stream: A Journey from the Present to the Past. Pictures and Words by R. ANDRÉ. Coloured Plates, 4to, 5*s.*

BOOKS BY JULES VERNE.

CELEBRATED TRAVELS and TRAVELLERS. 3 Vols., Demy 8vo, 600 pp., upwards of 100 full-page Illustrations, 12s. 6d.; gilt edges, 14s. each:—

I. The Exploration of the World.
II. The Great Navigators of the Eighteenth Century.
III. The Great Explorers of the Nineteenth Century.

☞ The letters appended to each book refer to the various Editions and Prices given at the foot of the page.

- *a e* **TWENTY THOUSAND LEAGUES UNDER THE SEA.**
- *a e* **HECTOR SERVADAC.**
- *a e* **THE FUR COUNTRY.**
- *a f* **FROM THE EARTH TO THE MOON, AND A TRIP ROUND IT.**
- *a e* **MICHAEL STROGOFF, THE COURIER OF THE CZAR.**
- *a e* **DICK SANDS, THE BOY CAPTAIN.**
- *b c d* **FIVE WEEKS IN A BALLOON.**
- *b c d* **ADVENTURES OF THREE ENGLISHMEN AND THREE RUSSIANS.**
- *b c d* **AROUND THE WORLD IN EIGHTY DAYS.**
- *b c* { *d* **A FLOATING CITY.**
       d **THE BLOCKADE RUNNERS.** }
- *b c* { *d* { **DR. OX'S EXPERIMENT.**
             MASTER ZACHARIUS. }
         d { **A DRAMA IN THE AIR.**
             A WINTER AMID THE ICE. } }
- *b c* { *d* **THE SURVIVORS OF THE "CHANCELLOR."**
         d **MARTIN PAZ.** }
- *b c d* **THE CHILD OF THE CAVERN.**

THE MYSTERIOUS ISLAND, 3 Vols.:—
- *b c d* I. **DROPPED FROM THE CLOUDS.**
- *b c d* II. **ABANDONED.**
- *b c d* III. **SECRET OF THE ISLAND.**
- *b c* { *d* **THE BEGUM'S FORTUNE.**
         THE MUTINEERS OF THE "BOUNTY." }
- *b c d* **THE TRIBULATIONS OF A CHINAMAN.**

THE STEAM HOUSE, 2 Vols.:—
- *b c* I. **DEMON OF CAWNPORE.**
- *b c* II. **TIGERS AND TRAITORS.**

THE GIANT RAFT, 2 Vols.:—
- *b* I. **EIGHT HUNDRED LEAGUES ON THE AMAZON.**
- *b* II. **THE CRYPTOGRAM.**
- *b* **GODFREY MORGAN.**

THE GREEN RAY. Cloth, gilt edges, 6s.; plain edges, 5s.

a Small 8vo, very numerous Illustrations, handsomely bound in cloth, with gilt edges, 10s. 6d.; ditto, plainer binding, 5s.
b Large imperial 16mo, very numerous Illustrations, handsomely bound in cloth, with gilt edges, 7s. 6d.
c Ditto, plainer binding, 3s. 6d.
d Cheaper Edition, 1 Vol., paper boards, with some of the Illustrations, 1s.; bound in cloth, gilt edges, 2s.
e Cheaper Edition as (*d*), in 2 Vols., 1s. each; bound in cloth, gilt edges, 1 Vol., 3s. 6d.
f Same as (*c*), except in cloth, 2 Vols., gilt edges, 2s. each.

VELAZQUEZ and Murillo. By C. B. CURTIS. With Original Etchings. Royal 8vo, 31s. 6d.; large paper, 63s.

Victoria (Queen) Life of. By GRACE GREENWOOD. With numerous Illustrations. Small post 8vo, 6s.

Vincent (F.) Norsk, Lapp, and Finn. By FRANK VINCENT, Jun., Author of "The Land of the White Elephant," "Through and Through the Tropics," &c. 8vo, cloth, with Frontispiece and Map, 12s.

Viollet-le-Duc (E.) Lectures on Architecture. Translated by BENJAMIN BUCKNALL, Architect. With 33 Steel Plates and 200 Wood Engravings. Super-royal 8vo, leather back, gilt top, with complete Index, 2 vols., 3l. 3s.

Vivian (A. P.) Wanderings in the Western Land. 3rd Edition, 10s. 6d.

Voyages. See MCCORMICK.

WALLACE (L.) Ben Hur: A Tale of the Christ. Crown 8vo, 6s.

Waller (Rev. C. H.) The Names on the Gates of Pearl, and other Studies. By the Rev. C. H. WALLER, M.A. New Edition. Crown 8vo, cloth extra, 3s. 6d.

—— *A Grammar and Analytical Vocabulary of the Words in* the Greek Testament. Compiled from Brüder's Concordance. For the use of Divinity Students and Greek Testament Classes. By the Rev. C. H. WALLER, M.A. Part I. The Grammar. Small post 8vo, cloth, 2s. 6d. Part II. The Vocabulary, 2s. 6d.

—— *Adoption and the Covenant.* Some Thoughts on Confirmation. Super-royal 16mo, cloth limp, 2s. 6d.

—— *Silver Sockets; and other Shadows of Redemption.* Eighteen Sermons preached in Christ Church, Hampstead. Small post 8vo, cloth, 6s.

Warner (C. D.) Back-log Studies. Boards, 1s. 6d.; cloth, 2s.

Washington Irving's Little Britain. Square crown 8vo, 6s.

Webster. (American Men of Letters.) 18mo, 2s. 6d.

Weismann (A.) Studies in the Theory of Descent. One of the most complete of recent contributions to the Theory of Evolution. With a Preface by the late CHARLES DARWIN, F.R.S., and numerous Coloured Plates. 2 vols., 8vo, 40s.

Wheatley (H. B.) and Delamotte (P. H.) Art Work in Porcelain. Large 8vo, 2s. 6d.

—— *Art Work in Gold and Silver. Modern.* Large 8vo, 2s. 6d.

White (Rhoda E.) From Infancy to Womanhood. A Book of Instruction for Young Mothers. Crown 8vo, cloth, 10s. 6d.

White (R. G.) England Without and Within. New Edition, crown 8vo, 10s. 6d.

Whittier (J. G.) The King's Missive, and later Poems. 18mo, choice parchment cover, 3s. 6d.

—— *The Whittier Birthday Book.* Extracts from the Author's writings, with Portrait and numerous Illustrations. Uniform with the "Emerson Birthday Book." Square 16mo, very choice binding, 3s. 6d.

—— *Life of.* By R. A. UNDERWOOD. Cr. 8vo, cloth, 10s. 6d.

Wild Flowers of Switzerland. With Coloured Plates, life-size, from living Plants, and Botanical Descriptions of each Example. Imperial 4to, 52s. 6d.

Williams (C. F.) The Tariff Laws of the United States. 8vo, cloth, 10s. 6d.

Williams (H. W.) Diseases of the Eye. 8vo, 21s.

Williams (M.) Some London Theatres: Past and Preesnt. Crown 8vo, 7s. 6d.

Wills, A Few Hints on Proving, without Professional Assistance. By a PROBATE COURT OFFICIAL. 5th Edition, revised, with Forms of Wills, Residuary Accounts, &c. Fcap. 8vo, cloth limp, 1s.

Winckelmann (John) History of Ancient Art. Translated by JOHN LODGE, M.D. With very numerous Plates and Illustrations. 2 vols., 8vo, 36s.

Winks (W. E.) Lives of Illustrious Shoemakers. With eight Portraits. Crown 8vo, 7s. 6d.

Woodbury (Geo. E.) History of Wood Engraving. Illustrated, 8vo, 18s.

Woolsey (C. D., LL.D.) Introduction to the Study of International Law; designed as an Aid in Teaching and in Historical Studies. 5th Edition, demy 8vo, 18s.

Woolson (Constance F.) See "Low's Standard Novels."

Wright (the late Rev. Henry) The Friendship of God. With Biographical Preface by the Rev. E. H. BICKERSTETH, Portrait, &c. Crown 8vo, 6s.

YRIARTE *(Charles) Florence: its History.* Translated by C. B. PITMAN. Illustrated with 500 Engravings. Large imperial 4to, extra binding, gilt edges, 63s.

History; the Medici; the Humanists; letters; arts; the Renaissance; illustrious Florentines; Etruscan art; monuments; sculpture; painting.

London:
SAMPSON LOW, MARSTON, SEARLE, & RIVINGTON,
CROWN BUILDINGS, 188, FLEET STREET, E.C.

www.ingramcontent.com/pod-product-compliance
Lightning Source LLC
Chambersburg PA
CBHW060351170426
43199CB00013B/1834